OG MANDINO

THREE VOLUMES IN ONE

OG MANDINO

THREE VOLUMES IN ONE

~

The Greatest Salesman in the World

The Greatest Secret in the World

The Greatest Miracle in the World

BONANZA BOOKS
New York

This 1991 edition is published by Bonanza Books,
distributed by Outlet Book Company, Inc., a Random House Company,
225 Park Avenue South, New York, New York 10003, by arrangement
with Frederick Fell Publishers, Inc.
Originally published as *Og Mandino's Great Trilogy*
Printed and bound in the United States of America
Library of Congress Cataloging-in-Publication Data

ISBN 0-517-05587-2
Cover illustration by Donna Diamond
8 7 6 5 4 3 2 1

A Special Message From
OG MANDINO . . .

I have never been one who could be faulted for possessing too little ego, at least not in recent years; however, the great honor of having my three bestselling works gathered together in this magnificent anthology is a humbling experience.

Only a few talented and distinguished writers, the likes of a Faulkner, Steinbeck, Cheever, or Shaw, are fortunate enough to live to see their short stories distinguished in such a fashion. One's lengthier efforts, such as the three books presented here, are rarely (if ever) corralled between the covers of a single volume until long after the author's obituary notices have faded to a sad shade of saffron.

The road to success, for me, was a long and arduous journey, strewn with obstacles and traps, pitfalls and hurdles—all created by myself. Painful as it is, I speak of those sad and frustrating times whenever I am invited to address sales gatherings, corporate conventions, and success rallies, in the hope that my personal experiences will serve as sufficient evidence for all who hear me that they have it in their own power to make their lives as glorious or as terrible as they choose. Hopefully, all of my writings reinforce that very theme—each book in its own way.

The will to write has been a part of me since early youth. To echo Lincoln's words, "All that I am, and all that I hope to be, I owe to my angel mother." I can close my eyes, even now, fifty years later, and still see my Irish mother's flaming red hair and, yes, I can even hear her voice as she would lean over my shoulder to correct a piece of homework on which I was making little progress. Somehow, and for reasons I shall never know, she had me convinced, early on, that the day would come when I would be a writer. Not just a writer, she would insist, but a *great* writer. And then, the year after I graduated from high school, her loving heart stopped beating and I fled from my youth—into the Army Air Force. The year was 1942.

Three years later I returned to the United States after flying thirty combat missions over Germany. I had a chestful of ribbons, twenty-six hundred dollars in cash and a single burning ambition—to write the great American novel. I rented a coldwater flat just off Times Square, bought a second-hand typewriter and spent the next year collecting rejection slip after rejection slip from scores of publishers. I never so much as sold a single sentence of my work to anyone.

Finally, my money ran out and I abandoned my dream,

returning to New England from whence I had come. I shall not recount the dreary saga of my next fifteen years, years when I married a lovely woman, bought a house, was blessed with a beautiful daughter—and struggled in job after job, failure after failure, until I tried to drown my frustrations and miseries in bottles of wine. Eventually I lost everything that was important to me, and one day, as a lonely bum peering at a small handgun in a Cleveland pawnshop window, found myself contemplating suicide. I didn't buy that gun, although its tiny yellow tag was marked "Only $29!" No guts.

Although I have been asked, several hundred times on radio, television, and press interviews through the years, I am unable to explain the miracle that turned my life around. Who can explain miracles? In any event, while working here and there around the country at any menial job I could find, just in order to survive, I began spending countless hours in public libraries. They were free, they were warm, and they were peaceful and quiet. Among all those books I began searching for some answers. Why had I failed? How did I come to ruin my life and the lives of those who loved me most? Where had I gone wrong? Most important, was it too late for a thirty-five-year-old loser to make something of his life?

I read the Bible many times. I became intimate with the old philosophers. I studied the great self-help authors such as Dale Carnegie, Norman Vincent Peale, Maxwell Maltz, Napoleon Hill, even Ralph Waldo Emerson. One day, in a library in Concord, New Hampshire, I discovered the ideas of W. Clement Stone, the insurance genius and philanthropist, through his mangnificent classic, *Success Through A Positive Mental Attitude*, which he co-authored with Napoleon Hill. Almost at the same time that I was trying to absorb Stone's wonderful philosophy for achieving success, I met a woman who had more faith in my potential than I had ever had and, with her encouragement and love to bolster me, I went to Boston and applied for an insurance salesman's job in Stone's Combined Group of Companies. They hired me—and I married Bette.

Still, through all that had happened to me, I never forgot our dream, my mother's and mine. Sometime during my second year of selling insurance in southern Maine, I took a week off from work, a week we could ill afford, and wrote a manual on how one could apply Stone's success system of selling in rural areas. I typed the final draft on a rented typewriter, Bette packaged it lovingly, and we mailed it to Stone's executive offices in Chicago with the prayer that someone there would read it and realize what a great writing talent they had in their employ back in New England. Someone did—and three months later, Bette and I packed our few belongings and our young son, Dana, into our car and moved to Chicago. There I was assigned the thrilling job, to me, of *writing*—writing sales promotion material for our people in the field. Soon afterwards, our second son, Matthew, arrived on the scene.

A year later, the position of executive editor of Stone's magazine, *Success Unlimited*, became open, and since I was now imbued with plenty of his positive mental attitude, I boldly applied for the job although I knew next to nothing about editing a magazine. The miracles continued. They accepted me after several interviews during which I had spelled out, in detail, what I would do to improve the magazine's quality and, most of all, its circulation.

Another miracle. One month, for an issue of the magazine that seemed quite "thin" to me, I wrote an article recounting the inspiring story of Ben Hogan, the great golfer, and of his brave comeback, after a terrible automobile accident, to win the United States Open again. Frederick Fell, a New York publisher, came across that particular issue and wrote to me, suggesting that he believed I had the talent to write a book and if I ever did he would be interested in seeing the manuscript first.

And so, in 1968, shortly before my forty-fifth birthday, my first book was published! It was a tiny thing, as books go, only one hundred and eight pages in length, with the unwieldy title of *The Greatest Salesman In The World*. Of course, since it was by an unknown author, it received little promotion or attention—but then another miracle occurred.

Since I had dedicated the book to W. Clement Stone, I presented an autographed copy to him and to his wife, Jessie. While the two were flying to London to spend Christmas with their son, Clem, and his family, Mrs. Stone reached into her travel bag, removed her copy of my book, and handed it to her husband to read.

On Christmas morning I received a cablegram from London. It read, "Your book the most inspiring I have read since *Magnificent Obsession*. Please see me as soon as I return."

Well, I saw him all right. When I walked into his office, soon after the New Year, he asked me to call my publisher, Frederick Fell, and tell him that W. Clement Stone wished to purchase 10,000 copies of *The Greatest Salesman In The World* to distribute to every employee and salesperson in his company and to its shareholders!

Those copies, dispersed to all points of the compass, eventually became more prolific than Johnny Appleseed's seedings. Soon, Rich DeVos, Amway Corporation's dynamic president, was singing the praises of *Greatest Salesman* to his hundreds of thousands of nationwide distributors, and the book became one of those rare publishing phenomenons that happens only once or twice in each generation—a bestseller generated by that most powerful of all advertising mediums, "word of mouth."

As I write this message to you, *The Greatest Salesman In The World* has surpassed more than four million copies in sales, in all editions, and has gone through more than one hundred and thirty printings in seventeen languages and Braille. Who, in their right mind, could have possibly imagined that a miserable failure such as I would literally crawl out of the gutter to write what is now acknowledged to be the bestselling book of all time, *in the entire world*, in the field of sales—and that the book would also appeal to countless thousands, from housewives to rock stars, whose lives have nothing to do with professional sales-manship? Even in a soap opera one would have trouble digesting such a plot.

The Greatest Secret In The World, the second book of this trilogy, was published by Frederick Fell Publishers, Inc., in 1972. It was a natural follow-up to the first. In *The Greatest Salesman In The World* you will discover ten scrolls of success and how to use them. The second book amplifies on techniques for using these scrolls to your greatest advantage and also provides you with a Success Recorder Diary on which you can chart your progress, daily, toward a better life.

The Greatest Miracle In The World, the third in this trilogy, was published by Frederick Fell Publishers, Inc., in 1975. It has a very special link with *The Greatest Salesman In The World* and I cannot urge you strongly enough to read *Salesman* before you read *Miracle*.

An essential ingredient of *The Greatest Miracle In The World* is a Memorandum from God—to you. God, I reasoned, hasn't contacted us directly for many thousands of years and the last time He did was when He chiseled Ten Commandments on two stone tablets. However, if He were trying to reach us directly, today, I was certain that He would use the most modern form of written communication and send us a memo—and so the book contains one—from Him to you.

A recording of the Memorandum, made exclusively for my use by an old friend, Don Allen, who I'm quite certain has the most magnificent male speaking voice in the world, is an integral part of a speech I deliver, more than fifty times each year, to groups throughout the Western Hemisphere. At a special point in my speech, after I have related the horror story of my early struggles, I light a candle resting on the lectern. When I do, every light in the auditorium or theater or ballroom is turned off. Then, with only the light from the flickering candle in a room of darkness, I introduce my audience to God—and over the facility's public address system they hear the resonant tones of God, through Don Allen's voice, speaking the words of the Memorandum from God.

As often as I have delivered that speech, I never cease to be amazed at the love and warmth and empathy that flows up from the crowd when the Memorandum ends and the lights gradually come up.

The three books in this anthology have sold, separately, more than seven million copies. There are times when I am certain that all seven million readers, plus seven million of their friends, have written to me at least once, each expressing gratitude for the change that one or more of the books has wrought in his or her life. Although it does cut into my golfing and loafing time considerably, I do, eventually, respond to every letter personally.

Many of those who write also include a question. "Did the events that you describe in *The Greatest Miracle In The World* actually happen to you or were they merely figments of your creative imagination?" To all of them, and to you before you ask, I have only one answer. Read John 4:48.

Not so long ago, I was fortunate enough to sign a long-term book contract providing me with more money than any amount I could have conceived of twenty years ago. After the signing was completed, I departed from the building where the legal ceremonies had taken place and decided to walk back to the New York Hilton, where I was staying, in order to clear my head and settle my stomach.

On the way, a sudden rain shower exploded over the city, and I dashed into a small church, whose name I regretfully cannot recall, to seek refuge from the storm. An organ was playing in the almost empty church and I walked slowly toward the altar as if I were being drawn there by a magnet. At last I was at the railing and I knelt to pray, thanking God in my own stumbling way for all the blessings He had bestowed on me, blessings I did not deserve.

Suddenly I felt myself sobbing, uncontrollably, while I repeated, over and over, half aloud, "Mom, wherever you are, I just want you to know that your little kid finally made it. I'm a writer, at last."

Og Mandino

The Greatest Salesman
in the World

This book is respectfully dedicated
to a great salesman
W. CLEMENT STONE

who has blended love, compassion, and a unique
system of salesmanship into a living philosophy for
success which motivates and guides countless thousands of individuals, each year, to discover greater
happiness, good mental and physical health, peace of
mind, power and wealth.

Chapter I

Hafid lingered before the bronze mirror and studied his reflected image in the polished metal.

"Only the eyes have retained their youth," he murmured as he turned away and moved slowly across the spacious marble floor. He passed between black onyx columns rising to support ceilings burnished with silver and gold and his aging legs carried him past tables carved from cyprus and ivory.

Tortoise shell gleamed from couches and divans and the walls, inlaid with gems, shimmered with brocades of the most painstaking design. Huge palms grew placidly in bronze vessels framing a fountain of alabaster nymphs while flower boxes, encrusted with gems, competed with their contents for attention. No visitor to Hafid's palace could doubt that he was, indeed, a person of great wealth.

The old man passed through an enclosed garden and entered his warehouse which extended beyond the mansion for five hundred paces. Erasmus, his chief book-keeper, waited uncertainly just beyond the entryway.

"Greetings, sire."

Hafid nodded and continued on in silence. Erasmus followed, his face unable to disguise concern at the master's unusual request for a meeting in this place. Near the loading platforms Hafid paused to watch goods being removed from baggage wagons and counted into separate stalls.

There were wools, fine linens, parchment, honey, carpets, and oil from Asia Minor; glass, figs, nuts, and balsam from his own country; textiles and drugs from Palmyra; ginger, cinnamon, and precious stones from Arabia; corn, paper, granite, alabaster, and basalt from Egypt; tapestries from Babylon; paintings from Rome; and statues from Greece. The smell of balsam was heavy in the air and Hafid's sensitive old nose detected the presence of sweet plums, apples, cheese, and ginger.

Finally he turned to Erasmus. "Old friend, how much wealth is there now accumulated in our treasury?"

Erasmus paled, "Everything, master?"

"Everything."

"I have not studied the numbers recently but I would estimate there is in excess of seven million gold talents."

"And were all the goods in all my warehouses and emporiums converted into gold, how much would they bring?"

"Our inventory is not yet complete for this season, sire, but I would calculate a minimum of another three million talents."

Hafid nodded, "Purchase no more goods. Institute immediately whatever plans are required to sell everything that is mine and convert all of it to gold."

The bookkeeper's mouth opened but no sound came forth. He fell back as if struck and when finally he could speak, the words came with effort.

"I do not understand, sire. This has been our most profitable year. Every emporium reports an increase in sales over the previous season. Even the Roman legions are now our customers for did you not sell the Procurator in Jerusalem two hundred Arabian stallions within the fortnight? Forgive my boldness for seldom have I questioned your orders but this command I cannot comprehend. . . ."

Hafid smiled and gently grasped Erasmus' hand.

"My trusted comrade, is your memory of sufficient strength to recall the first command you received from me when you entered my employ many years ago?"

Erasmus frowned momentarily and then his face brightened. "I was enjoined by you to remove, each year, half the profit from our treasury and dispense it to the poor."

"Did you not, at that time, consider me a foolish man of business?"

"I had great forebodings, sire."

Hafid nodded and spread his arms toward the loading platforms. "Will you now admit that your concern was without ground?"

"Yes, sire."

"Then let me encourage you to maintain faith in this

decision until I explain my plans. I am now an old man and my needs are simple. Since my beloved Lisha has been taken from me, after so many years of happiness, it is my desire to distribute all of my wealth among the poor of this city. I shall keep only enough to complete my life without discomfort. Besides disposing of our inventory, I wish you to prepare the necessary documents which will transfer the ownership of every emporium to he who now manages each for me. I also wish you to distribute five thousand gold talents to these managers as a reward for their years of loyalty and so that they may restock their shelves in any manner that they desire."

Erasmus began to speak but Hafid's raised hand silenced him. "Does this assignment seem unpleasant to you?"

The bookkeeper shook his head and attempted to smile. "No, sire, it is only that I cannot understand your reasoning. Your words are those of a man whose days are numbered."

"It is your character, Erasmus, that your concern should be for me instead of yourself. Have ye no thoughts for your own future when our trade empire is disbanded?"

"We have been comrades together for many years. How can I, now, think only of myself?"

Hafid embraced his old friend and replied, "It is not necessary. I ask that you immediately transfer fifty thousand gold talents to your name and I beg that you remain with me until a promise I made long ago is fulfilled. When that promise is kept I will then bequeath this palace and warehouse to you for I will then be ready to rejoin Lisha."

The old bookkeeper stared at his master unable to comprehend the words heard. "Fifty thousand gold talents, the palace, the warehouse . . . I am not deserving. . . ."

Hafid nodded. "I have always counted your friendship as my greatest asset. What I now bestow on you is of little measure compared to your unending loyalty. You have mastered the art of living not for yourself alone, but for others, and this concern has stamped thee above all, as a man among men. Now I urge you to hasten with the consummation of my plans. Time is the most precious commodity I possess and the hour glass of my life is nearly filled."

Erasmus turned his face to hide his tears. His voice broke as he asked, "And what of your promise, yet to keep? Although we have been as brothers never have I heard you talk of such a matter."

Hafid folded his arms and smiled. "I will meet with you again when you have discharged my commands of this morning. Then I will disclose a secret which I have shared with no one, except my beloved wife, for over thirty years."

Chapter II

And so it came to pass that a heavily guarded caravan soon departed from Damascus carrying certificates of ownership and gold for those who managed each of Hafid's trade emporiums. From Obed in Joppa to Reuel at Petra, each of the ten managers received word of Hafid's retirement and gift in stunned silence. Eventually, after making its last stop at the emporium in Antipatris, the caravan's mission was complete.

The most powerful trade empire of its time was no more.

His heart heavy with sadness, Erasmus sent word to his master that the warehouse was now empty and the emporiums no longer bore the proud banner of Hafid. The messenger returned with a request that Erasmus meet with his master by the fountain in the peristyle, immediately.

Hafid studied his friend's face and asked, "Is it done?"

"It is done."

"Grieve not, kind friend, and follow me."

Only the sound of their sandals echoed in the giant chamber as Hafid led Erasmus toward the marble stairway at the rear. His steps momentarily slowed as he neared a solitary murrhine vase on a tall stand of citrus wood and he watched as the sunlight changed the glass from white to purple. His old face smiled.

Then the two old friends began to climb the inner steps that led to the room inside the palace dome. Erasmus took notice that the armed guard, always present at the foot of the steps, no longer was there. Finally they reached a landing and paused since both were without breath from the exertion of the climb. Then they continued on to a second landing and Hafid removed a small key from his belt. He unlocked the heavy oak door and leaned against it until it creaked inwards. Erasmus hesitated until his master beckoned him inside and then he stepped timidly into the room to which no one had been allowed admission for over three decades.

Gray and dusty light seeped down from turrets above and Erasmus gripped Hafid's arm until his eyes became accustomed to the semi-darkness. With a faint smile, Hafid watched as Erasmus turned slowly in a room that was bare expect for a small cedar chest spotlighted in a shaft of sunlight in one corner.

"Are you not disappointed, Erasmus?"

"I know not what to say, sire."

"Are you not disappointed in the furnishings? Certainly the contents of this room have been a conversation

11

piece among many. Have you not wondered or concerned yourself with the mystery of what is contained
here which I have guarded so zealously for so long?"

Erasmus nodded, "It is true. There has been much
talk and many rumors through the years as to what our
master kept hidden here in the tower."

"Yes, my friend, and most of them I have heard. It has
been said that barrels of diamonds were here, and gold
ingots, or wild animals, or rare birds. Once a Persian rug
merchant hinted that perhaps I maintained a small
harem here. Lisha laughed at the thought of me with a
collection of concubines. But, as you can observe, there
is nothing here except a small chest. Now, come forward."

The two men crouched beside the chest and Hafid
carefully proceeded to unroll the leather strapping which
encircled it. He inhaled deeply of the cedar fragrance
from the wood and finally he pushed against the cover
and it quietly sprung open. Erasmus leaned forward and
stared over Hafid's shoulder at the trunk's contents. He
looked at Hafid and shook his head in bewilderment.
There was nothing inside the trunk but scrolls . . .
leather scrolls.

Hafid reached inside and gently removed one of the
rolls. Momentarily he clasped it to his breast and closed
his eyes. A quiet calmness settled over his face, brushing
away the lines of age. Then he rose to his feet and
pointed toward the chest.

"Were this room filled to its beams with diamonds, its

value could not surpass what your eyes behold in this simple wooden box. All the success, happiness, love, peace of mind, and wealth that I have enjoyed is directly traceable to what is contained in these few scrolls. My debt to them and to the wise one who entrusted them to my care can never be repaid."

Frightened by the tone in Hafid's voice, Erasmus stepped back and asked, "Is this the secret to which you have referred? Is this chest connected in some way with the promise you have yet to keep?"

"The answer is 'yes' to both of your questions."

Erasmus passed his hand across his perspiring forehead and looked at Hafid with disbelief. "What is written on these scrolls that places their value beyond that of diamonds?"

"All but one of these scrolls contain a principle, a law, or a fundamental truth written in a unique style to help the reader understand its meaning. To become a master in the art of sales one must learn and practice the secret of each scroll. When one masters these principles one has the power to accumulate all the wealth he desires."

Erasmus stared at the old scrolls with dismay. "As wealthy even, as you?"

"Far wealthier, if he chooses."

"You have stated that all but one of these scrolls contain selling principles. What is contained on the last scroll?"

"The last scroll, as you call it, is the first scroll which must be read, since each is numbered to be read in a special sequence. And the first scroll contains a secret which has been given to a mere handful of wise men throughout history. The first scroll, in truth, teaches the most effective way to learn what is written on the others."

"It seems to be a task that anyone can master."

"It is, indeed, a simple task provided one is willing to pay the price in time and concentration until each principle becomes a part of one's personality; until each principle becomes a habit in living."

Erasmus reached into the chest and removed a scroll. Holding it gently between his fingers and his thumb, he shook it toward Hafid. "Forgive me, master, but why is it that you have not shared these principles with others, especially those who have labored long in your employ? You have always shown such generosity in all other matters, how is it that all who have sold for you did not receive the opportunity to read these words of wisdom and thus become wealthy too? At the very least, all would have been better sellers of goods with such valuable knowledge. Why have you kept these principles to yourself for all these years?"

"I had no choice. Many years ago when these scrolls were entrusted to my care, I was made to promise under oath that I would share their contents with only one person. I do not yet understand the reasoning behind this strange request. However, I was commanded to apply the principles of the scrolls to my own life, until one day someone would appear who had need for the help and guidance contained in these scrolls far more than I did when I was a youth. I was told that through some sign I would recognize the individual to whom I was to pass the scrolls even though it was possible that the individual would not know that he was seeking the scrolls.

"I have waited patiently, and while I waited I applied these principles as I was given permission to do. With their knowledge I became what many call the greatest salesman in the world just as he who bequeathed these scrolls to me was acclaimed as the greatest salesman of his time. Now, Erasmus, perhaps you will understand, at last, why some of my actions through the years seemed peculiar and unworkable to you, yet they proved successful. Always were my deeds and decisions guided by these scrolls; therefore, it was not through my wisdom that we acquired so many gold talents. I was only the instrument of fulfillment."

"Do you still believe that he who is to receive these scrolls from thee will appear after all this time?"

"Yes."

Hafid gently replaced the scrolls and closed the chest. He spoke softly from his knees, "Will you stay with me until that day, Erasmus?"

The bookkeeper reached through soft light until their hands clasped. He nodded once and then withdrew from the room as if from an unspoken command from his master. Hafid replaced the leather strapping on the chest and then stood and walked to a small turret. He stepped through it out onto the scaffold that surrounded the great dome.

A wind from the East blew into the old man's face carrying with it the smell of the lakes and the desert beyond. He smiled as he stood high above the rooftops of Damascus and his thoughts leaped backwards through time. . . .

Chapter III

It was winter and the chill was bitter on the Mount of Olives. From Jerusalem, across the narrow cleft of the Kidron Valley, came the smell of smoke, incense, and burning flesh from the Temple and its foulness mixed with the turpentine odor of terebinth trees on the mountain.

On an open slope, only a short descent from the village of Bethpage, slumbered the immense trade caravan of Pathros of Palmyra. The hour was late and even the great merchant's favorite stallion had ceased munching on the low pistachio bushes and settled down against a soft hedge of laurel.

Beyond the long row of silent tents, strands of thick hemp curled around four ancient olive trees. They formed a square corral enclosing shapeless forms of camels and asses huddled together to draw warmth from each other's body. Except for two guards, patrolling near the baggage wagons, the only movement in the camp was the tall and moving shadow outlined against the goat's hair wall of Pathros' great tent.

Inside, Pathros paced angrily back and forth, pausing occasionally to frown and shake his head at the youth kneeling timidly near the tent opening. Finally he lowered his ailing body to the gold-woven rug and beckoned the lad to move closer.

"Hafid, you have always been as my own. I am perplexed and puzzled by your strange request. Are you not content with your work?"

The boy's eyes were fixed on the rug. "No, sire."

"Perhaps the ever-increasing size of our caravans has made your task of tending to all our animals too great?"

"No, sire."

"Then kindly repeat your request. Include also, in thy words, the reasoning behind such an unusual request."

"It is my desire to become a seller of your goods instead of only your camel boy. I wish to become as Hadad, Simon, Caleb, and the others who depart from our baggage wagons with animals barely able to crawl from the weight of your goods and who return with gold for thee and gold also for themselves. I desire to improve my lowly position in life. As a camel boy I am nothing, but as a salesman for you I can acquire wealth and success."

"How do you know this?"

"Often have I heard you say that no other trade or profession has more opportunity for one to rise from poverty to great wealth than that of salesman."

Pathros began to nod but thought better of it and continued to question the youth. "Dost thou believe you are capable of performing as Hadad and the other sellers?"

Hafid stared intently at the old man and replied, "Many times have I overheard Caleb complain to you about misfortunes that accounted for his lack of sales and many times have I heard you remind him that anyone could sell all the goods in your warehouse within a small passing of time if he but applied himself to learn the principles and laws of selling. If you believe that Caleb, whom everyone calls a fool, can learn these principles, then cannot I also acquire this special knowledge?"

"If you should master these principles what would be your goal in life?"

Hafid hesitated and then said, "It has been repeated throughout the land that you are a great salesman. The world has never seen a trade empire such as you have built through your mastery of salesmanship. My ambition is to become even greater than you, the greatest merchant, the wealthiest man, and the greatest salesman in all the world!"

Pathros leaned back and studied the young, dark face. The smell from the animals was still on his clothes but the youth displayed little humility in his manner. "And what will you do with all this great wealth and the fearsome power that will surely accompany it?"

"I will do as you do. My family will be provided with the finest of worldly goods and the rest I will share with those in need."

Pathros shook his head. "Wealth, my son, should never

be your goal in life. Your words are eloquent but they are mere words. True wealth is of the heart, not of the purse."

Hafid persisted, "Art thou not wealthy, sire?"

The old man smiled at Hafid's boldness. "Hafid, so far as material wealth is concerned, there is only one difference between myself and the lowliest beggar outside Herod's palace. The beggar thinks only of his next meal and I think only of the meal that will be my last. No, my son, do not aspire for wealth and labor not only to be rich. Strive instead for happiness, to be loved and to love, and most important, to acquire peace of mind and serenity."

Hafid continued to persist. "But these things are impossible without gold. Who can live in poverty with peace of mind? How can one be happy with an empty stomach? How can one demonstrate love for one's family if he is unable to feed and clothe and house them? You, yourself, have said that wealth is good when it brings joy to others. Why then is my ambition to be wealthy not a good one? Poverty may be a privilege and even a way of life for the monk in the desert, for he has only himself to sustain and none but his god to please, but I consider poverty to be the mark of a lack of ability or a lack of ambition. I am not deficient in either of these qualities!"

Pathros frowned, "What has caused this sudden outburst of ambition? You speak of providing for a family yet you have no family lest it be I who have adopted you since the pestilence removed thy mother and father."

Hafid's sun-darkened skin could not hide the sudden flush in his cheeks. "While we encamped in Hebron before journeying here I met the daughter of Calneh. She . . . she. . . ."

"Oh, ho, now the truth emergeth. Love, not noble ideals, has changed my camel boy into a mighty soldier ready to battle the world. Calneh is a very wealthy man. His daughter and a camel boy? Never! But his daughter and a rich, young, and handsome merchant . . . ah, that is another matter. Very well, my young soldier, I will help you begin your career as a salesman."

The lad fell to his knees and grasped Pathros' robe. "Sire, sire! How can I say the words to show my thanks?"

Pathros freed himself from Hafid's grip and stepped back. "I would suggest you withhold thy thanks for the present. Whatever aid I give thee will be as a grain of sand compared to the mountains you must move for yourself."

Hafid's joy immediately subsided as he asked, "Will you not teach me the principles and laws that will transform me into a great salesman?"

"I will not. No more than I have made your early youth soft and easy through pampering. I have been criticized often for condemning my adopted son to the life of a camel boy but I believed that if the right fire was burning inside it would eventually emerge . . . and when it did you would be far more a man for your years of difficult toil. Tonight, your request has made me happy for the fire of ambition glows in your eyes and your face shines with burning desire. This is good and my judgment is vindicated but you must still prove that there is more behind your words than air."

Hafid was silent and the old man continued, "First, you must prove to me, and more important to yourself, that you can endure the life of a salesman for it is not an easy lot you have chosen. Truly, many times have you heard me say that the rewards are great if one succeeds but the rewards are great only because so few succeed. Many succumb to despair and fail without realizing that they already possess all the tools needed to acquire great wealth. Many others face each obstacle in their path with fear and doubt and consider them as enemies when, in truth, these obstructions are friends and helpers. Obstacles are necessary for success because in selling, as in all careers of importance, victory comes only after many struggles and countless defeats. Yet each struggle, each defeat, sharpens your skills and strengths, your courage and your endurance, your ability and your confidence and thus each obstacle is a comrade-in-arms forcing you to become better . . . or quit. Each rebuff is an opportunity to move forward; turn away from them, avoid them, and you throw away your future."

The youth nodded and made as if to speak but the old man raised his hand and continued, "Furthermore, you are embarking on the loneliest profession in the world. Even the despised tax collectors return to their homes at sundown and the legions of Rome have a barracks to call home. But you will witness many setting suns far from all friends and loved ones. Nothing can bring the hurt of loneliness upon a man so swiftly as to pass a strange house in the dark and witness, in the lamplight from within, a family breaking evening bread together.

"It is in these periods of loneliness that temptations will confront thee," Pathros continued. "How you meet these temptations will greatly affect your career. When you are on the road with only your animal it is a strange and often frightening sensation. Often our perspectives and our values are temporarily forgotten and we become like children, longing for the safety and love of our own. What we find as a substitute has ended the career of many including thousands who were considered to have great potential in the art of selling. Furthermore, there will be no one to humor you or console you when you have sold no goods; no one except those who seek to separate you from your money pouch."

"I will be careful and heed thy words of warning."

"Then let us begin. For the present you will receive no more advice. You stand before me as a green fig. Until the fig is ripe it cannot be called a fig and until you have been exposed to knowledge and experience you cannot be called a salesman."

"How shall I begin?"

"In the morning you are to report to Silvio at the baggage wagons. He will release, in your charge, one of our finest seamless robes. It is woven from the hair of a goat

THE GREATEST SALESMAN IN THE WORLD

and will withstand even the heaviest rains and it is dyed red from the roots of the madder plant so that the color will always hold fast. Near the hem you will find sewn on the inside, a small star. This is the mark of Tola whose guild makes the finest robes in all the world. Next to the star is my mark, a circle within a square. Both these marks are known and respected throughout the land and we have sold countless thousands of these robes. I have dealt with the Jews so long that I only know their name for such a garment as this. It is called an *abeyah*.

"Take the robe and a donkey and depart at dawn for Bethlehem, the village which our caravan passed through before arriving here. None of our sellers ever visit there. They report that it is a waste of their time because the people are so poor, yet many years ago I sold hundreds of robes among the shepherds there. Remain in Bethlehem until you have sold the robe."

Hafid nodded, attempting in vain to conceal his excitement. "At what price shall I sell the robe, master?"

"I will enter a charge of one silver denarius against your name on my ledger. When you return you will remit one silver denarius to me. Keep all that you receive in excess of this as your commission, so, in fact, you set the price of the robe yourself. You may visit the market place which is at the south entry of town or you may wish to consider calling on each dwelling in the town itself, of which I am certain there are over a thousand. Certainly it is conceivable that one robe can be sold there, do you not agree?"

Hafid nodded again, his mind already on the morrow.

Pathros placed his hand gently on the lad's shoulder. "I will place no one in your position until you return. If you discover that your stomach is not for this profession I will understand and you must not consider yourself in disgrace. Never feel shame for trying and failing for he who has never failed is he who has never tried. Upon your return I will question you at length concerning your experiences. Then I will decide how I shall proceed with helping you to make your outlandish dreams come true."

Hafid bowed and turned to leave but the old man was not finished. "Son, there is one precept that you must remember as you begin this new life. Keep it always in your mind and you will overcome seemingly impossible obstacles that are certain to confront you as they do everyone with ambition."

Hafid waited, "Yes, sire?"

"Failure will never overtake you if your determination to succeed is strong enough."

Pathros stepped close to the youth. "Do you comprehend the full meaning of my words?"

"Yes, sire."

"Then repeat them to me!"

"Failure will never overtake me if my determination to succeed is strong enough."

Chapter IV

Hafid pushed aside the half-eaten loaf of bread and considered his unhappy fate. Tomorrow would be his fourth day in Bethlehem and the single red robe that he had carried so confidently away from the caravan was still in the pack on the back of his animal, now tethered to a stake in the cave behind the inn.

He heard not the noise that surrounded him in the overcrowded dining hall as he scowled at his unfinished meal. Doubts that have assailed every seller since the beginning of time passed through his mind:

"Why will the people not listen to my story? How does one command their attention? Why do they close their door before I have said five words? Why do they lose interest in my talk and walk away? Is everyone poor in this town? What can I say when they tell me they like the robe but cannot afford it? Why do so many tell me to return at a later date? How do others sell when I cannot? What is this fear that seizes me when I approach a closed door and how can I overcome it? Is my price not in line with the other sellers?"

He shook his head in disgust at his failure. Perhaps this was not the life for him. Perhaps he should remain a camel boy and continue earning only coppers for each day's labor. As a seller of goods he would indeed be fortunate if he returned to the caravan with any profit at all. What had Pathros called him? A young soldier? He wished, momentarily, that he were back with his animals.

Then his thoughts turned to Lisha and to her stern father, Calneh, and the doubts quickly left his mind. Tonight he would again sleep in the hills to conserve his funds and tomorrow he would sell the robe. Furthermore, he would speak with such eloquence that the robe would bring a good price. He would begin early, just after dawn, and station himself near the town well. He would address everyone that approached and within a short time he would be returning to the Mount of Olives with silver in his purse.

He reached for the unfinished bread and began to eat while he thought of his master. Pathros would be proud of him because he had not despaired and returned as a failure. In truth, four days was much too long a time to consummate the sale of but one simple robe but if he could accomplish the deed in four days he knew he could learn, from Pathros, how to accomplish it in three days, then two days. In time he would become so proficient that he would sell many robes every hour! Then he would indeed be a salesman of repute.

He departed from the noisy inn and headed toward the cave and his animal. The chilled air had stiffened the grass with a thin coating of frost and each blade crackled with complaint from the pressure of his sandals. Hafid decided not to ride into the hills tonight. Instead, he would rest in the cave with his animal.

Tomorrow, he knew, would be a better day although now he understood why the others always bypassed this unprosperous village. They had said that no sales could be made here and he had recalled their words every time someone had refused to buy his robe. Yet, Pathros had sold hundreds of robes here many years ago. Perhaps times had been different then and, after all, Pathros was a great salesman.

A flickering light from the cave caused him to hasten his steps for fear that a thief was within. He rushed through the opening in the limestone ready to overcome the criminal and recover his possessions. Instead, the tenseness immediately left his body at the sight that confronted him.

A small candle, forced between a cleft in the cave wall, shone faintly on a bearded man and a young woman huddled closely together. At their feet, in a hollowed-out stone that usually held cattle fodder, slept an infant. Hafid knew little of such things but he sensed that the baby was newborn from the child's wrinkled and crimson skin. To protect the sleeping infant from the cold, both the man's and the woman's cloaks covered all but the small head.

The man nodded in Hafid's direction while the woman moved closer to the child. No one spoke. Then the woman trembled and Hafid saw that her thin garment offered little protection against the dampness of the cave. Hafid looked again at the infant. He watched, fascinated, as the small mouth opened and closed, almost in a smile, and a strange sensation passed through him. For some unknown reason he thought of Lisha. The woman trembled again from the cold and her sudden movement returned Hafid from his daydreaming.

After painful moments of indecision the would-be seller of goods walked to his animal. He carefully untied the knots, opened his pack, and withdrew the robe. He unrolled it and rubbed his hands over the material. The red dye glowed in the candlelight and he could see the mark of Pathros and the mark of Tola on its underside. The circle in the square and the star. How many times had he held this robe in his tired arms in the past three days? It seemed as if he knew every weave and fiber of it. This was indeed a robe of quality. With care it would last a lifetime.

Hafid closed his eyes and sighed. Then he walked swiftly toward the small family, knelt on the straw beside the infant, and gently removed first the father's tattered cloak and then the mother's from the manger. He handed each back to its owner. Both were too shocked at Hafid's boldness to react. Then Hafid opened his precious red robe and wrapped it gently around the sleeping child.

Moisture from the young mother's kiss was still on Hafid's cheek as he led his animal out of the cave. Directly above him was the brightest star Hafid had ever seen. He stared up at it until his eyes filled with tears and then he headed his animal through the path that led toward the main road back to Jerusalem and the caravan on the mountain.

Chapter V

Hafid rode slowly, his head bowed so that he no longer noticed the star spreading its path of light before him. Why had he committed such a foolish act? He knew not those people in the cave. Why had he not attempted to sell the robe to them? What would he tell Pathros? And the others? They would roll on the ground with laughter when they learned he had given away a robe with which he had been charged. And to a strange baby in a cave. He searched his mind for a tale that would deceive Pathros. Perhaps he could say that the robe had been stolen from his animal while he was in the dining hall. Would Pathros believe such a tale? After all, there were many bandits in the land. And should Pathros believe him would he not then be condemned for carelessness?

All too soon he reached the path that led through the Garden of Gethsemane. He dismounted and walked wearily ahead of the mule until he arrived at the caravan. The light from above made it seem as daylight and the confrontation he had been dreading was quickly upon him as he saw Pathros, outside his tent, staring into the heavens. Hafid remained motionless but the old man noticed him almost immediately.

There was awe in the voice of Pathros as he approached the youth and asked, "Have you come directly from Bethlehem?"

"Yes, master."

"Are you not alarmed that a star should follow you?"

"I had not noticed, sire."

"Had not noticed? I have been unable to move from this spot since I first saw that star rise over Bethlehem nearly two hours ago. Never have I seen one with more color and brightness. Then as I watched, it began to move in the heavens and approach our caravan. Now that it is directly overhead, you appear, and by the gods, it moves no more."

Pathros approached Hafid and studied the youth's face closely as he asked, "Did you participate in some extraordinary event while in Bethlehem?"

"No, sire."

The old man frowned as if deep in thought, "I have never known a night or an experience such as this."

Hafid flinched, "This night I shall never forget either, master."

"Oh, ho, then something did indeed happen this evening. How is it that thou returneth at such a late hour?"

Hafid was silent as the old man turned and prodded at the pack on Hafid's mule. "It is empty! Success at last.

32

Come into my tent and tell me of your experiences. Since the gods have turned night into day I cannot sleep and perhaps your words will furnish some clue as to why a star should follow a camel boy."

Pathros reclined on his cot and listened with closed eyes to Hafid's long tale of endless refusals, rebuffs, and insults which had been encountered in Bethlehem. Occasionally he would nod as when Hafid described the pottery merchant who had thrown him bodily from his shop and he smiled when told of the Roman soldier who had flung the robe back in Hafid's face when the young seller had refused to reduce his price.

Finally Hafid, his voice hoarse and muffled, was describing all the doubts that had beset him in the inn this very evening. Pathros interrupted him, "Hafid, as well as you can recall, relate to me every doubt that passed through your mind as you sat feeling sorry for yourself."

When Hafid had named them all to the best of his recollection, the old man asked, "Now, what thought finally entered your mind which drove away the doubts and gave you new courage to decide to try again to sell the robe on the morrow?"

Hafid considered his reply for a moment and then said, "I thought only of the daughter of Calneh. Even in that foul inn I knew that I could never face her again if I failed." Then Hafid's voice broke, "But I failed her, anyway."

"You failed? I do not understand. The robe did not return with thee."

In a voice so low that Pathros found it necessary to

lean forward in order to hear, Hafid related the incident of the cave, the infant, and the robe. As the youth spoke, Pathros glanced again and again at the open tent flap and the brightness beyond which still illuminated the camp grounds. A smile began to form on his puzzled face and he did not notice that the lad had ceased with his story and was now sobbing.

Soon the sobs subsided and there was only silence in the great tent. Hafid dared not look up at his master. He had failed and proven that he was ill-equipped to be anything more than a camel boy. He fought back the urge to leap up and run from the tent. Then he felt the great salesman's hand on his shoulder and forced himself to look into the eyes of Pathros.

"My son, this trip has not been of much profit to you."

"No, sire."

"But to me it has. The star which followed you has cured me of a blindness that I am reluctant to admit. I will explain this matter to you only after we return to Palmyra. Now I make a request of thee."

"Yes, master."

"Our sellers will begin returning to the caravan before sundown tomorrow and their animals will need your care. Are you willing to return to your duties as camel boy for the present?"

Hafid rose resignedly and bowed toward his benefactor. "Whatever you ask of me, that I will do . . . and I am sorry that I have failed you."

"Go then, and prepare for the return of our men and we shall meet again when we are in Palmyra."

As Hafid stepped through the tent opening, bright light from above momentarily blinded him. He rubbed his eyes and heard Pathros call from inside the tent.

The youth turned and stepped back inside, waiting for the old man to speak. Pathros pointed toward him and said, "Sleep in peace for you have not failed."

The bright star remained above throughout the night.

Chapter VI

Nearly a fortnight after the caravan had returned to its headquarters in Palmyra, Hafid was awakened from his straw cot in the stable, and summoned to appear before Pathros.

He hastened to the bed chamber of the master and stood uncertainly before the huge bed which dwarfed its occupant. Pathros opened his eyes and struggled with his coverings until he was sitting upright. His face was gaunt and blood vessels bulged in his hands. It was difficult for Hafid to believe that this was the same man with whom he had spoken only twelve days ago.

Pathros motioned toward the lower half of the bed and the youth sat carefully on its edge, waiting for the old man to speak. Even Pathros' voice was different in sound and pitch from their last meeting.

"My son, ye have had many days to reconsider your ambitions. Is it still within thee to become a great salesman?"

"Yes, sire."

The ancient head nodded. "So be it. I had planned to spend much time with you but as you can see there are other plans for me. Although I consider myself a good salesman I am unable to sell death on departing from my door. He has been waiting for days like a hungry dog at our kitchen door. Like the dog, he knows that eventually the door will be left unguarded. . . ."

Coughing interrupted Pathros and Hafid sat motionless as the old man gasped for air. Finally the coughs ceased and Pathros smiled weakly, "Our time together is brief so let us begin. First, remove the small cedar chest which is beneath this bed."

Hafid knelt and pulled out a small leather-strapped box. He placed it below the contour made by Pathros' legs on the bed. The old man cleared his throat, "Many years ago when I possessed less status than even a camel boy, I was privileged to rescue a traveler from the East who had been set upon by two bandits. He insisted that I had saved his life and wished to reward me although I sought none. Since I had neither a family nor funds he enjoined me to return with him to his home and kin where I was accepted as one of his own.

"One day, after I had grown accustomed to my new life, he introduced me to this chest. Inside were ten leather scrolls, each one numbered. The first contained the secret of learning. The others contained all the secrets and principles necessary to become a great success in the art of selling. For the next year I was tutored each day on the wise words of the scrolls and with the secret of learning from the first scroll I eventually memorized every word on every scroll until they had become a part of my thinking and my life. They became habit.

"At last I was presented with the chest containing all ten scrolls, a sealed letter, and a purse containing fifty gold pieces. The sealed letter was not to be opened until my adopted home was out of sight. I bade the family farewell and waited until I had reached the trade route to Palmyra before opening the letter. The contents commanded me to take the gold pieces, apply what I had learned from the scrolls, and begin a new life. The letter further commanded me to always share half of whatever wealth I would acquire with others less fortunate, but the leather scrolls were neither to be given nor shared with anyone until the day when I would be given a special sign that would tell me who was next chosen to receive these scrolls."

Hafid shook his head, "I do not understand, sire."

"I will explain. I have remained on watch for this person with a sign for many years and while I watched I applied what I learned from the scrolls to amass a great fortune. I had almost come to believe that no such person would ever appear before my death until you returned from your trip to Bethlehem. My first inkling that you were the chosen one to receive the scrolls came upon me when you appeared under the bright star that had followed you from Bethlehem. In my heart I have tried to comprehend the meaning of this event but I am resigned not to challenge the actions of the gods. Then when you told me of giving up the robe, which meant so much to you, something within my heart spoke and told me that my long search was ended. I had finally found he who was ordained to next receive the chest. Strangely, as soon as I knew I had found the right one, my life's energy began to slowly drain away. Now I am near the end but my long search is over and I can depart from this world in peace."

The old man's voice grew faint but he clenched his bony fists and leaned closer to Hafid. "Listen closely, my son, for I will have no strength to repeat these words."

Hafid's eyes were moist as he moved nearer to his master. Their hands touched and the great salesman inhaled with effort. "I now pass on this chest and its valuable contents to thee but first there are certain conditions to which you must agree. In the chest is a purse with one hundred gold talents. This will enable you to live and purchase a small supply of rugs with which you can enter the business world. I could bestow on you great wealth but this would do you a terrible disservice. Far better is it that you become the world's wealthiest and greatest salesman on your own. You see, I have not forgotten your goal.

"Depart from this city immediately and go to Damascus. There you will find unlimited opportunities to apply what the scrolls will teach. After you have secured lodging you will open only the scroll marked One. You are to read this over and over until you understand fully the secret method which it relates and which you will use in learning the principles of selling success contained on all the other scrolls. As you learn from each scroll you can begin to sell the rugs you have purchased, and if you combine what you lean with the experience you acquire, and continue to study each scroll as instructed, your sales will grow in number each day. My first condition then is that you must swear under oath that you will follow the instructions contained in the scroll marked One. Do you agree?"

"Yes, sire."

"Good, good . . . and when you apply the principles of the scrolls you will become far wealthier than you have ever dreamed. My second condition is that you must constantly dispose of half your earnings to those less fortunate than you. There must be no deviation from this condition. Will you agree?"

"Yes, sire."

"And now the most important condition of all. You are forbidden to share the scrolls or the wisdom they contain with anyone. One day there will appear a person who will transmit to you a sign just as the star and your unselfish actions were the sign I sought. When this happens you will recognize this sign even though the person transmitting it may be ignorant that he is the chosen person. When your heart assures you that you are correct you will pass over to him, or her, the chest and its contents and when this is done there need be no conditions imposed on the receiver such as were imposed on me and which I now impose on you. The letter which I received so long ago commanded that the third to receive the scrolls could share their message with the world if he so desires. Will you promise to carry out this third condition?"

"I will."

Pathros sighed in relief as if a heavy weight had been removed from his body. He smiled weakly and cupped Hafid's face in his bony hands. "Take the chest and depart. I will see thee no more. Go with my love and with my wishes for success and may your Lisha eventually share all the happiness your future will bring you."

Tears unashamedly rolled down Hafid's cheeks as he took the chest and carried it through the open bedroom door. He paused outside, placed the chest on the floor, and turned back toward his master, "Failure will never overtake me if my determination to succeed is strong enough?"

The old man smiled faintly and nodded. He raised his hand in farewell.

Chapter VII

Hafid, with his animal, entered the walled city of Damascus through the East gate. He rode along the street called Straight with doubts and trepidations, and the noise and shoutings from hundreds of bazaars did little to ease his fear. It was one thing to arrive in a large city with a powerful trade caravan such as that of Pathros; it was another to be unprotected and alone. Street merchants rushed at him from all sides holding up merchandise, each screaming louder than the next. He passed cell-like shops and bazaars displaying craftsmanship of coppersmiths, silversmiths, saddlers, weavers, carpenters; and each step of his mule brought him face to face with another vender, hands outstretched, wailing words of self-pity.

Directly ahead of him, beyond the western wall of the city, rose Mt. Hermon. Although the season was summer, its top was still capped with white and it seemed to look

down on the cacophony of the market place with toler-
ance and forbearance. Eventually Hafid turned off the
famous street and inquired about lodging which he had
no difficulty finding in an inn called Moscha. His room
was clean and he paid his rent for a month in advance
which immediately established his standing with Anto-
nine, the owner. Then he stabled his animal behind the
inn, bathed himself in the waters of the Barada and returned to his room.

He placed the small cedar chest at the foot of his cot
and proceeded to unroll the leather strappings. The
cover opened easily and he gazed down at the leather
scrolls. Finally he reached inside and touched the
leather. It gave under his fingers as if it were alive and
he hurriedly withdrew his hand. He arose and stepped
toward the latticed window through which sounds
poured from the noisy market place nearly half a mile
distant. Fear and doubt returned again as he looked in
the direction of the muffled voices and he felt his confidence waning. He closed his eyes, leaned his head
against the wall, and cried aloud, "How foolish I am to
dream that I, a mere camel boy, will one day be acclaimed as the greatest salesman in the world when I
have not even the courage to ride through the stalls of
the hawkers in the street. Today mine eyes have witnessed hundreds of salesmen, all far better equipped for
their profession than I. All had boldness, enthusiasm,
and persistence. All seemed equipped to survive in the

jungle of the market. How stupid and presumptuous to think I can compete with and surpass them. Pathros, my Pathros, I fear that I will fail you again."

He threw himself on his cot and weary from his travels he sobbed until he slept.

When he awoke it was morning. Even before he opened his eyes he heard the chirp. Then he sat up and stared in disbelief at the sparrow perched on the open cover of the chest containing the scrolls. He ran to the window. Outside, thousands of sparrows clustered in the fig trees and sycamores, each welcoming the day with song. As he watched, some landed on the window ledge but quickly flew away when Hafid moved even slightly. Then he turned and looked at the chest again. His feathered visitor cocked its head and stared back at the youth.

Hafid walked slowly to the chest, his hand extended. The bird leaped into his palm. "Thousands of your kind are outside and afraid. But you had the courage to come through the window."

The bird pecked sharply at Hafid's skin and the youth carried him toward the table where his knapsack contained bread and cheese. He broke off chunks and placed them beside his small friend who began to eat.

A thought came to Hafid and he returned to the window. He rubbed his hand against the openings in the lattice. They were so small that it seemed almost impossible for the sparrow to have entered. Then he remembered the voice of Pathros and he repeated the words aloud, "Failure will never overtake you if your determination to succeed is strong enough."

He returned to the chest and reached inside. One leather scroll was more worn than the rest. He removed it from the box and gently unrolled it. The fear he had known was gone. Then he looked toward the sparrow. He too was gone. Only crumbs of bread and cheese remained as evidence of his visit from the little bird with courage. Hafid glanced down at the scroll. Its heading read *The Scroll Marked I.* He began to read. . . .

Chapter VIII

The Scroll Marked I

Today I begin a new life.

Today I shed my old skin which hath, too long, suffered the bruises of failure and the wounds of mediocrity.

Today I am born anew and my birthplace is a vineyard where there is fruit for all.

Today I will pluck grapes of wisdom from the tallest and fullest vines in the vineyard, for these were planted by the wisest of my profession who have come before me, generation upon generation.

Today I will savor the taste of grapes from these vines and verily I will swallow the seed of success buried in each and new life will sprout within me.

The career I have chosen is laden with opportunity yet it is fraught with heartbreak and despair, and the bodies of those who have failed, were they piled one atop another, would cast its shadow down upon all the pyramids of the earth.

Yet I will not fail, as the others, for in my hands I now hold the charts which will guide me through perilous waters to shores which only yesterday seemed but a dream.

Failure no longer will be my payment for struggle. Just as nature made no provision for my body to tolerate pain neither has it made any provision for my life to suffer failure. Failure, like pain, is alien to my life. In the past I accepted it as I accepted pain. Now I reject it and I am prepared for wisdom and principles which will guide me out of the shadows into the sunlight of wealth, position, and happiness far beyond my most extravagant dreams until even the golden apples in the Garden of Hesperides will seem no more than my just reward.

Time teaches all things to he who lives forever but I have not the luxury of eternity. Yet, within my allotted time I must practice the art of patience for nature acts never in haste. To create the olive, king of all trees, a hundred years is required. An onion plant is old in nine weeks. I have lived as an onion plant. It has not pleased me. Now I wouldst become the greatest of olive trees and, in truth, the greatest of salesmen.

And how will this be accomplished? For I have neither the knowledge nor the experience to achieve greatness and already I have stumbled in ignorance and fallen into pools of self-pity. The answer is simple. I will commence my journey unencumbered with either the weight of unnecessary knowledge or the handicap of meaningless experience. Nature already has supplied me with knowledge and instinct far greater than any beast in the forest and the value of experience is overrated, usually by old men who nod wisely and speak stupidly.

In truth, experience teaches thoroughly yet her course of instruction devours men's years so the value of her lessons diminishes with the time necessary to acquire her special wisdom. The end finds it wasted on dead men. Furthermore, experience is comparable to fashion; an action that proved successful today will be unworkable and impractical tomorrow.

Only principles endure and these I now possess, for the laws that will lead me to greatness are contained in the words of these scrolls. What they will teach me is more to prevent failure than to gain success, for what is success other than a state of mind? Which two, among a thousand wise men, will define success in the same words; yet failure is always described but one way. *Failure is man's inability to reach his goals in life, whatever they may be.*

In truth, the only difference between those who have failed and those who have succeeded lies in the difference of their habits. Good habits are the key to all success. Bad habits are the unlocked door to failure. Thus, the first law I will obey, which precedeth all others is— *I will form good habits and become their slaves.*

As a child I was slave to my impulses; now I am slave to my habits, as are all grown men. I have surrendered my free will to the years of accumulated habits and the past deeds of my life have already marked out a path which threatens to imprison my future. My actions are ruled by appetite, passion, prejudice, greed, love, fear, environment, habit, and the worst of these tyrants is habit. Therefore, if I must be a slave to habit let me be a slave to good habits. My bad habits must be destroyed and new furrows prepared for good seed.

I will form good habits and become their slave.

And how will I accomplish this difficult feat? Through these scrolls, it will be done, for each scroll contains a principle which will drive a bad habit from my life and replace it with one which will bring me closer to success. For it is another of nature's laws that only a habit can subdue another habit. So, in order for these written words to perform their chosen task, I must discipline myself with the first of my new habits which is as follows:

I will read each scroll for thirty days in this prescribed manner, before I proceed to the next scroll.

First, I will read the words in silence when I arise. Then, I will read the words in silence after I have partaken of my midday meal. Last, I will read the words again just before I retire at day's end, and most important, on this occasion I will read the words aloud.

On the next day I will repeat this procedure, and I will continue in like manner for thirty days. Then, I will turn to the next scroll and repeat this procedure for another thirty days. I will continue in this manner until I have lived with each scroll for thirty days and my reading has become habit.

And what will be accomplished with this habit?

Herein lies the hidden secret of all man's accomplishments. As I repeat the words daily they will soon become a part of my active mind, but more important, they will also seep into my other mind, that mysterious source which never sleeps, which creates my dreams, and often makes me act in ways I do not comprehend.

As the words of these scrolls are consumed by my mysterious mind I will begin to awake, each morning, with a vitality I have never known before. My vigor will increase, my enthusiasm will rise, my desire to meet the world will overcome every fear I once knew at sunrise, and I will be happier than I ever believed it possible to be in this world of strife and sorrow.

Eventually I will find myself reacting to all situations which confront me as I was commanded in the scrolls to react, and soon these actions and reactions will become easy to perform, for any act with practice becomes easy.

Thus a new and good habit is born, for when an act becomes easy through constant repetition it becomes a pleasure to perform and if it is a pleasure to perform it is man's nature to perform it often. When I perform it often it becomes a habit and I become its slave and since it is a good habit this is my will.

Today I begin a new life.

And I make a solemn oath to myself that nothing will retard my new life's growth. I will lose not a day from these readings for that day cannot be retrieved nor can I substitute another for it. I must not, I will not, break this habit of daily reading from these scrolls and, in truth, the few moments spent each day on this new habit are but a small price to pay for the happiness and success that will be mine.

As I read and re-read the words in the scrolls to follow, never will I allow the brevity of each scroll nor the simplicity of its words to cause me to treat the scroll's message lightly. Thousands of grapes are pressed to fill one jar with wine, and the grapeskin and pulp are tossed to the birds. So it is with these grapes of wisdom from the ages. Much has been filtered and tossed to the wind. Only the pure truth lies distilled in the words to come. I will drink as instructed and spill not a drop. And the seed of success I will swallow.

Today my old skin has become as dust. I will walk tall among men and they will know me not, for today I am a new man, with a new life.

Chapter IX

The Scroll Marked II

I will greet this day with love in my heart.

For this is the greatest secret of success in all ventures. Muscle can split a shield and even destroy life but only the unseen power of love can open the hearts of men and until I master this art I will remain no more than a peddler in the market place. I will make love my greatest weapon and none on whom I call can defend against its force.

My reasoning they may counter; my speech they may distrust; my apparel they may disapprove; my face they may reject; and even my bargains may cause them suspicion; yet my love will melt all hearts liken to the sun whose rays soften the coldest clay.

I will greet this day with love in my heart.

And how will I do this? Henceforth will I look on all things with love and I will be born again. I will love the sun for it warms my bones; yet I will love the rain for it cleanses my spirit. I will love the light for it shows me the way; yet I will love the darkness for it shows me the stars. I will welcome happiness for it enlarges my heart; yet I will endure sadness for it opens my soul. I will acknowledge rewards for they are my due; yet I will welcome obstacles for they are my challenge.

I will greet this day with love in my heart.

And how will I speak? I will laud mine enemies and they will become friends; I will encourage my friends and they will become brothers. Always will I dig for reasons to applaud; never will I scratch for excuses to gossip. When I am tempted to criticize I will bite on my tongue; when I am moved to praise I will shout from the roofs.

Is it not so that birds, the wind, the sea and all nature speaks with the music of praise for their creator? Cannot I speak with the same music to his children? Henceforth will I remember this secret and it will change my life.

I will greet this day with love in my heart.

And how will I act? I will love all manners of men for each has qualities to be admired even though they be hidden. With love I will tear down the wall of suspicion and hate which they have built round their hearts and in its place will I build bridges so that my love may enter their souls.

I will love the ambitious for they can inspire me; I will love the failures for they can teach me. I will love the kings for they are but human; I will love the meek for they are divine. I will love the rich for they are yet lonely; I will love the poor for they are so many. I will love the young for the faith they hold; I will love the old for the wisdom they share. I will love the beautiful for their eyes of sadness; I will love the ugly for their souls of peace.

I will greet this day with love in my heart.

But how will I react to the actions of others? With love. For just as love is my weapon to open the hearts of men, love is also my shield to repulse the arrows of hate and the spears of anger. Adversity and discouragement will beat against my new shield and become as the softest of rains. My shield will protect me in the market place and sustain me when I am alone. It will uplift me in moments of despair yet it will calm me in time of exultation. It will become stronger and more protective with use until one day I will cast it aside and walk unencumbered among all manners of men and, when I do, my name will be raised high on the pyramid of life.

I will greet this day with love in my heart.

And how will I confront each whom I meet? In only one way. In silence and to myself I will address him and say I Love You. Though spoken in silence these words will shine in my eyes, unwrinkle my brow, bring a smile to my lips, and echo in my voice; and his heart will be opened. And who is there who will say nay to my goods when his heart feels my love?

I will greet this day with love in my heart.

And most of all I will love myself. For when I do I will zealousy inspect all things which enter my body, my mind, my soul, and my heart. Never will I overindulge the requests of my flesh, rather I will cherish my body with cleanliness and moderation. Never will I allow my mind to be attracted to evil and despair, rather I will uplift it with the knowledge and wisdom of the ages. Never will I allow my soul to become complacent and satisfied, rather I will feed it with meditation and prayer. Never will I allow my heart to become small and bitter, rather I will share it and it will grow and warm the earth.

I will greet this day with love in my heart.

Henceforth will I love all mankind. From this moment all hate is let from my veins for I have not time to hate, only time to love. From this moment I take the first step required to become a man among men. With love I will increase my sales a hundredfold and become a great salesman. If I have no other qualities I can succeed with love alone. Without it I will fail though I possess all the knowledge and skills of the world.

I will greet this day with love, and I will succeed.

Chapter X

The Scroll Marked III

I will persist until I succeed.

In the Orient young bulls are tested for the fight arena in a certain manner. Each is brought to the ring and allowed to attack a picador who pricks them with a lance. The bravery of each bull is then rated with care according to the number of times he demonstrates his willingness to charge in spite of the sting of the blade. Henceforth will I recognize that each day I am tested by life in like manner. If I persist, if I continue to try, if I continue to charge forward, I will succeed.

I will persist until I succeed.

I was not delivered unto this world in defeat, nor does failure course in my veins. I am not a sheep waiting to be prodded by my shepherd. I am a lion and I refuse to talk, to walk, to sleep with the sheep. I will hear not those who weep and complain, for their disease is contagious. Let them join the sheep. The slaughterhouse of failure is not my destiny.

I will persist until I succeed.

The prizes of life are at the end of each journey, not near the beginning; and it is not given to me to know how many steps are necessary in order to reach my goal. Failure I may still encounter at the thousandth step, yet success hides behind the next bend in the road. Never will I know how close it lies unless I turn the corner.

Always will I take another step. If that is of no avail I will take another, and yet another. In truth, one step at a time is not too difficult.

I will persist until I succeed.

Henceforth, I will consider each day's effort as but one blow of my blade against a mighty oak. The first blow may cause not a tremor in the wood, nor the second, nor the third. Each blow, of itself, may be trifling, and seem of no consequence. Yet from childish swipes the oak will eventually tumble. So it will be with my efforts of today.

I will be liken to the rain drop which washes away the mountain; the ant who devours a tiger; the star which brightens the earth; the slave who builds a pyramid. I will build my castle one brick at a time for I know that small attempts, repeated, will complete any undertaking.

I will persist until I succeed.

I will never consider defeat and I will remove from my vocabulary such words and phrases as quit, cannot, unable, impossible, out of the question, improbable, failure, unworkable, hopeless, and retreat; for they are the words of fools. I will avoid despair but if this disease of the mind should infect me then I will work on in despair. I will toil and I will endure. I will ignore the obstacles at my feet and keep mine eyes on the goals above my head, for I know that where dry desert ends, green grass grows.

I will persist until I succeed.

I will remember the ancient law of averages and I will bend it to my good. I will persist with knowledge that each failure to sell will increase my chance for success at the next attempt. Each nay I hear will bring me closer to the sound of yea. Each frown I meet only prepares me for the smile to come. Each misfortune I encounter will carry in it the seed of tomorrow's good luck. I must have the night to appreciate the day. I must fail often to succeed only once.

I will persist until I succeed.

I will try, and try, and try again. Each obstacle I will consider as a mere detour to my goal and a challenge to my profession. I will persist and develop my skills as the mariner develops his, by learning to ride out the wrath of each storm.

I will persist until I succeed.

Henceforth, I will learn and apply another secret of those who excel in my work. When each day is ended, not regarding whether it has been a success or a failure, I will attempt to achieve one more sale. When my thoughts beckon my tired body homeward I will resist the temptation to depart. I will try again. I will make one more attempt to close with victory, and if that fails I will make another. Never will I allow any day to end with a failure. Thus will I plant the seed of tomorrow's success and gain an insurmountable advantage over those who cease their labor at a prescribed time. When others cease their struggle, then mine will begin, and my harvest will be full.

I will persist until I succeed.

Nor will I allow yesterday's success to lull me into today's complacency, for this is the great foundation of failure. I will forget the happenings of the day that is gone, whether they were good or bad, and greet the new sun with confidence that this will be the best day of my life.

So long as there is breath in me, that long will I persist. For now I know one of the greatest principles of success; if I persist long enough I will win.

I will persist.

I will win.

Chapter XI

The Scroll Marked IV

I am nature's greatest miracle.

Since the beginning of time never has there been another with my mind, my heart, my eyes, my ears, my hands, my hair, my mouth. None that came before, none that live today, and none that come tomorrow can walk and talk and move and think exactly like me. All men are my brothers yet I am different from each. I am a unique creature.

I am nature's greatest miracle.

Although I am of the animal kingdom, animal rewards alone will not satisfy me. Within me burns a flame which has been passed from generations uncounted and its heat is a constant irritation to my spirit to become better than I am, and I will. I will fan this flame of dissatisfaction and proclaim my uniqueness to the world.

None can duplicate my brush strokes, none can make my chisel marks, none can duplicate my handwriting, none can produce my child, and, in truth, none has the ability to sell exactly as I. Henceforth, I will capitalize on this difference for it is an asset to be promoted to the fullest.

I am nature's greatest miracle.

Vain attempts to imitate others no longer will I make. Instead will I place my uniqueness on display in the market place. I will proclaim it, yea, I will sell it. I will begin now to accent my differences; hide my similarities. So too will I apply this principle to the goods I sell. Salesman and goods, different from all others, and proud of the difference.

I am a unique creature of nature.

I am rare, and there is value in all rarity; therefore, I am valuable. I am the end product of thousands of years of evolution; therefore, I am better equipped in both mind and body than all the emperors and wise men who preceded me.

But my skills, my mind, my heart, and my body will stagnate, rot, and die lest I put them to good use. I have unlimited potential. Only a small portion of my brain do I employ; only a paltry amount of my muscles do I flex. A hundredfold or more can I increase my accomplishments of yesterday and this I will do, beginning today.

Nevermore will I be satisfied with yesterday's accomplishments nor will I indulge, anymore, in self-praise for deeds which in reality are too small to even acknowledge. I can accomplish far more than I have, and I will, for why should the miracle which produced me end with my birth? Why can I not extend that miracle to my deeds of today?

I am nature's greatest miracle.

I am not on this earth by chance. I am here for a purpose and that purpose is to grow into a mountain, not to shrink to a grain of sand. Henceforth will I apply all my efforts to become the highest mountain of all and I will strain my potential until it cries for mercy.

I will increase my knowledge of mankind, myself, and the goods I sell, thus my sales will multiply. I will practice, and improve, and polish the words I utter to sell my goods, for this is the foundation on which I will build my career and never will I forget that many have attained great wealth and success with only one sales talk, delivered with excellence. Also will I seek constantly to improve my manners and graces, for they are the sugar to which all are attracted.

I am nature's greatest miracle.

I will concentrate my energy on the challenge of the moment and my actions will help me forget all else. The problems of my home will be left in my home. I will think naught of my family when I am in the market place for this will cloud my thoughts. So too will the problems of the market place be left in the market place and I will think naught of my profession when I am in my home for this will dampen my love.

There is no room in the market place for my family, nor is there room in my home for the market. Each I will divorce from the other and thus will I remain wedded to both. Separate must they remain or my career will die. This is a paradox of the ages.

I am nature's greatest miracle.

I have been given eyes to see and a mind to think and now I know a great secret of life for I perceive, at last, that all my problems, discouragements, and heart-aches are, in truth, great opportunities in disguise. I will no longer be fooled by the garments they wear for mine eyes are open. I will look beyond the cloth and I will not be deceived.

I am nature's greatest miracle.

No beast, no plant, no wind, no rain, no rock, no lake had the same beginning as I, for I was conceived in love and brought forth with a purpose. In the past I have not considered this fact but it will henceforth shape and guide my life.

I am nature's greatest miracle.

And nature knows not defeat. Eventually, she emerges victorious and so will I, and with each victory the next struggle becomes less difficult.

I will win, and I will become a great salesman, for I am unique.

I am nature's greatest miracle.

Chapter XII

The Scroll Marked V

I will live this day as if it is my last.

And what shall I do with this last precious day which remains in my keeping? First, I will seal up its container of life so that not one drop spills itself upon the sand. I will waste not a moment mourning yesterday's misfortunes, yesterday's defeats, yesterday's aches of the heart, for why should I throw good after bad?

Can sand flow upward in the hour glass? Will the sun rise where it sets and set where it rises? Can I relive the errors of yesterday and right them? Can I call back yesterday's wounds and make them whole? Can I become younger than yesterday? Can I take back the evil that was spoken, the blows that were struck, the pain that was caused? No. Yesterday is buried forever and I will think of it no more.

I will live this day as if it is my last.

And what then shall I do? Forgetting yesterday neither will I think of tomorrow. Why should I throw *now* after *maybe?* Can tomorrow's sand flow through the glass before today's? Will the sun rise twice this morning? Can I perform tomorrow's deeds while standing in today's path? Can I place tomorrow's gold in today's purse? Can tomorrow's child be born today? Can tomorrow's death cast its shadow backward and darken today's joy? Should I concern myself over events which I may never witness? Should I torment myself with problems that may never come to pass? No! Tomorrow lies buried with yesterday, and I will think of it no more.

I will live this day as if it is my last.

This day is all I have and these hours are now my eternity. I greet this sunrise with cries of joy as a prisoner who is reprieved from death. I lift mine arms with thanks for this priceless gift of a new day. So too, I will beat upon my heart with gratitude as I consider all who greeted yesterday's sunrise who are no longer with the living today. I am indeed a fortunate man and today's hours are but a bonus, undeserved. Why have I been allowed to live this extra day when others, far better than I, have departed? Is it that they have accomplished their purpose while mine is yet to be achieved? Is this another opportunity for me to become the man I know I can be? Is there a purpose in nature? Is this my day to excel?

I will live this day as if it is my last.

I have but one life and life is naught but a measurement of time. When I waste one I destroy the other, If I waste today I destroy the last page of my life. Therefore, each hour of this day will I cherish for it can never return. It cannot be banked today to be withdrawn on the morrow, for who can trap the wind? Each minute of this day will I grasp with both hands and fondle with love for its value is beyond price. What dying man can purchase another breath though he willingly give all his gold? What price dare I place on the hours ahead? I will make them priceless!

I will live this day as if it is my last.

I will avoid with fury the killers of time. Procrastination I will destroy with action; doubt I will bury under faith; fear I will dismember with confidence. Where there are idle mouths I will listen not; where there are idle hands I will linger not; where there are idle bodies I will visit not. Henceforth I know that to court idleness is to steal food, clothing, and warmth from those I love. I am not a thief. I am a man of love and today is my last chance to prove my love and my greatness.

I will live this day as if it is my last.

The duties of today I shall fulfill today. Today I shall fondle my children while they are young; tomorrow they will be gone, and so will I. Today I shall embrace my woman with sweet kisses; tomorrow she will be gone, and so will I. Today I shall lift up a friend in need; tomorrow he will no longer cry for help, nor will I hear his cries. Today I shall give myself in sacrifice and work; tomorrow I will have nothing to give, and there will be none to receive.

I will live this day as if it is my last.

And if it is my last, it will be my greatest monument. This day I will make the best day of my life. This day I will drink every minute to its full. I will savor its taste and give thanks. I will maketh every hour count and each minute I will trade only for something of value. I will labor harder than ever before and push my muscles until they cry for relief, and then I will continue. I will make more calls than ever before. I will sell more goods than ever before. I will earn more gold than ever before. Each minute of today will be more fruitful than hours of yesterday. My last must be my best.

I will live this day as if it is my last.

And if it is not, I shall fall to my knees and give thanks.

Chapter XIII

The Scroll Marked VI

Today I will be master of my emotions.

The tides advance; the tides recede. Winter goes and summer comes. Summer wanes and the cold increases. The sun rises; the sun sets. The moon is full; the moon is black. The birds arrive; the birds depart. Flowers bloom; flowers fade. Seeds are sown; harvests are reaped. All nature is a circle of moods and I am a part of nature and so, like the tides, my moods will rise; my moods will fall.

Today I will be master of my emotions.

It is one of nature's tricks, little understood, that each day I awaken with moods that have changed from yesterday. Yesterday's joy will become today's sadness; yet today's sadness will grow into tomorrow's joy. Inside me is a wheel, constantly turning from sadness to joy, from exultation to depression, from happiness to melancholy. Like the flowers, today's full bloom of joy will fade and wither into despondency, yet I will remember that as today's dead flower carries the seed of tomorrow's bloom so, too, does today's sadness carry the seed of tomorrow's joy.

Today I will be master of my emotions.

And how will I master these emotions so that each day will be productive? For unless my mood is right the day will be a failure. Trees and plants depend on the weather to flourish but I make my own weather, yea I transport it with me. If I bring rain and gloom and darkness and pessimism to my customers then they will react with rain and gloom and darkness and pessimism and they will purchase naught. If I bring joy and enthusiasm and brightness and laughter to my customers they will react with joy and enthusiasm and brightness and laughter and my weather will produce a harvest of sales and a granary of gold for me.

Today I will be master of my emotions.

And how will I master my emotions so that every day is a happy day, and a productive one? I will learn this secret of the ages: *Weak is he who permits his thoughts to control his actions; strong is he who forces his actions to control his thoughts.* Each day, when I awake, I will follow this plan of battle before I am captured by the forces of sadness, self-pity and failure—

If I feel depressed I will sing.
If I feel sad I will laugh.
If I feel ill I will double my labor.
If I feel fear I will plunge ahead.

If I feel inferior I will wear new garments.
If I feel uncertain I will raise my voice.
If I feel poverty I will think of wealth to come.
If I feel incompetent I will remember past success.
If I feel insignificant I will remember my goals.
Today I will be master of my emotions.

Henceforth, I will know that only those with inferior ability can always be at their best, and I am not inferior. There will be days when I must constantly struggle against forces which would tear me down. Those such as despair and sadness are simple to recognize but there are others which approach with a smile and the hand of friendship and they can also destroy me. Against them, too, I must never relinquish control—

If I become overconfident I will recall my failures.
If I overindulge I will think of past hungers.
If I feel complacency I will remember my competition.
If I enjoy moments of greatness I will remember moments of shame.
If I feel all-powerful I will try to stop the wind.
If I attain great wealth I will remember one unfed mouth.
If I become overly proud I will remember a moment of weakness.
If I feel my skill is unmatched I will look at the stars.
Today I will be master of my emotions.

And with this new knowledge I will also understand and recognize the moods of he on whom I call. I will make allowances for his anger and irritation of today for he knows not the secret of controlling his mind. I can withstand his arrows and insults for now I know that tomorrow he will change and be a joy to approach.

No longer will I judge a man on one meeting; no longer will I fail to call again tomorrow on he who meets me with hate today. This day he will not buy gold chariots for a penny, yet tomorrow he would exchange his home for a tree. My knowledge of this secret will be my key to great wealth.

Today I will be master of my emotions.

Henceforth I will recognize and identify the mystery of moods in all mankind, and in me. From this moment I am prepared to control whatever personality awakes in me each day. I will master my moods through positive action and when I master my moods I will control my destiny.

Today I control my destiny, and my destiny is to become the greatest salesman in the world!

I will become master of myself.

I will become great.

Chapter XIV

The Scroll Marked VII

I will laugh at the world.

No living creature can laugh except man. Trees may bleed when they are wounded, and beasts in the field will cry in pain and hunger, yet only I have the gift of laughter and it is mine to use whenever I choose. Henceforth I will cultivate the habit of laughter.

I will smile and my digestion will improve; I will chuckle and my burdens will be lightened; I will laugh and my life will be lengthened for this is the great secret of long life and now it is mine.

I will laugh at the world.

And most of all, I will laugh at myself for man is most comical when he takes himself too seriously. Never will I fall into this trap of the mind. For though I be nature's greatest miracle am I not still a mere grain tossed about by the winds of time? Do I truly know whence I came or whither I am bound? Will my concern for this day not seem foolish ten years hence? Why should I permit the petty happenings of today to disturb me? What can take place before this sun sets which will not seem insignificant in the river of centuries?

I will laugh at the world.

And how can I laugh when confronted with man or deed which offends me so as to bring forth my tears or my curses? Four words I will train myself to say until they become a habit so strong that immediately they will appear in my mind whenever good humor threatens to depart from me. These words, passed down from the ancients, will carry me through every adversity and maintain my life in balance. These four words are: *This too shall pass.*

I will laugh at the world.

For all worldly things shall indeed pass. When I am heavy with heartache I shall console myself that this too shall pass; when I am puffed with success I shall warn myself that this too shall pass. When I am strangled in poverty I shall tell myself that this too shall pass; when I am burdened with wealth I shall tell myself that this too shall pass. Yea, verily, where is he who built the pyramid? Is he not buried within its stone? And will the pyramid, one day, not also be buried under sand? If all things shall pass why should I be of concern for today?

I will laugh at the world.

I will paint this day with laughter; I will frame this night in song. Never will I labor to be happy; rather will I remain too busy to be sad. I will enjoy today's happiness today. It is not grain to be stored in a box. It is not wine to be saved in a jar. It cannot be saved for the morrow. It must be sown and reaped on the same day and this I will do, henceforth.

I will laugh at the world.

And with my laughter all things will be reduced to their proper size. I will laugh at my failures and they will vanish in clouds of new dreams; I will laugh at my successes and they will shrink to their true value. I will laugh at evil and it will die untasted; I will laugh at goodness and it will thrive and abound. Each day will be triumphant only when my smiles bring forth smiles from others and this I do in selfishness, for those on whom I frown are those who purchase not my goods.

I will laugh at the world.

Henceforth will I shed only tears of sweat, for those of sadness or remorse or frustration are of no value in the market place whilst each smile can be exchanged for gold and each kind word, spoken from my heart, can build a castle.

Never will I allow myself to become so important, so wise, so dignified, so powerful, that I forget how to laugh at myself and my world. In this matter I will always remain as a child, for only as a child am I given the ability to look up to others; and so long as I look up to another I will never grow too long for my cot.

I will laugh at the world.

And so long as I can laugh never will I be poor. This then, is one of nature's greatest gifts, and I will waste it no more. Only with laughter and happiness can I truly become a success. Only with laughter and happiness can I enjoy the fruits of my labor. Were it not so, far better would it be to fail, for happiness is the wine that sharpens the taste of the meal. To enjoy success I must have happiness, and laughter will be the maiden who serves me.

I will be happy.

I will be successful.

I will be the greatest salesman the world has ever known.

Chapter XV

The Scroll Marked VIII

Today I will multiply my value a hundredfold.

A mulberry leaf touched with the genius of man becomes silk.

A field of clay touched with the genius of man becomes a castle.

A cyprus tree touched with the genius of man becomes a shrine.

A cut of sheep's hair touched with the genius of man becomes raiment for a king.

If it is possible for leaves and clay and wood and hair to have their value multiplied a hundred, yea a thousandfold by man, cannot I do the same with the clay which bears my name?

Today I will multiply my value a hundredfold.

I am liken to a grain of wheat which faces one of three futures. The wheat can be placed in a sack and dumped in a stall until it is fed to swine. Or it can be ground to flour and made into bread. Or it can be placed in the

earth and allowed to grow until its golden head divides
and produces a thousand grains from the one.

I am liken to a grain of wheat with one difference. The
wheat cannot choose whether it be fed to swine, ground
for bread, or planted to multiply. I have a choice and I
will not let my life be fed to swine nor will I let it be
ground under the rocks of failure and despair to be
broken open and devoured by the will of others.

Today I will multiply my value a hundredfold.

To grow and multiply it is necessary to plant the
wheat grain in the darkness of the earth and my failures,
my despairs, my ignorance, and my inabilities are the
darkness in which I have been planted in order to ripen.
Now, like the wheat grain which will sprout and blossom
only if it is nurtured with rain and sun and warm winds,
I too must nurture my body and mind to fulfill my
dreams. But to grow to full stature the wheat must wait
on the whims of nature. I need not wait for I have the
power to choose my own destiny.

Today I will multiply my value a hundredfold.

And how will I accomplish this? First I will set goals
for the day, the week, the month, the year, and my life.
Just as the rain must fall before the wheat will crack its
shell and sprout, so must I have objectives before my
life will crystallize. In setting my goals I will consider
my best performance of the past and multiply it a hundredfold. This will be the standard by which I will live
in the future. Never will I be of concern that my goals
are too high for is it not better to aim my spear at the

moon and strike only an eagle than to aim my spear at the eagle and strike only a rock?

Today I will multiply my value a hundredfold.

The height of my goals will not hold me in awe though I may stumble often before they are reached. If I stumble I will rise and my falls will not concern me for all men must stumble often to reach the hearth. Only a worm is free from the worry of stumbling. I am not a worm. I am not an onion plant. I am not a sheep. I am a man. Let others build a cave with their clay. I will build a castle with mine.

Today I will multiply my value a hundredfold.

And just as the sun must warm the earth to bring forth the seedling of wheat so, too, will the words on these scrolls warm my life and turn my dreams into reality. Today I will surpass every action which I performed yesterday. I will climb today's mountain to the utmost of my ability yet tomorrow I will climb higher than today, and the next will be higher than tomorrow. To surpass the deeds of others is unimportant; to surpass my own deeds is all.

Today I will multiply my value a hundredfold.

And just as the warm wind guides the wheat to maturity, the same winds will carry my voice to those who will listen and my words will announce my goals. Once spoken I dare not recall them lest I lose face. I will be as my own prophet and though all may laugh at my utterances they will hear my plans, they will know my dreams; and thus there will be no escape for me until my words become accomplished deeds.

Today I will multiply my value a hundredfold.

I will commit not the terrible crime of aiming too low.

I will do the work that a failure will not do.

I will always let my reach exceed my grasp.

I will never be content with my performance in the market.

I will always raise my goals as soon as they are attained.

I will always strive to make the next hour better than this one.

I will always announce my goals to the world.

Yet, never will I proclaim my accomplishments. Let the world, instead, approach me with praise and may I have the wisdom to receive it in humility.

Today I will multiply my value a hundredfold.

One grain of wheat when multiplied a hundredfold will produce a hundred stalks. Multiply these a hundredfold, ten times, and they will feed all the cities of the earth. Am I not more than a grain of wheat?

Today I will multiply my value a hundredfold.

And when it is done I will do it again, and again, and there will be astonishment and wonder at my greatness as the words of these scrolls are fulfilled in me.

Chapter XVI

The Scroll Marked IX

My dreams are worthless, my plans are dust, my goals are impossible.

All are of no value unless they are followed by action. I will act now.

Never has there been a map, however carefully executed to detail and scale, which carried its owner over even one inch of ground. Never has there been a parchment of law, however fair, which prevented one crime. Never has there been a scroll, even such as the one I hold, which earned so much as a penny or produced a single word of acclamation. Action, alone, is the tinder which ignites the map, the parchment, this scroll, my dreams, my plans, my goals, into a living force. Action is the food and drink which will nourish my success.

I will act now.

My procrastination which has held me back was born of fear and now I recognize this secret mined from the depths of all courageous hearts. Now I know that to conquer fear I must always act without hesitation and the flutters in my heart will vanish. Now I know that action reduces the lion of terror to an ant of equanimity.

I will act now.

Henceforth, I will remember the lesson of the firefly who gives off its light only when it is on the wing, only when it is in action. I will become a firefly and even in the day my glow will be seen in spite of the sun. Let others be as butterflies who preen their wings yet depend on the charity of a flower for life. I will be as the firefly and my light will brighten the world.

I will act now.

I will not avoid the tasks of today and charge them to tomorrow for I know that tomorrow never comes. Let me act now even though my actions may not bring happiness or success for it is better to act and fail than not to act and flounder. Happiness, in truth, may not be the fruit plucked by my action yet without action all fruit will die on the vine.

I will act now.

I will act now. I will act now. I will act now. Henceforth, I will repeat these words again and again and again, each hour, each day, every day, until the words become as much a habit as my breathing and the actions which follow become as instinctive as the blinking of my eyelids. With these words I can condition my mind to perform every act necessary for my success. With these words I can condition my mind to meet every challenge which the failure avoids.

I will act now.

I will repeat these words again and again and again.

When I awake I will say them and leap from my cot while the failure sleeps yet another hour.

I will act now.

When I enter the market place I will say them and immediately confront my first prospect while the failure ponders yet his possibility of rebuff.

I will act now.

When I face a closed door I will say them and knock while the failure waits outside with fear and trepidation.

I will act now.

When I face temptation I will say them and immediately act to remove myself from evil.

I will act now.

When I am tempted to quit and begin again tomorrow I will say them and immediately act to consummate another sale.

I will act now.

Only action determines my value in the market place and to multiply my value I will multiply my actions. I will walk where the failure fears to walk. I will work when the failure seeks rest. I will talk when the failure remains silent. I will call on ten who can buy my goods while the failure makes grand plans to call on one. I will say it is done before the failure says it is too late.

I will act now.

For now is all I have. Tomorrow is the day reserved for the labor of the lazy. I am not lazy. Tomorrow is the day when the evil become good. I am not evil. Tomorrow is the day when the weak become strong. I am not weak. Tomorrow is the day when the failure will succeed. I am not a failure.

I will act now.

When the lion is hungry he eats. When the eagle has thirst he drinks. Lest they act, both will perish.

I hunger for success. I thirst for happiness and peace of mind. Lest I act I will perish in a life of failure, misery, and sleepless nights.

I will command, and I will obey mine own command.

I will act now.

Success will not wait. If I delay she will become betrothed to another and lost to me forever.

This is the time. This is the place. I am the man.

I will act now.

Chapter XVII

The Scroll Marked X

Who is of so little faith that in a moment of great disaster or heartbreak has not called to his God? Who has not cried out when confronted with danger, death, or mystery beyond his normal experience or comprehension? From where has this deep instinct come which escapes from the mouth of all living creatures in moments of peril?

Move your hand in haste before another's eyes and his eyelids will blink. Tap another on his knee and his leg will jump. Confront another with dark horror and his mouth will say, "My God" from the same deep impulse.

My life need not be filled with religion in order for me to recognize this greatest mystery of nature. All creatures that walk the earth, including man, possess the instinct to cry for help. Why do we possess this instinct, this gift?

Are not our cries a form of prayer? Is it not incomprehensible in a world governed by nature's laws to give a lamb, or a mule, or a bird, or man the instinct to cry out for help lest some great mind has also provided that the cry should be heard by some superior power having the ability to hear and to answer our cry? Henceforth I will pray, but my cries for help will only be cries for guidance.

Never will I pray for the material things of the world. I am not calling to a servant to bring me food. I am not ordering an innkeeper to provide me with room. Never will I seek delivery of gold, love, good health, petty victories, fame, success, or happiness. Only for guidance will I pray, that I may be shown the way to acquire these things, and my prayer will always be answered.

The guidance I seek may come, or the guidance I seek may not come, but are not both of these an answer? If a child seeks bread from his father and it is not forthcoming has not the father answered?

I will pray for guidance, and I will pray as a salesman, in this manner—

Oh creator of all things, help me. For this day I go out into the world naked and alone, and without your hand to guide me I will wander far from the path which leads to success and happiness.

I ask not for gold or garments or even opportunities equal to my ability; instead, guide me so that I may acquire ability equal to my opportunities.

You have taught the lion and the eagle how to hunt and prosper with teeth and claw. Teach me how to hunt with words and prosper with love so that I may be a lion among men and an eagle in the market place.

Help me to remain humble through obstacles and failures; yet hide not from mine eyes the prize that will come with victory.

Assign me to tasks which others have failed; yet guide me to pluck the seeds of success from their failures. Confront me with fears that will temper my spirit; yet endow me with courage to laugh at my misgivings.

Spare me sufficient days to reach my goals; yet help me to live this day as though it be my last.

Guide me in my words that they may bear fruit; yet silence me from gossip that none be maligned.

Discipline me in the habit of trying and trying again; yet show me the way to make use of the law of averages. Favor me with alertness to recognize opportunity; yet endow me with patience which will concentrate my strength.

Bathe me in good habits that the bad ones may drown; yet grant me compassion for weaknesses in others. Suffer me to know that all things shall pass; yet help me to count my blessings of today.

Expose me to hate so it not be a stranger; yet fill my cup with love to turn strangers into friends.

But all these things be only if thy will. I am a small and a lonely grape clutching the vine yet thou hast made me different from all others. Verily, there must be a special place for me. Guide me. Help me. Show me the way.

Let me become all you planned for me when my seed was planted and selected by you to sprout in the vine-yard of the world.

Help this humble salesman.
Guide me, God.

Chapter XVIII

And so it came to pass that Hafid waited in his lonely palace for he who was to receive the scrolls. The old man, with only his trusted bookkeeper for a companion, watched the seasons come and go, and the infirmities of old age soon prevented him from doing little except sit quietly in his covered garden.

He waited.

He waited nearly three full years after the disposal of his worldly wealth and the disbanding of his trade empire.

And then from out of the desert to the East there appeared a slight, limping figure of a stranger who entered Damascus and made straightway through the streets until he stood before the palace of Hafid. Erasmus, usually a model of courtesy and propriety remained resolutely in the doorway as the caller repeated his request, "I wouldst speak with thy master."

The stranger's appearance was not one to inspire confidence. His sandals were ripped and mended with rope, his brown legs were cut and scratched and had sores in many places, and above them hung a loose and tattered camel's hair loincloth. The man's hair was snarled and long and his eyes, red from the sun, seemed to burn from within.

Erasmus held tightly to the door handle, "What is it thou seeketh of my sire?"

The stranger allowed his sack to fall from his shoulders and clenched both hands in prayer toward Erasmus. "Please, kind man, grant me an audience with thy master. I mean him no harm nor seek I alms. Let him hear my words and then I will go in haste if I offend him."

Erasmus, still unsure, slowly opened the door and nodded toward the interior. Then he turned without looking back and walked swiftly toward the garden with his visitor limping behind.

In the garden, Hafid dozed, and Erasmus hesitated before his master. He coughed and Hafid stirred. He coughed again and the old man opened his eyes.

"Forgive this disturbance, master, but there is a caller."

Hafid, now awake, sat up and shifted his gaze to the stranger who bowed and spoke. "Art thou he who has been called the greatest salesman in the world?"

Hafid frowned but nodded, "I have been called that in years now gone. No longer is that crown on my old head. What seeketh thee of me?"

The small visitor stood self-consciously before Hafid

and rubbed his hands over his matted chest. He blinked his eyes in the soft light and replied, "I am called Saul and I return now, from Jerusalem, to my birthplace in Tarsus. However, I beg you, let not my appearance deceive you. I am not a bandit from the wilderness nor am I a beggar of the streets. I am a citizen of Tarsus and also a citizen of Rome. My people are Pharisees of the Jewish tribe of Benjamin and although I am a tentmaker by trade, I have studied under the great Gamaliel. Some call me Paul." He swayed as he spoke and Hafid, not fully awake until this moment, apologetically motioned for his visitor to sit.

Paul nodded but remained standing, "I come to thee for guidance and help which only you can give. Will you permit me, sire, to tell my story?"

Erasmus, standing behind the stranger, shook his head violently, but Hafid pretended not to notice. He studied the intruder of his sleep carefully and then nodded, "I am too old to continue to look up at thee. Sit at my feet and I will hear you through."

Paul pushed his sack aside and knelt near the old man who waited in silence.

"Four years ago, because the accumulated knowledge of too many years of study had blinded my heart to truth, I was the official witness to the stoning, in Jerusalem, of a holy man called Stephen. He had been condemned to death by the Jewish Sanhedrin for blasphemy against our God."

Hafid interrupted with puzzlement in his voice, "I do

not understand how I am connected with this activity."

Paul raised his hand as if to calm the old man. "I will explain quickly. Stephen was a follower of a man called Jesus, who less than a year before the stoning of Stephen, was crucified by the Romans for sedition against the state. Stephen's guilt was his insistence that Jesus was the Messiah whose coming had been foretold by the Jewish prophets, and that the Temple had conspired with Rome to murder this son of God. This rebuke to those in authority could only be punishable with death and as I have already told thee, I participated.

"Furthermore, with my fanaticism and youthful zeal, I was supplied with letters from the high priest of the Temple and entrusted with the mission of journeying here to Damascus to search out every follower of Jesus and return them in chains to Jerusalem for punishment. This was, as I have said, four years ago."

Erasmus glanced at Hafid and was startled, for there was a look in the old man's eyes which had not been seen by the faithful bookkeeper in many years. Only the splash of fountain water could be heard in the garden until Paul spoke once more.

"Now as I approached Damascus with murder in my heart there was a sudden flash of light from the heavens. I remember not having been struck but I found myself on the ground and although I could not see, I could hear, and I heard a voice in my ear say, 'Saul, Saul, why do you persecute me?' I answered, 'Who are you?' and the voice replied, 'I am Jesus, whom you are persecuting;

but rise and enter the city, and you will be told what to do.'

"I arose and was led by the hands of my companions into Damascus and there I was not able to eat or drink for three days while I remained in the house of a follower of the crucified one. Then I was visited by another called Ananias, who said he had been visited in a vision and told to come to me. Then he laid his hands upon my eyes and I could see again. Then I ate, and I drank, and my strength returned."

Hafid now leaned forward from his bench and inquired, "What then took place?"

"I was brought to the synagogue and my presence as a persecutor of the followers of Jesus struck fear into the hearts of all his followers but I preached nevertheless and my words confounded them, for now I spoke that he who had been crucified was indeed the Son of God.

"And all who listened suspected a trick of deceit on my part for had I not caused havoc in Jerusalem? I could not convince them of my change of heart and many plotted my death so I escaped over the walls and returned to Jerusalem.

"In Jerusalem the happenings of Damascus repeated themselves. None of the followers of Jesus would come near me although word had been received of my preaching in Damascus. Nevertheless, I continued to preach in the name of Jesus but it was of no avail. Everywhere I spoke I antagonized those who listened until one day I went to the Temple and in the courtyard, as I watched the sale of doves and lambs for sacrifice, the voice came to me again."

"This time what did it say?" Erasmus spoke before he could stop himself. Hafid smiled at his old friend and nodded for Paul to continue.

"The voice said, 'Thou hast had the Word for nearly four years but thou hast shown few the light. Even the word of God must be sold to the people or they will hear it not. Did not I speak in parables so that all might understand? Thou wilt catch few flies with vinegar. Return to Damascus and seek out he who is acclaimed as the greatest salesman in the world. If thou wouldst spread my word to the world let him show you the way.' "

Hafid glanced quickly at Erasmus and the old bookkeeper sensed the unspoken question. Was this the one for whom he had waited so long? The great salesman leaned forward and placed his hand on Paul's shoulder. "Tell me about this Jesus."

Paul, his voice now alive with new strength and volume, told of Jesus and his life. While the two listened, he spoke of the long Jewish wait for a Messiah who would come and unite them within a new and independent kingdom of happiness and peace. He told of John the Baptist and the arrival, on the stage of history, of one called Jesus. He told of the miracles performed by this man, his lectures to the crowds, his raising of the dead, his treatment of the money changers, and he told of the crucifixion, burial, and resurrection. Finally, as if to give further impact to his story, Paul reached into the sack at his side and removed a red garment which he placed in the lap of Hafid. "Sire, you hold in your arms all the worldly goods left behind by this Jesus. All that he possessed he shared with the world, even unto his life. And at the foot of his cross, Roman soldiers cast lots for this robe. It has come into my possession through much diligence and searching when I was last in Jerusalem."

Hafid's face paled and his hands shook as he turned the robe stained with blood. Erasmus, alarmed at his master's appearance moved closer to the old man. Hafid continued to turn the garment until he found the small star sewn into the cloth . . . the mark of Tola, whose guild made the robes sold by Pathros. Next to the star was a circle sewn within a square . . . the mark of Pathros.

As Paul and Erasmus watched, the old man raised the robe and rubbed it gently against his cheek. Hafid shook his head. Impossible. Thousands of other robes were made by Tola and sold by Pathros in the years of his great trade route.

Still clutching the robe and speaking in a hoarse whisper, Hafid said, "Tell me what is known of the birth of this Jesus."

Paul said, "He left our world with little. He had entered it with less. He was born in a cave, in Bethlehem, during the time of the census of Tiberius."

Hafid's smile seemed almost childish to the two men,

and they looked on with puzzlement, for tears also flowed down his wrinkled cheeks. He brushed them away with his hand and asked, "And was there not the brightest star that man has ever seen which shone above the birthplace of this baby?"

Paul's mouth opened yet he could not speak, nor was it necessary. Hafid raised his arms and embraced Paul, and this time the tears of both were mingled.

Finally the old man arose and beckoned toward Erasmus. "Faithful friend, go to the tower and return with the chest. We have found our salesman at last."

The Greatest Secret
in the World

To the greatest "success recorder"
in my life, with love . . .
. . . my wife, Bette

The most valuable result of all education is to make you do the thing you have to do, when it ought to be done, whether you like it or not. It is the first lesson that ought to be learned. And however early a man's training begins, it is probably the last lesson that he learns thoroughly.

Thomas Huxley

The Legend Of The Ten Scrolls

From

THE GREATEST SALESMAN IN THE WORLD

Once upon a time, nearly two thousand years ago, a young camel boy named Hafid fell in love with a wealthy merchant's daughter.

To improve his lowly station in life, in order that he could ask for the fair Lisha's hand in marriage, Hafid convinced his master, the great caravan merchant, Pathros, to give him an opportunity to prove his ability as a salesman.

From the caravan's supply wagon Pathros presented the youth with one new robe, which he challenged him to sell in the nearby village of Bethlehem. For three days in that poor hamlet Hafid failed in his every attempt to sell the robe . . . and finally, in a moment of pity, he gave the robe to warm a newborn baby in a cave near the village inn.

The young man returned to the caravan so full of shame and self-pity with his failure at becoming a salesman that he did not notice the bright star shining above his head which accompanied him on his return journey from Bethlehem.

But Pathros noticed . . . and the old man interpreted the brightness above as a sign from the gods . . . a sign he had been awaiting for many years . . . a sign which would release him from his secret possession of The Ten Great Scrolls For Success which he had received when he had also been a poor youth.

The old merchant, before his death, presented the ten scrolls to Hafid, who employed their principles to eventually become the wealthiest, the most successful, The Greatest Salesman In The World.

Several decades later Hafid passed the ten scrolls on to a very special person.

Now you hold them in *your* hands . . . and in this book you will be taught how to read them and how to apply their wisdom to your own life plus how to chart your day-to-day progress with your own Success Recorder so that you can achieve lasting wealth, health, happiness, and most important . . . peace of mind.

Chapter I

Before you and I become involved in the Ten Great Scrolls For Success, let's have a heart to heart talk.

I'll talk.

You listen!

The money spent on this book has been wasted.

Whether someone who cares for you, who wants you to "make it" big, who perhaps even loves you, gave you *The Greatest Secret In The World* . . . or whether you purchased it yourself . . . the money has been wasted.

The money has been wasted unless you are willing to accept, and try, a plan which has already worked for thousands of others.

The money has been wasted unless you have the guts, the persistence, and the will-power to follow the plan through to its fruition.

The money has been wasted unless you are willing to give the plan just ten minutes of your time *each day* of your work week . . . for forty-five weeks.

If I were a Nick the Greek-type-oddsmaker I'd say the odds were about 75 to 1 against your letting this system for doubling or tripling your income within a year help you as much as it can.

"But I'm different!" you remind me.

Really? If you made any New Year's resolutions last January 1st how long did you keep them? What about those excess pounds you were going to lose, or those cigarettes you were going to quit using . . . or that second drink you were going to stop having?

How long are you going to keep kidding yourself?

Perhaps you really do have a burning desire to succeed. Perhaps the added responsibility of marriage, or parenthood, or the desire for a new home, even a new car, or a mounting pile of debts have forced you to come to terms with yourself and acknowledge that the solution to all your needs and desires is really dependent on no one but you.

But a burning desire to succeed is not enough. As the Executive Editor of *Success Unlimited*, a magazine devoted to helping individuals improve their business and personal life, I long ago recognized the fact that there are two types of burning desire . . . and one type is phony and hypocritical. This phony type of burning desire is found in the person who is constantly telling his wife, his boss, and (worst of all) himself, that he really wants to succeed. He reads all the self-help books published and he gets his "kicks" from reading about others succeeding just as there are individuals who get their "kicks" from reading pornographic books. Unfortunately for our friends who read either types of these books they never get into action. They live their lives vicariously through their imagined participation in the lives and activities of others.

Tomorrow, to this type of dreamer, will be a great day.

Tomorrow never comes.

If I have struck a little nerve within you don't be concerned. Let me wipe that frown from your brow by assuring you that all of us possess some of that phony kind of burning desire. We make promises to others, promises that we know we can't keep, in order to get our boss or our wife off our backs . . . little realizing the harm we are doing to our own personality, because we *know* we're lying.

Today is the day you wipe that slate clean. No more phony promises, no more great plans in the evening which vanish when the sun rises, no more kidding yourself.

As you move, day by day, through this simple success program, you will slowly come to realize one important truth. *You are nature's greatest miracle.* Just to duplicate the computer you possess, called a brain, would require sufficient electronic equipment to fill the entire interior of the Empire State Building. You are rare and unique and the ultimate product of several million years of evolution. Both in mind, and body, you are far better equipped than Solomon or Caesar or Plato to make something beautiful and meaningful of your life.

You have a greater potential than anyone who has ever lived before you!

But you'll never "make it" by sitting on your duff and telling the world how great you're going to be, starting tomorrow. Sooner or later that friendly bill collector or landlord will shake his head at your promises. Sooner or later "credit" runs out. Sooner or later you "put up . . . or shut up."

This book will show you how to "put up" . . . if you will give it a chance to work for you.

The Greatest Salesman In The World, the book from which this guide was developed, has been a publishing phenomenon since its first edition in 1968. Few books, especially books on salesmanship, ever attain hardcover sales of a quarter of a million copies, and neither the author nor its publisher dared to imagine that a small volume about a salesman living in the time of Christ would be met with the enthusiastic reception that it has enjoyed. Even more amazing . . . sales have increased each year since its publication.

Executives responsible for the supervision of sales groups throughout the country quickly recognized the potential impact of *The Greatest Salesman In The World* as a motivational tool. Soon after its publication one firm purchased 30,000 copies! Copies have been purchased in volume by several hundred firms and sales organizations including such corporate giants as Coca Cola, Amway Corporation, Combined Insurance Company of America, Kraft Foods, Success Motivation Institute, Parke, Davis & Company, Sperry Hutchinson,

Volkswagen, Valley Steel Company, Genesco, Stanley Home Products, Norton International, The Southwestern Company, Stratford Squire International, American General Insurance Company of Delaware, Steamatic, Life Insurance of Kentucky, and Steak & Ale Restaurants of America, Inc.

Soon after publication, both the author and publisher received another pleasant surprise. *The Greatest Salesman In The World,* written primarily for sales people, had somehow filtered far beyond its intended market. Letters, seeking more information about the scrolls, began to arrive from individuals and organizations representing such widely diversified groups as: an artist colony, prison heads concerned with rehabilitation, management consultants, politicians, college professors, armed forces personnel, the medical profession, students, professional athletes . . . even a national center for brain-damaged children.

One salesman, after purchasing a gun to end his life because he had taken company funds, wrote that the book saved his life. He went to his firm, confessed his mistake, made restitution . . . and was given another chance.

Many wrote that the book's title was misleading. *The Greatest Salesman In The World* sounded like a "salesman's book" whereas it was a book for anyone searching for his or her niche in life. The book became, and still is, a popular gift item. Sales managers to their salesmen, parents to their children, wives to husbands who are still struggling.

Hopefully, with my "name-dropping" of all those corporations and the other examples cited in the past few paragraphs I have sold you on the fact that you are not holding just another "how-to" sales book loaded with complicated theories, charts, and selling techniques that look and sound terrific but won't do much for you, tomorrow . . . or next week.

Each Success Scroll will be beneficial to you, no matter what your profession may be . . . providing you make one sincere promise to yourself . . . that you will give it just *ten minutes* of your time, each work day, for the next forty-five weeks. Ten minutes . . . about the time it takes you to shower each day. Is that too much to ask to double or triple your income in the next ten months? When have you ever had a deal like this before?

Now, I'm not going to ask you what you want from life. I'm not sure you could answer me. And I'm not going to ask you to list your assets as they are now and then make a second list showing what you'd like them to be a year from now, five years from now . . . and so on. We don't need to go through all that "pipe dream success bookkeeping" you find in most self-help books.

All we both need to know are four facts. What is your job title and what is your weekly income, today . . . plus what would you like your job title to be and what do you want to be earning forty-five weeks from now when you complete your Success Recorder.

So . . . on a piece of paper, which I want you to keep in the privacy of your home, I'd like you to write a memo to yourself:

To: John Smith   Date:
My present job title is ....
My present weekly income is ....
My job title, 45 weeks from now ....
My weekly income, 45 weeks from now ....

That's all! Sign it . . . and tuck it away. Don't even
discuss it with anyone, except perhaps your wife. Do it
now . . . right now! Procrastination is one of your habits
we can't start working on any too soon.

Why didn't I ask you for a long list of the things you
wanted to achieve and acquire in the next 10 months?
Things like a new home, perhaps, or the beginning of
a college fund for your children, or maybe that movie
camera with a 10 to 1 zoom lens you've wanted for so
long? Because it wasn't necessary. If you have improved
your job title and your weekly income as much as I
think you've indicated on that private memo to yourself then all the material things you want will begin to
come your way. Any long list of your dreams is unnecessary! You know what you want . . . and your Success
Recorder Diary will help keep you on the right course.

Chapter II

You can begin your Success Recorder on any Monday during the year . . . but once you commence you must not let anything except a serious illness prevent you from following through, each day.

One exception. If a vacation is on your schedule while you're working on this program go off and enjoy yourself. Then, on your first day back to work, just pick up where you left off.

You are about to read The First Great Scroll For Success. This scroll contains the instructions on how and when you are to read the scrolls that follow. Read this scroll several times during the week-end prior to the Monday you begin this program.

Warning! Don't let the simplicity of the scrolls' instructions turn you off. Simplicity is the keynote of success in any endeavor. Remember Vince Lombardi and his uncomplicated game plans relying on basic fundamentals and the minimum of plays. Remember the letters K.I.S.S. . . . "Keep it simple, stupid!"

You are about to learn how to tangle with the worst enemy you have . . . your bad habits. The Scroll Marked I contains the secret for getting rid of them. Read slowly.

Read with a pen or pencil in your hand, if you like, and underline ideas which you feel are most meaningful and relevant to you.

As you proceed you will discover that you have company. ME! I'll be with you all the way:

The Scroll Marked I

Today I begin a new life.

Today I shed my old skin which hath, too long, suffered the bruises of failure and the wounds of mediocrity.

Today I am born anew and my birthplace is a vineyard where there is fruit for all.

Today I will pluck grapes of wisdom from the tallest and fullest vines in the vineyard, for these were planted by the wisest of my profession who have come before me, generation upon generation.

Today I will savor the taste of grapes from these vines and verily I will swallow the seed of success buried in each and new life will sprout within me.

The career I have chosen is laden with opportunity yet it is fraught with heartbreak and despair, and the bodies of those who have failed, were they piled one atop another, would cast its shadow down upon all the pyramids of the earth.

Yet I will not fail, as the others, for in my hands I now hold the charts which will guide me through perilous waters to shores which only yesterday seemed but a dream.

Failure no longer will be my payment for struggle. Just

as nature made no provision for my body to tolerate pain neither has it made any provision for my life to suffer failure. Failure, like pain, is alien to my life. In the past I accepted it as I accepted pain. Now I reject it and I am prepared for wisdom and principles which will guide me out of the shadows into the sunlight of wealth, position, and happiness far beyond my most extravagant dreams until even the golden apples in the Garden of Hesperides will seem no more than my just reward.

Time teaches all things to he who lives forever but I have not the luxury of eternity. Yet, within my allotted time I must practice the art of patience for nature acts never in haste. To create the olive, king of all trees, a hundred years is required. An onion plant is old in nine weeks. I have lived as an onion plant. It has not pleased me. Now I wouldst become the greatest of olive trees and, in truth, the greatest of salesmen.

And how will this be accomplished? For I have neither the knowledge nor the experience to achieve greatness and already I have stumbled in ignorance and fallen into pools of self-pity. The answer is simple. I will commence my journey unencumbered with either the weight of unnecessary knowledge or the handicap of meaningless experience. Nature already has supplied me with knowledge and instinct far greater than any beast in the forest and the value of experience is overrated, usually by old men who nod wisely and speak stupidly.

In truth experience teaches thoroughly yet her course of instruction devours men's years so the value of her lessons diminishes with the time necessary to acquire her special wisdom. The end finds it wasted on dead men. Furthermore, experience is comparable to fashion; an action that proved successful today will be unworkable and impractical tomorrow.

Only principles endure and these I now possess, for the laws that will lead me to greatness are contained in the words of these scrolls. What they will teach me is more to prevent failure than to gain success, for what is success other than a state of mind? Which two, among a thousand wise men, will define success in the same words; yet failure is always described but one way. *Failure is man's inability to reach his goals in life, whatever they may be.*

In truth, the only difference between those who have failed and those who have succeeded lies in the difference of their habits. Good habits are the key to all success. Bad habits are the unlocked door to failure. Thus, the first law I will obey, which precedeth all others is—*I will form good habits and become their slaves.*

As a child I was slave to my impulses; now I am slave to my habits, as are all grown men. I have surrendered my free will to the years of accumulated habits and the past deeds of my life have already marked out a path which threatens to imprison my future. My actions are ruled by appetite, passion, prejudice, greed, love, fear, environment, habit, and the worst of these tyrants is habit. Therefore, if I must be a slave to habit let me be a slave to good habits. My bad habits must be destroyed and new furrows prepared for good seed.

I will form good habits and become their slave.

And how will I accomplish this difficult feat? Through these scrolls, it will be done, for each scroll contains a principle which will drive a bad habit from my life and replace it with one which will bring me closer to success. For it is another of nature's laws that only a habit can subdue another habit. So, in order for these written words to perform their chosen task, I must discipline myself with the first of my new habits which is as follows:

I will read each scroll for thirty days in this prescribed manner, before I proceed to the next scroll.

First, I will read the words in silence when I arise. Then, I will read the words in silence after I have partaken of my midday meal. Last, I will read the words again just before I retire at day's end, and most important, on this occasion I will read the words aloud.

On the next day I will repeat this procedure, and I will continue in like manner for thirty days. Then, I will turn to the next scroll and repeat this procedure for another thirty days. I will continue in this manner until I have lived with each scroll for thirty days and my reading has become habit.

And what will be accomplished with this habit? Herein lies the hidden secret of man's accomplishments. As I repeat the words daily they will soon become a part of my active mind, but more important, they will also seep into my other mind, that mysterious source which never sleeps, which creates my dreams, and often makes me act in ways I do not comprehend.

As the words of these scrolls are consumed by my mysterious mind I will begin to awake, each morning, with a vitality I have never known before. My vigor will increase, my enthusiasm will rise, my desire to meet the world will overcome every fear I once knew at sunrise, and I will be happier than I ever believed it possible to be in this world of strife and sorrow.

Eventually I will find myself reacting to all situations which confront me as I was commanded in the scrolls to react, and soon these actions and reactions will become easy to perform, for any act with practice becomes easy.

Thus a new and good habit is born, for when an act becomes easy through constant repetition it becomes a pleasure to perform and if it is a pleasure to perform it is man's nature to perform it often. When I perform it often it becomes a habit and I become its slave and since it is a good habit this is my will.

Today I begin a new life.

And I make a solemn oath to myself that nothing will retard my new life's growth. I will lose not a day from these readings for that day cannot be retrieved nor can I substitute another for it. I must not, I will not, break this habit of daily reading from these scrolls and, in truth, the few moments spent each day on this new habit are but a small price to pay for the happiness and success that will be mine.

As I read and re-read the words in the scrolls to follow, never will I allow the brevity of each scroll nor the simplicity of its words to cause me to treat the scroll's message lightly. Thousands of grapes are pressed to fill one jar with wine, and the grapeskin and pulp are tossed to the birds. So it is with these grapes of wisdom from the ages. Much has been filtered and tossed to the wind. Only the pure truth lies distilled in the words to come. I will drink as instructed and spill not a drop. And the seed of success I will swallow.

Today my old skin has become as dust. I will walk tall among men and they will know me not, for today I am a new man, with a new life.

Now, before you continue, go back and read the scroll again. It contains one key sentence that I want you to underline:

"As I repeat the words daily they will soon become a

part of my active mind, but more important, they will also seep into my other mind, that mysterious source which never sleeps, which creates my dreams, and often makes me act in ways I do not comprehend."

In modern terminology what that key sentence means is that you are about to mind-condition yourself. You are about to begin the process of imprinting new relays and transistors onto your sub-conscious mind . . . that "control box" which mysteriously directs many of our actions and our ambitions. There's nothing weird or "far-out" about this technique. Many of the nation's outstanding examples of success constantly "program" themselves so that they instinctively react to various situations in a manner that will provide them with the greatest possible benefit. W. Clement Stone, Chairman of the Combined Insurance Company of America, and the country's outstanding expert on the motivation of others, used this technique on himself to amass a personal and self-made fortune of more than $400,000,000.

Perhaps your goal is not that high . . . but let's make a run for it, anyway.

Chapter III

Downhill ski racing is a battle of the individual against his environment . . . and the clock. What has always caused me to shake my head in sympathy for the losers is the infinitesimal difference in time between the winner and the also-rans.

The winner is clocked in 1:37:22 . . . one minute, thirty-seven and twenty-two one-hundreths seconds.

Second place is clocked in 1:37:25 . . . one minute, thirty-seven and twenty-five one-hundredths seconds.

In this case, the difference between being a champion and just another skier is *three one-hundreths of a second!* We can't even blink our eyes that fast.

What really was the difference between the champion and the also-ran? A lucky break? Maybe. But perhaps the champion practiced just a little bit harder . . . and just a little bit longer. Perhaps the champion worked on one bad habit, monotonous as this work is, until it was removed from his performance . . . saving him a fraction of a second on each downhill run . . . enough to spell success.

Now let's get to you . . . and let's start off by admitting that we both know you've got some, or many, bad

habits. Furthermore you know exactly what they are . . .
. . . perhaps procrastination, or over-indulgence, or lazi-
ness, or sloppiness, or a bad temper or an inability to follow through. I'm sure you can add to this list . . . and
I'm sure you also recognize that you're not going to get
very far so long as these vices are fouling up your
pistons.

I've always pictured George Washington as he looks
on my dollar bills . . . white coiffured wig framing a
face both calm, confident, and the personification of self-
control. My image of this great man was altered considerably when I read, recently, that George, in his
younger days, had a flaming crop of red hair . . . and a
temper to match.

Had George not learned to replace this bad habit with
one of self-control, which must have been extremely
difficult for him as he tried to lead an undisciplined and
untrained civilians' army against the forces of King
George, the odds are great that he would never have
become our first President.

Benjamin Franklin was probably the greatest and most
influential individual this country has ever produced.
He was "a man for any season," patriot, scientist, author,
diplomat, inventor, printer, and philosopher. He taught
himself to read French, Spanish, Italian, and Latin and
without his skillful guidance the United States might
never have attained its independence.

But even Benjamin Franklin had bad habits . . . and
he knew it. Unlike most of us, however, he determined

to do something about his. Inventor that he was, he worked out a "magic formula" to rid himself of his bad habits. First, he listed what he believed were the thirteen virtues necessary for true success: temperance, silence, order, resolution, frugality, industry, sincerity, justice, moderation, cleanliness, tranquility, chastity, and humility.

In his great autobiography he explained how he used the magic formula. "My intention being to acquire the habit of all these virtues, I judged it would be well not to distract my attention by attempting the whole at once, but to fix it *on one of them at a time;* and when I should be master of that, then to proceed to another; and so on, until I should have gone through the thirteen."

For another ingredient in his "magic formula" Franklin reached back to the advice of Pythagoras that it was necessary to examine one's actions each day. He designed the first Success Recorder:

"I made a little book in which I allotted a page for each of the virtues . . . and in its proper column, I might mark, by a little black spot, every fault I found upon examination to have been committed respecting that virtue upon that day."

Did the magic formula work for this great man?

Frank Bettger, author of one of the all-time classic books on self-motivation in the selling profession, *How I Raised Myself From Failure To Success In Selling* (published by Prentice-Hall) says, "When he was seventy-nine years old, Benjamin Franklin wrote more about this idea than anything else that ever happened to him in his entire life—fifteen pages—for to this one thing he felt he owed all his success and happiness."

Franklin wrote, "I hope, therefore, that some of my descendants may follow the example and reap the benefit."

Frank Bettger followed Franklin's examples, applied the magic formula to what had been a mediocre career as a salesman, and became the leading life insurance producer in the country.

Will the magic formula work for you?

Let's ask someone who can speak from experience and results. Let's ask the man we mentioned earlier, W Clement Stone:

"Benjamin Franklin's magic formula has motivated many failures to subsequently succeed when they recognized, related, assimilated and used his formula. You can use it. Anyone can use it. I have never met a person who employed the principles in Benjamin Franklin's magic formula daily who failed to make progress toward the goals he was striving for. You have an absolute guarantee that any year can be your record year if you follow the principles of his formula daily."

In point of time it's a long journey from the ten scrolls which The Greatest Salesman In The World followed during the time of Christ, to Benjamin Franklin's formula, to the present day success of great achievers such as W. Clement Stone and Frank Bettger. And yet the principles have not been altered, even in the smallest way, by the passage of centuries.

The Magic Formula, or Success Recorder, or whatever name you want to give it, lives on . . . a proven and simple method which can change your life . . . if you give it the chance.

It always comes back to you, doesn't it?

Chapter IV

Push-ups.

Let's think about them, for a moment, before we get involved in the next scroll.

If you got down on the floor, right now, how many push-ups could you do? Six, ten, twelve. Let's say you can do ten. Then, wait two weeks and try it again. How many? Probably ten, again.

But, if you do ten today, and try again, tomorrow, and the next day, and next, how many do you think you could be doing after two weeks? Probably thirty, forty, fifty, or more. Why? Because the muscles in your shoulders and your arms become stronger with each day's attempt. You are *conditioning* them to respond to a greater challenge each day and the daily increase in the number of push-ups you can do is only a small example of what you can accomplish in a specific period of time which, today, seems almost impossible. You are, indeed, a miracle of nature, and what applies to your shoulder muscles also applies to that big gray muscle between your two ears. And you are about to begin to make it do things which, at this moment, seem impossible to you.

Are you ready to begin?

Okay. Let's review the rules as they were spelled out for you in The Scroll Marked I. On the Monday which commences this program, sometime between your arising and departure for work you are to read The Scroll Marked II which you will find at the end of this chapter. Sometime around noon you are to read it again, which means you must take this book with you. Toss it in your brief case, perhaps, or leave it in your car if you use "wheels" in your business. In the evening, prior to your retiring, you are to read the scroll for the third time, and this time you should read it aloud. (You may have to explain this seemingly curious behavior to your spouse, but she's on your side and certainly wants you to make good.)

Following the scroll you will find your Success Recorder for the week, and the four weeks to follow, to help you live up to the injunction in The Scroll Marked I that each scroll is to be read, thought about, and acted on for thirty days.

Your Success Recorder was purposely designed to enable you to quickly conduct that "daily self-examination" which Benjamin Franklin insisted was an absolute necessity in a program such as this. In capsule form it summarizes the virtues, the qualities, the good habits, and the powers you are working to put into your life each day.

When your first day's work is done turn to your Success Recorder and place a date in the Monday section. Then, in the proper box, indicate how many times you read the scroll, that day. (Three, I hope.) Finally, read the review paragraph and consider how well you did in following the scroll's principles since you awoke. Rate yourself with 1 for "poor," 2 for "good," 3 for "very good," and 4 for "excellent." Be honest with yourself. Place your rating in the box . . . and tally the two boxes for the day. The highest rating you can have, for any day, is 7. This rating will serve as a daily and weekly accounting to yourself on your effort and your improvement.

Continue with this same procedure for the other four work days and then place the total number of points you earned for the week in its proper box. Then go on to the next week and continue this practice for five weeks . . . at which time you will begin a new chapter . . . and a new scroll.

Isn't that simple?

I'll let you in on a secret. It's so simple that it's going to "turn off" a lot of your reading companions of the moment who believe that nothing can be very worthwhile unless it's expensive or complicated. But then, they wouldn't be doing many push-ups either, if that was our program's purpose, so let them drop out with no regrets on our part. Mediocrity will always be their way of life.

As the first few weeks pass you will note a gradual change in both your attitude and your treatment of others, those you love and even casual acquaintances. You will begin hearing remarks like, "What's come over you?" or "That's not the old Smith I know!"

When that begins to happen you'll know the message of the scrolls and your daily Success Recorder review are beginning to work and your subconscious mind has been imprinted with new personality tracings that will disclose themselves time and time again in your future life . . . and you are on the way to a great year!

Now it's that first Monday.

As you begin this important day in your life I ask only that you remember these words:

"Failure will never overtake thee if thy determination to succeed is strong enough."

The Scroll Marked II

I will greet this day with love in my heart.

For this is the greatest secret of success in all ventures. Muscle can split a shield and even destroy life but only the unseen power of love can open the hearts of men and until I master this art I will remain no more than a peddler in the market place. I will make love my greatest weapon and none on whom I call can defend against its force.

My reasoning they may counter; my speech they may distrust; my apparel they may disapprove; my face they may reject; and even my bargains may cause them suspicion; yet my love will melt all hearts liken to the sun whose rays soften the coldest clay.

I will greet this day with love in my heart.

And how will I do this? Henceforth will I look on all things with love and I will be born again. I will love the sun for it warms my bones; yet I will love the rain for it cleanses my spirit. I will love the light for it shows me the way; yet I will love the darkness for it shows me the stars. I will welcome happiness for it enlarges my heart; yet I will endure sadness for it opens my soul. I will acknowledge rewards for they are my due; yet I will welcome obstacles for they are my challenge.

I will greet this day with love in my heart.

And how will I speak? I will laud mine enemies and they will become friends; I will encourage my friends and they will become brothers. Always will I dig for reasons to applaud; never will I scratch for excuses to gossip. When I am tempted to criticize I will bite on my tongue; when I am moved to praise I will shout from the roofs.

Is it not so that birds, the wind, the sea and all nature speaks with the music of praise for their creator? Cannot I speak with the same music to his children? Henceforth will I remember this secret and it will change my life.

I will greet this day with love in my heart.

And how will I act? I will love all manners of men for each has qualities to be admired even though they be hidden. With love I will tear down the wall of suspicion and hate which they have built around their hearts and in its place will I build bridges so that my love may enter their souls.

I will love the ambitious for they can inspire me; I will love the failures for they can teach me. I will love the kings for they are but human; I will love the meek for they are divine. I will love the rich for they are yet lonely; I will love the poor for they are so many. I will love the young for the faith they hold; I will love the old for the wisdom they share. I will love the beautiful for their eyes of sadness; I will love the ugly for their souls of peace.

I will greet this day with love in my heart.

But how will I react to the actions of others? With love. For just as love is my weapon to open the hearts of men, love is also my shield to repulse the arrows of hate and the spears of anger. Adversity and discouragement will beat against my new shield and become as the softest of rains. My shield will protect me in the market place and sustain me when I am alone. It will uplift me in moments of despair yet it will calm me in time of exultation. It will become stronger and more protective with use until one day I will cast it aside and walk unencumbered among all manners of men and, when I do, my name will be raised high on the pyramid of life.

I will greet this day with love in my heart.

And how will I confront each whom I meet? In only one way. In silence and to myself I will address him and say I Love You. Though spoken in silence these words will shine in my eyes, unwrinkle my brow, bring a smile to my lips, and echo in my voice; and his heart will be opened. And who is there who will say nay to my goods when his heart feels my love?

I will greet this day with love in my heart.

And most of all I will love myself. For when I do I will zealously inspect all things which enter my body, my mind, my soul, and my heart. Never will I overdindulge the re-quests of my flesh, rather I will cherish my body with clean-liness and moderation. Never will I allow my mind to be attracted to evil and despair, rather I will uplift it with the knowledge and wisdom of the ages. Never will I allow my soul to become complacent and satisfied, rather I will feed it with meditation and prayer. Never will I allow my heart to become small and bitter, rather I will share it and it will grow and warm the earth.

I will greet this day with love in my heart,

Henceforth will I love all mankind. From this moment all

hate is let from my veins for I have not time to hate, only time to love. From this moment I take the first step required to become a man among men. With love I will increase my sales a hundredfold and become a great salesman. If I have no other qualities I can succeed with love alone. Without it I will fail though I possess all the knowledge and skills of the world.

I will greet this day with love, and I will succeed.

SUCCESS RECORDER
The First Week

****

Monday   **Date**............................   No. of times daily

1. I read The Scroll Marked II
        Review Paragraph for the Week
2. I greeted this day with love in my heart; I praised my   Rating
   enemies; I thought "I love you" silently to all I met and
   I loved myself enough to protect my body from overin-
   dulgence and my mind from evil and despair.   Total

                (Insert number in each box)

Tuesday   **Date**............................   No. of times daily

1. I read The Scroll Marked II
2. I read the review paragraph above   Rating

                     Total

Wednesday   **Date**............................   No. of times daily

1. I read The Scroll Marked II
2. I read the review paragraph above   Rating

                     Total

Thursday   **Date**............................   No. of times daily

1. I read The Scroll Marked II
2. I read the review paragraph above   Rating

                     Total

Friday   **Date**............................   No. of times daily

1. I read The Scroll Marked II
2. I read the review paragraph above   Rating

                     Total

                Total points for the week

*Appointments for the week*_____

Monday_____
_____
_____
_____
_____

Tuesday_____
_____
_____
_____
_____

Wednesday_____
_____
_____
_____
_____

Thursday_____
_____
_____
_____
_____

Friday_____
_____
_____
_____
_____

*Achievements of the week*_____
_____
_____
_____
_____
_____

Reflection For The Week

Love is never lost. If not reciprocated, it will flow
back and soften and purify the heart. —*Washington Irving*

SUCCESS RECORDER
The Second Week

❖❖❖

Monday   **Date**........................   No. of times daily

1. I read The Scroll Marked II
            Review Paragraph for the Week   [ ]
2. I greeted this day with love in my heart; I praised my   Rating
   enemies; I thought "I love you" silently to all I met and
   I loved myself enough to protect my body from overin-   [ ]
   dulgence and my mind from evil and despair.   Total
                    (Insert number in each box)   [ ]

Tuesday   **Date**........................   No. of times daily

1. I read The Scroll Marked II   [ ]
2. I read the review paragraph above   Rating

                                                             [ ]

                                              Total   [ ]

Wednesday   **Date**........................   No. of times daily

1. I read The Scroll Marked II   [ ]
2. I read the review paragraph above   Rating

                                                             [ ]

                                              Total   [ ]

Thursday   **Date**........................   No. of times daily

1. I read The Scroll Marked II   [ ]
2. I read the review paragraph above   Rating

                                                             [ ]

                                              Total   [ ]

Friday   **Date**........................   No. of times daily

1. I read The Scroll Marked II   [ ]
2. I read the review paragraph above   Rating

                                                             [ ]

                                              Total   [ ]

                          Total points for the week   [ ]

*Appointments for the week*_____

Monday_____
_____
_____
_____
_____

Tuesday_____
_____
_____
_____
_____

Wednesday_____
_____
_____
_____
_____

Thursday_____
_____
_____
_____
_____

Friday_____
_____
_____
_____
_____

*Achievements of the week*_____
_____
_____
_____
_____
_____

Reflection For The Week

To each and every one of us, love gives the power of
working miracles if we will.   —*Lydia M. Child*

SUCCESS RECORDER
The Third Week

****

Monday   **Date**...................................   No. of times daily

1. I read The Scroll Marked II

       Review Paragraph for the Week

2. I greeted this day with love in my heart; I praised my   **Rating**
   enemies; I thought "I love you" silently to all I met and
   I loved myself enough to protect my body from overin-
   dulgence and my mind from evil and despair.   **Total**

                                 (Insert number in each box)

Tuesday   **Date**...........................   No. of times daily

1. I read The Scroll Marked II
2. I read the review paragraph above   **Rating**

                                     Total

Wednesday   **Date**...........................   No. of times daily

1. I read The Scroll Marked II
2. I read the review paragraph above   **Rating**

                                     Total

Thursday   **Date**...........................   No. of times daily

1. I read The Scroll Marked II
2. I read the review paragraph above   **Rating**

                                     Total

Friday   **Date**...........................   No. of times daily

1. I read The Scroll Marked II
2. I read the review paragraph above   **Rating**

                                     Total

                         Total points for the week

*Appointments for the week*_____

Monday_____
_____
_____
_____
_____
_____

Tuesday_____
_____
_____
_____
_____
_____

Wednesday_____
_____
_____
_____
_____
_____

Thursday_____
_____
_____
_____
_____
_____

Friday_____
_____
_____
_____
_____
_____

*Achievements of the week*_____
_____
_____
_____
_____
_____

Reflection For The Week

It is possible that a man can be so changed by love as
hardly to be recognized as the same person.　**—Terence**

SUCCESS RECORDER
The Fourth Week

****

Monday   Date.................. ....   No. of times daily

1. I read The Scroll Marked II   ▢
        Review Paragraph for the Week
2. I greeted this day with love in my heart; I praised my   Rating
   enemies; I thought "I love you" silently to all I met and
   I loved myself enough to protect my body from overin-   ▢
   dulgence and my mind from evil and despair.   Total
                        (Insert number in each box)   ▢

Tuesday   Date................................   No. of times daily

1. I read The Scroll Marked II   ▢
2. I read the review paragraph above   Rating
                                                                  ▢
                                            Total   ▢

Wednesday   Date................................   No. of times daily

1. I read The Scroll Marked II   ▢
2. I read the review paragraph above   Rating
                                                                  ▢
                                            Total   ▢

Thursday   Date................................   No. of times daily

1. I read The Scroll Marked II   ▢
2. I read the review paragraph above   Rating
                                                                  ▢
                                            Total   ▢

Friday   Date................................   No. of times daily

1. I read The Scroll Marked II   ▢
2. I read the review paragraph above   Rating
                                                                  ▢
                                            Total   ▢

                            Total points for the week   ▢

*Appointments for the week*_____

Monday_____
_____
_____
_____
_____

Tuesday_____
_____
_____
_____
_____

Wednesday_____
_____
_____
_____
_____

Thursday_____
_____
_____
_____
_____

Friday_____
_____
_____
_____
_____

*Achievements of the week*_____
_____
_____
_____
_____
_____

Reflection For The Week

Love, and you shall be loved. All love is mathematically just, as much as the two sides of an algebraic equation. —*Emerson*

SUCCESS RECORDER
The Fifth Week

✱✱✱

Monday   Date............................   No. of times daily

1. I read The Scroll Marked II

          Review Paragraph for the Week

2. I greeted this day with love in my heart; I praised my   Rating
   enemies; I thought "I love you" silently to all I met and
   I loved myself enough to protect my body from overin-
   dulgence and my mind from evil and despair.   Total

                          (Insert number in each box)

Tuesday   Date............................   No. of times daily

1. I read The Scroll Marked II
2. I read the review paragraph above   Rating

                                        Total

Wednesday   Date............................   No. of times daily

1. I read The Scroll Marked II
2. I read the review paragraph above   Rating

                                        Total

Thursday   Date............................   No. of times daily

1. I read The Scroll Marked II
2. I read the review paragraph above   Rating

                                        Total

Friday   Date............................   No. of times daily

1. I read The Scroll Marked II
2. I read the review paragraph above   Rating

                                        Total

                    Total points for the week

Appointments for the week_____

Monday_____
_____
_____
_____
_____
_____

Tuesday_____
_____
_____
_____
_____

Wednesday_____
_____
_____
_____
_____

Thursday_____
_____
_____
_____
_____

Friday_____
_____
_____
_____
_____

Achievements of the week_____
_____
_____
_____
_____
_____

Reflection For The Week

It is the duty of men to love even those who injure them. —*Marcus Antonius*

Chapter V

Still with us?

Look around you. The group has thinned out considerably. Those that have already dropped out all came up with at least one excuse not to continue with their Success Recorder and it is not coincidental that this is the same group whose past performance shows the same "drop-out" habit in their previous attempts to make something of themselves. These are the individuals with the "phony" type of burning desire which I mentioned earlier. All talk . . . no action.

Of course, when you stop feeling sorry for them, the realization suddenly hits you that what they have done is make it easier for you. The competition is less. William Danforth, in his great self-help classic, "I Dare You," wrote that 95% of all individuals lack the determination to call on their unused capacities. This tremendous majority quickly settle on the plateau of mediocrity . . . and bewail their misfortune and "bad breaks" for the rest of their lives while the daring 5% continue on to leadership levels. He speaks to that small and surviving band of gutsy individuals, including you, when he says:

"The day of defending your present possessions is

gone. From now on you are not going to worry about
holding your job. Put the worry on the fellow above you
about holding his. From this day onward wrong things
are put on the defense. You have marshalled right things
for the attack. Your eyes are turned toward your strength,
not your weakness. Henceforth, you will wake in the
morning thinking of ways to do things, rather than reasons why they cannot be done!"

And henceforth, for the next five weeks, you will
awake each morning to read and absorb the principles
in:

The Scroll Marked III

I will persist until I succeed.

In the Orient young bulls are tested for the fight arena
in a certain manner. Each is brought to the ring and allowed
to attack a picador who pricks them with a lance. The
bravery of each bull is then rated with care according to
the number of times he demonstrates his willingness to
charge in spite of the sting of the blade. Henceforth will I
recognize that each day I am tested by life in like manner.
If I persist, if I continue to charge forward, I will succeed.

I will persist until I succeed.

I was not delivered unto this world in defeat, nor does
failure course in my veins. I am not a sheep waiting to be
prodded by my shepherd. I am a lion and I refuse to talk,
to walk, to sleep with the sheep. I will hear not those who
weep and complain, for their disease is contagious. Let them
join the sheep. The slaughterhouse of failure is not my
destiny.

I will persist until I succeed.

The prizes of life are at the end of each journey, not near the beginning; and it is not given to me to know how many steps are necessary in order to reach my goal. Failure I may still encounter at the thousandth step, yet success hides behind the next bend in the road. Never will I know how close it lies unless I turn the corner.

Always will I take another step. If that is of no avail I will take another, and yet another. In truth, one step at a time is not too difficult.

I will persist until I succeed.

Henceforth, I will consider each day's effort as but one blow of my blade against a mighty oak. The first blow may cause not a tremor in the wood, nor the second, nor the third. Each blow, of itself, may be trifling, and seem of no consequence. Yet from childish swipes the oak will eventually tumble. So it will be with my efforts of today.

I will be liken to the rain drop which washes away the mountain; the ant who devours a tiger; the star which brightens the earth; the slave who builds a pyramid. I will build my castle one brick at a time for I know that small attempts, repeated, will complete any undertaking.

I will persist until I succeed.

I will never consider defeat and I will remove from my vocabulary such words and phrases as quit, cannot, unable, impossible, out of the question, improbable, failure, unworkable, hopeless, and retreat; for they are the words of fools. I will avoid despair but if this disease of the mind should infect me then I will work on in despair. I will toil and I will endure. I will ignore the obstacles at my feet and keep mine eyes on the goals above my head, for I know that where dry desert ends, green grass grows.

I will persist until I succeed.

I will remember the ancient law of averages and I will bend it to my good. I will persist with knowledge that each failure to sell will increase my chance for success at the next attempt. Each nay I hear will bring me closer to the sound of yea. Each frown I meet only prepares me for the smile to come. Each misfortune I encounter will carry in it the seed of tomorrow's good luck. I must have the night to appreciate the day. I must fail often to succeed only once.

I will persist until I succeed.

I will try, and try, and try again. Each obstacle I will consider as a mere detour to my goal and a challenge to my profession. I will persist and develop my skills as the mariner develops his, by learning to ride out the wrath of each storm.

I will persist until I succeed.

Henceforth, I will learn and apply another secret of those who excel in my work. When each day is ended, not regarding whether it has been a success or failure, I will attempt to achieve one more sale. When my thoughts beckon my tired body homeward I will resist the temptation to depart. I will try again. I will make one more attempt to close with victory, and if that fails I will make another. Never will I allow any day to end with a failure. Thus will I plant the seed of tomorrow's success and gain an insurmountable advantage over those who cease their labor at a prescribed time. When others cease their struggle, then mine will begin, and my harvest will be full.

I will persist until I succeed.

Nor will I allow yesterday's success to lull me into today's complacency, for this is the great foundation of failure. I will forget the happenings of the day that is gone, whether they were good or bad, and greet the new sun with confidence that this will be the best day of my life.

So long as there is breath in me, that long will I persist. For now I know one of the greatest principles of success; if I persist long enough I will win.

I will persist.

I will win.

SUCCESS RECORDER
The Sixth Week

✦✦

Monday　　　　　　　**Date** ....　　No. of times daily

1. I read The Scroll Marked III
　　　　　Review Paragraph for the Week
2. I kept myself away from the sheep whose weeping and　　**Rating**
　　complaining are contagious; I avoided negative thoughts
　　or words; I tried for just one more sale or completed one
　　more task when it was time to journey home and I did
　　not allow the day to end with a failure.　　　　　　**Total**
　　　　　　　　　　(Insert number in each box)

Tuesday　　　　　　**Date** ....　　No. of times daily

1. I read The Scroll Marked III
2. I read the review paragraph above　　　　　　　　**Rating**

　　　　　　　　　　　　　　　　　　Total

Wednesday　　　　**Date** ....　　No. of times daily

1. I read The Scroll Marked III
2. I read the review paragraph above　　　　　　　　**Rating**

　　　　　　　　　　　　　　　　　　Total

Thursday　　　　　**Date** ....　　No. of times daily

1. I read The Scroll Marked III
2. I read the review paragraph above　　　　　　　　**Rating**

　　　　　　　　　　　　　　　　　　Total

Friday　　　　　　　**Date** ....　　No. of times daily

1. I read The Scroll Marked III
2. I read the review paragraph above　　　　　　　　**Rating**

　　　　　　　　　　　　　　　　　　Total

　　　　　　　　　　Total points for the week

*Appointments for the week*_____

Monday_____

_____

_____

_____

_____

Tuesday_____

_____

_____

_____

_____

Wednesday_____

_____

_____

_____

_____

Thursday_____

_____

_____

_____

_____

Friday_____

_____

_____

_____

_____

*Achievements of the week*_____

_____

_____

_____

_____

_____

Reflection For The Week

Every noble work is at first impossible.　　—*Carlyle*

SUCCESS RECORDER
The Seventh Week

✦✦✦

Monday **Date**.. No. of times daily

1. I read The Scroll Marked III
   Review Paragraph for the Week
2. I kept myself away from the sheep whose weeping and   **Rating**
   complaining are contagious; I avoided negative thoughts
   or words; I tried for just one more sale or completed one
   more task when it was time to journey home and I did
   not allow the day to end with a failure.   **Total**
   (Insert number in each box)

Tuesday **Date**.. No. of times daily

1. I read The Scroll Marked III
2. I read the review paragraph above   **Rating**

Total

Wednesday **Date**.. No. of times daily

1. I read The Scroll Marked III
2. I read the review paragraph above   **Rating**

Total

Thursday **Date**.. No. of times daily

1. I read The Scroll Marked III
2. I read the review paragraph above   **Rating**

Total

Friday **Date**.. No. of times daily

1. I read The Scroll Marked III
2. I read the review paragraph above   **Rating**

Total

Total points for the week

*Appointments for the week*_____

Monday_____
_____
_____
_____
_____

Tuesday_____
_____
_____
_____
_____

Wednesday_____
_____
_____
_____
_____

Thursday_____
_____
_____
_____
_____

Friday_____
_____
_____
_____
_____

*Achievements of the week*_____
_____
_____
_____
_____

Reflection For The Week

The conditions of conquest are always easy. We have but to toil awhile, endure awhile, believe always, and never turn back. —*Simms*

SUCCESS RECORDER
The Eighth Week

✦✦✦

Monday   **Date** ....   No. of times daily

1. I read The Scroll Marked III

        Review Paragraph for the Week

2. I kept myself away from the sheep whose weeping and   Rating
   complaining are contagious; I avoided negative thoughts
   or words; I tried for just one more sale or completed one
   more task when it was time to journey home and I did
   not allow the day to end with a failure.   Total

                        (Insert number in each box)

Tuesday   **Date**..............................   No. of times daily

1. I read The Scroll Marked III
2. I read the review paragraph above   Rating

                            Total

Wednesday   **Date**..............................   No. of times daily

1. I read The Scroll Marked III
2. I read the review paragraph above   Rating

                            Total

Thursday   **Date**..............................   No. of times daily

1. I read The Scroll Marked III
2. I read the review paragraph above   Rating

                            Total

Friday   **Date**..............................   No. of times daily

1. I read The Scroll Marked III
2. I read the review paragraph above   Rating

                            Total

                        Total points for the week

*Appointments for the week*_____

Monday_____
_____
_____
_____
_____

Tuesday_____
_____
_____
_____
_____

Wednesday_____
_____
_____
_____
_____

Thursday_____
_____
_____
_____
_____

Friday_____
_____
_____
_____
_____

*Achievements of the week*_____
_____
_____
_____
_____

Reflection For The Week

I hold a doctrine, to which I owe not much, indeed, but all the little I ever had, namely, that with ordinary talent and extraordinary perseverance, all things are attainable.   —*T. F. Buxton*

SUCCESS RECORDER
The Ninth Week

◆◆

Monday Date................................... No. of times daily

1. I read The Scroll Marked III
      Review Paragraph for the Week
2. I kept myself away from the sheep whose weeping and   Rating
   complaining are contagious; I avoided negative thoughts
   or words; I tried for just one more sale or completed one
   more task when it was time to journey home and I did
   not allow the day to end with a failure.   Total

(Insert number in each box)

_____

Tuesday Date................................... No. of times daily

1. I read The Scroll Marked III
2. I read the review paragraph above   Rating

Total

_____

Wednesday Date................................... No. of times daily

1. I read The Scroll Marked III
2. I read the review paragraph above   Rating

Total

_____

Thursday Date................................... No. of times daily

1. I read The Scroll Marked III
2. I read the review paragraph above   Rating

Total

_____

Friday Date................................... No. of times daily

1. I read The Scroll Marked III
2. I read the review paragraph above   Rating

Total

Total points for the week

*Appointments for the week*_____

Monday_____

_____

_____

_____

_____

Tuesday_____

_____

_____

_____

_____

Wednesday_____

_____

_____

_____

_____

Thursday_____

_____

_____

_____

_____

Friday_____

_____

_____

_____

_____

*Achievements of the week*_____

_____

_____

_____

_____

_____

Reflection For The Week

Persistent people begin their success where others end in failure.
—*Edward Eggleston*

SUCCESS RECORDER
The Tenth Week

✦✦✦

Monday   Date ....   No. of times daily

1. I read The Scroll Marked III
            Review Paragraph for the Week

2. I kept myself away from the sheep whose weeping and   Rating
complaining are contagious; I avoided negative thoughts
or words; I tried for just one more sale or completed one
more task when it was time to journey home and I did
not allow the day to end with a failure.
                 (Insert number in each box)   Total

Tuesday   Date...............................   No. of times daily

1. I read The Scroll Marked III
2. I read the review paragraph above   Rating

                              Total

Wednesday   Date...............................   No. of times daily

1. I read The Scroll Marked III
2. I read the review paragraph above   Rating

                              Total

Thursday   Date...............................   No. of times daily

1. I read The Scroll Marked III
2. I read the review paragraph above   Rating

                              Total

Friday   Date...............................   No. of times daily

1. I read The Scroll Marked III
2. I read the review paragraph above   Rating

                              Total

                      Total points for the week

*Appointments for the week*_____

Monday_____
_____
_____
_____
_____

Tuesday_____
_____
_____
_____
_____

Wednesday_____
_____
_____
_____
_____

Thursday_____
_____
_____
_____
_____

Friday_____
_____
_____
_____
_____

*Achievements of the week*_____
_____
_____
_____
_____
_____

Reflection For The Week

No road is too long for the man who advances deliberately and without undue haste; and no honors are too distant for the man who prepares himself for them with patience.　　　**—Bruyere**

Chapter VI

Isn't this simple?

If you've come this far you already have the habit of reading your scroll three times a day. Nothing to it . . . just as there would be nothing to your doing a hundred push-ups by now if you had started that ten weeks ago. What a difference ten weeks makes!

And completing each day's Success Recorder . . . that's simple, too, isn't it? So simple that you can't even get out of doing it with the excuse that you're too busy . . . or too tired.

But do you realize what you have already done for yourself by simply reading and imprinting on your subconscious mind the words from The Scroll Marked II and The Scroll Marked III three times each day . . . for five weeks each? You are, no doubt, already communicating better with those around you, you have relieved friction from some quarters, and you have hardened that spine so that you continue to try, and try again when, in the past, you would have headed home afer a few failures, with your tail between your legs.

Now your personality is more open, you are a warmer person, you make friends easier, and yet you know how

THE GREATEST SECRET IN THE WORLD

to hang in there until you make sales or complete tasks which you would never have come close to completing before you started this program. Furthermore, your sales or your duties are coming easier, because you're a friendlier and more likeable person, so you rarely have to call upon that new persistence you've developed. The scrolls, you are discovering, as with all virtues, are not separate, but related. When you improve on one they all improve. When one bad habit is subdued, the next is overcome with less struggle.

I told you that you were a miracle of nature . . . and now I'll prove it to you in:

The Scroll Marked IV

I am nature's greatest miracle.

Since the beginning of time never has there been another with my mind, my heart, my eyes, my ears, my hands, my hair, my mouth. None that came before, none that live today, and none that come tomorrow can walk and talk and move and think exactly like me. All men are my brothers yet I am different from each. I am a unique creature.

Although I am of the animal kingdom, animal rewards alone will not satisfy me. Within me burns a flame which has been passed from generations uncounted and its heat is a constant irritation to my spirit to become better than I am, and I will. I will fan this flame of dissatisfaction and proclaim my uniqueness to the world.

None can duplicate my brush strokes, none can make my chisel marks, none can duplicate my handwriting, none

157

can produce my child, and, in truth, none has the ability to sell exactly as I. Henceforth, I will capitalize on this difference for it is an asset to be promoted to the fullest.

I am nature's greatest miracle.

Vain attempts to imitate others no longer will I make. Instead will I place my uniqueness on display in the market place. I will proclaim it, yea, I will sell it. I will begin now to accent my differences; hide my similarities. So too will I apply this principle to the goods I sell. Salesman and goods, different from all others, and proud of the difference.

I am a unique creature of nature.

I am rare, and there is value in all rarity; therefore, I am valuable. I am the end product of thousands of years of evolution; therefore, I am better equipped in both mind and body than all the emperors and wise men who preceded me.

But my skills, my mind, my heart, and my body will stagnate, rot, and die lest I put them to good use. I have unlimited potential. Only a small portion of my brain do I employ; only a paltry amount of my muscles do I flex. A hundredfold or more can I increase my accomplishments of yesterday and this I will do, beginning today.

Nevermore will I be satisfied with yesterday's accomplishments nor will I indulge, anymore, in self-praise for deeds which in reality are too small to even acknowledge. I can accomplish far more than I have, and I will, for why should the miracle which produced me end with my birth? Why can I not extend that miracle to my deeds of today?

I am nature's greatest miracle.

I am not on this earth by chance. I am here for a purpose and that purpose is to grow into a mountain, not to shrink to a grain of sand. Henceforth will I apply all my efforts to become the highest mountain of all and I will strain my potential until it cries for mercy.

I will increase my knowledge of mankind, myself, and the goods I sell, thus my sales will multiply. I will practice, and improve, and polish the words I utter to sell my goods, for this is the foundation on which I will build my career and never will I forget that many have attained great wealth and success with only one sales talk, delivered with excellence. Also will I seek constantly to improve my manners and graces, for they are the sugar to which all are attracted.

I am nature's greatest miracle.

I will concentrate my energy on the challenge of the moment and my actions will help me forget all else. The problems of my home will be left in my home. I will think naught of my family when I am in the market place for this will cloud my thoughts. So too will the problems of the market place be left in the market place and I will think naught of my profession when I am in my home for this will dampen my love.

There is no room in the market place for my family, nor is there room in my home for the market. Each I will divorce from the other and, thus will I remain wedded to both. Separate must they remain or my career will die. This is a paradox of the ages.

I am nature's greatest miracle.

I have been given eyes to see and a mind to think and now I know a great secret of life for I perceive, at last, that all my problems, discouragements, and heartaches are, in truth, great opportunities in disguise. I will no longer be fooled by the garments they wear for my eyes are open. I will look beyond the cloth and I will not be deceived.

I am nature's greatest miracle.

No beast, no plant, no wind, no rain, no rock, no lake had the same beginning as I, for I was conceived in love and brought forth with a purpose. In the past I have not considered this fact but it will henceforth shape and guide my life.

I am nature's greatest miracle.

And nature knows not defeat. Eventually, she emerges victorious and so will I, and with each victory the next struggle becomes less difficult.

I will win, and I will become a great salesman, for I am unique.

I am nature's greatest miracle.

SUCCESS RECORDER
The Eleventh Week

✦✦

Monday   Date..................   No. of times daily

1. I read The Scroll Marked IV
         Review Paragraph for the Week

2. I refrained from all self-praise; I learned at least one new   Rating
   benefit or feature about the product I handle; I concentrated on making each project or sales presentation better
   than the last; I worked on my manners and I kept the
   market place and home separate from each other in my
   thoughts.   Total

                    (Insert number in each box)

Tuesday   Date..................   No. of times daily

1. I read The Scroll Marked IV
2. I read the review paragraph above   Rating

                                        Total

Wednesday   Date..................   No. of times daily

1. I read The Scroll Marked IV
2. I read the review paragraph above   Rating

                                        Total

Thursday   Date..................   No. of times daily

1. I read The Scroll Marked IV
2. I read the review paragraph above   Rating

                                        Total

Friday   Date..................   No. of times daily

1. I read The Scroll Marked IV
2. I read the review paragraph above   Rating

                                        Total

                    Total points for the week

*Appointments for the week*_____

Monday_____
_____
_____
_____

Tuesday_____
_____
_____
_____

Wednesday_____
_____
_____
_____

Thursday_____
_____
_____
_____

Friday_____
_____
_____
_____

*Achievements of the week*_____
_____
_____
_____
_____

Reflection For The Week

Man is an animal which alone among the animals re-
fuses to be satisfied by the fulfillment of animal desires.
—*Alexander Graham Bell*

SUCCESS RECORDER
The Twelfth Week

◆◆◆

Monday   **Date**................................ No. of times daily

1. I read The Scroll Marked IV
          Review Paragraph for the Week
2. I refrained from all self-praise; I learned at least one new   Rating
   benefit or feature about the product I handle; I concentrated on making each project or sales presentation better
   than the last; I worked on my manners and I kept the
   market place and home separate from each other in my
   thoughts.   Total
                          (Insert number in each box)

_____

Tuesday   **Date**................................ No. of times daily

1. I read The Scroll Marked IV
2. I read the review paragraph above   Rating

                                                      Total

_____

Wednesday   **Date**................................ No. of times daily

1. I read The Scroll Marked IV
2. I read the review paragraph above   Rating

                                                      Total

_____

Thursday   **Date**................................ No. of times daily

1. I read The Scroll Marked IV
2. I read the review paragraph above   Rating

                                                      Total

_____

Friday   **Date**................................ No. of times daily

1. I read The Scroll Marked IV
2. I read the review paragraph above   Rating

                                                      Total

_____

                              Total points for the week

*Appointments for the week*_____

Monday_____
_____
_____
_____
_____

Tuesday_____
_____
_____
_____
_____

Wednesday_____
_____
_____
_____
_____

Thursday_____
_____
_____
_____
_____

Friday_____
_____
_____
_____
_____

*Achievements of the week*_____
_____
_____
_____
_____
_____

Reflection For The Week

Whoever considers the study of anatomy, I believe, will never be an atheist; the frame of man's body, and coherence of his parts, being so strange and paradoxical, that I hold it to be the greatest miracle of nature. **—Lord Herbert**

SUCCESS RECORDER
The Thirteenth Week

❖❖

Monday   **Date** ....   No. of times daily

1. I read The Scroll Marked IV
          Review Paragraph for the Week
2. I refrained from all self-praise; I learned at least one new   **Rating**
   benefit or feature about the product I handle; I concentrated on making each project or sales presentation better
   than the last; I worked on my manners and I kept the
   market place and home separate from each other in my
   thoughts.   **Total**

                              (Insert number in each box)

Tuesday   **Date** ....   No. of times daily

1. I read The Scroll Marked IV
2. I read the review paragraph above   **Rating**

                                              Total

Wednesday   **Date** ....   No. of times daily

1. I read The Scroll Marked IV
2. I read the review paragraph above   **Rating**

                                              Total

Thursday   **Date** ....   No. of times daily

1. I read The Scroll Marked IV
2. I read the review paragraph above   **Rating**

                                              Total

Friday   **Date** ....   No. of times daily

1. I read The Scroll Marked IV
2. I read the review paragraph above   **Rating**

                                              Total

                    Total points for the week

*Appointments for the week*_____

Monday_____
_____
_____
_____
_____

Tuesday_____
_____
_____
_____
_____

Wednesday_____
_____
_____
_____
_____

Thursday_____
_____
_____
_____
_____

Friday_____
_____
_____
_____
_____

*Achievements of the week*_____
_____
_____
_____
_____
_____

Reflection For The Week

The way of a superior man is threefold: virtuous, he
is free from anxieties; wise, he is free from perplexities;
bold, he is free from fear. —Confucius

SUCCESS RECORDER
The Fourteenth Week

✦✦

Monday   Date ....   No. of times daily

1. I read The Scroll Marked IV
        Review Paragraph for the Week
2. I refrained from all self-praise; I learned at least one new
   benefit or feature about the product I handle; I concentrated on making each project or sales presentation better
   than the last; I worked on my manners and I kept the
   market place and home separate from each other in my
   thoughts.

Rating

(Insert number in each box)   **Total**

Tuesday   Date ....   No. of times daily

1. I read The Scroll Marked IV
2. I read the review paragraph above

Rating

     Total

Wednesday   Date ....   No. of times daily

1. I read The Scroll Marked IV
2. I read the review paragraph above

Rating

     Total

Thursday   Date ....   No. of times daily

1. I read The Scroll Marked IV
2. I read the review paragraph above

Rating

     Total

Friday   Date ....   No. of times daily

1. I read The Scroll Marked IV
2. I read the review paragraph above

Rating

     Total

        Total points for the week

*Appointments for the week*_____

Monday_____
_____
_____
_____
_____

Tuesday_____
_____
_____
_____
_____

Wednesday_____
_____
_____
_____
_____

Thursday_____
_____
_____
_____
_____

Friday_____
_____
_____
_____
_____

*Achievements of the week*_____
_____
_____
_____
_____
_____

Reflection For The Week

I mean to make myself a man, and if I succeed in
that, I shall succeed in everything else.　　*—Garfield*

SUCCESS RECORDER
The Fifteenth Week

✦✦

Monday   Date....................................   No. of times daily

1. I read The Scroll Marked IV
               Review Paragraph for the Week
2. I refrained from all self-praise; I learned at least one new   **Rating**
    benefit or feature about the product I handle; I concen-
    trated on making each project or sales presentation better
    than the last; I worked on my manners and I kept the
    market place and home separate from each other in my
    thoughts.   Total

                              (Insert number in each box)

Tuesday   Date....................................   No. of times daily

1. I read The Scroll Marked IV
2. I read the review paragraph above   **Rating**

                                                          Total

---

Wednesday   Date....................................   No. of times daily

1. I read The Scroll Marked IV
2. I read the review paragraph above   **Rating**

                                                          Total

---

Thursday   Date....................................   No. of times daily

1. I read The Scroll Marked IV
2. I read the review paragraph above   **Rating**

                                                          Total

---

Friday   Date....................................   No. of times daily

1. I read The Scroll Marked IV
2. I read the review paragraph above   **Rating**

                                                          Total

                              Total points for the week

*Appointments for the week*_____

Monday_____
_____
_____
_____
_____

Tuesday_____
_____
_____
_____
_____

Wednesday_____
_____
_____
_____
_____

Thursday_____
_____
_____
_____
_____

Friday_____
_____
_____
_____
_____

*Achievements of the week*_____
_____
_____
_____
_____
_____

Reflection For The Week

Man himself is the crowning wonder of creation; the
study of his nature the noblest study the world affords.

—Gladstone

Chapter VII

Fifteen weeks have now passed.

You have come a long way, my good friend.

If you have read the scrolls three times a day; if you have taken a few moments each evening to examine your actions of the day . . . then without doubt you are a changed person from the individual you were. And isn't it amazing . . . everyone around you seems to have changed, too.

Perhaps this old legend will help you understand what has happened to you:

There was an old Quaker who stood at the village well, greeting weary travelers who passed along the way. And to each who asked, "What manner of people live hereabouts?" he would respond with another question, "What manner of people did thee find in thy last abode?"

If the traveler said that he had left a community where people were bright and gay; genial and fun-loving, the Quaker would answer confidently that the questing one would find them much the same in his community. But to travelers who complained that they left a community where people were ugly, quarrelsome, and ill-tempered, the patriarch would sadly shake his head and say "Alas, here thee will find them much the same."

You are about to embark on five very interesting weeks. More than any other scroll, I promise you that as you begin to live the injunctions in The Scroll Marked V you will be noticed by strangers, friends, and foes alike.

Henry Van Dyke once wrote that some people are so afraid to die that they never begin to live. For the next five weeks you are being asked to imagine that each day, when you arise, will be your last day on earth . . . and you are to act accordingly.

Those with little faith, and less courage, would shrivel up in a corner if they knew this was really their last day on earth . . . but since you have persisted to this point with your Success Recorder I have little doubt of your abundance of faith . . . or courage.

You may wish to keep additional notes about how others react to you during these next five weeks . . . especially those above you in the "pecking order" of your company. Along with what you have *already* accomplished in transforming your personality, these weeks usually produce confrontations with superiors which lead to interesting developments . . . like promotions and raises.

So let's get started with this important scroll:

The Scroll Marked V

I will live this day as if it is my last.

And what shall I do with this last precious day which remains in my keeping? First, I will seal up its container of life so that not one drop spills itself upon the sand. I will waste not a moment mourning yesterday's misfortunes, yesterday's defeats, yesterday's aches of the heart, for why should I throw good after bad?

Can sand flow upward in the hour glass? Will the sun rise where it sets and set where it rises? Can I relive the errors of yesterday and right them? Can I call back yesterday's wounds and make them whole? Can I become younger than yesterday? Can I take back the evil that was spoken, the blows that were struck, the pain that was caused? No. Yesterday is buried forever and I will think of it no more.

I will live this day as if it is my last.

And what then shall I do? Forgetting yesterday neither will I think of tomorrow. Why should I throw *now* after *maybe?* Can tomorrow's sand flow through the glass before today's? Will the sun rise twice this morning? Can I perform tomorrow's deeds while standing in today's path? Can I place tomorrow's gold in today's purse? Can tomorrow's child be born today? Can tomorrow's death cast its shadow backward and darken today's joy? Should I concern myself over events which I may never witness? Should I torment myself with problems that may never come to pass? No! Tomorrow lies buried with yesterday, and I will think of it no more.

I will live this day as if it is my last.

This day is all I have and these hours are now my eternity. I greet this sunrise with cries of joy as a prisoner who is reprieved from death. I lift mine arms with thanks for this priceless gift of a new day. So too, I will beat upon my heart with gratitude as I consider all who greeted yesterday's sunrise who are no longer with the living today. I am indeed a fortunate man and today's hours are but a bonus, undeserved. Why have I been allowed to live this extra day when others,

far better than I, have departed? Is it that they have accomplished their purpose while mine is yet to be achieved?
Is this another opportunity for me to become the man I
know I can be? Is there a purpose in nature? Is this my day
to excel?

I will live this day as if it is my last.

I have but one life and life is naught but a measurement
of time. When I waste one I destroy the other. If I waste
today I destroy the last page of my life. Therefore, each
hour of this day will I cherish for it can never return. It
cannot be banked today to be withdrawn on the morrow,
for who can trap the wind? Each minute of this day will I
grasp with both hands and fondle with love for its value is
beyond price. What dying man can purchase another breath
though he willingly give all his gold? What price dare I place
on the hours ahead? I will make them priceless!

I will live this day as if it is my last.

I will avoid with fury the killers of time. Procrastination
I will destroy with action; doubt I will bury under faith;
fear I will dismember with confidence. Where there are idle
mouths I will listen not; where there are idle hands I will
linger not; where there are idle bodies I will visit not. Henceforth I know that to court idleness is to steal food, clothing,
and warmth from those I love. I am not a thief. I am a man
of love and today is my last chance to prove my love and
my greatness.

I will live this day as if it is my last.

The duties of today I shall fulfill today. Today I shall
fondle my children while they are young; tomorrow they will
be gone, and so will I. Today I shall embrace my woman
with sweet kisses; tomorrow she will be gone, and so will
I. Today I shall lift up a friend in need; tomorrow he will

no longer cry for help, nor will I hear his cries. Today I shall give myself in sacrifice and work; tomorrow I will have nothing to give, and there will be none to receive.

I will live this day as if it is my last.

And if it is my last, it will be my greatest monument. This day I will make the best day of my life. This day I will drink every minute to its full. I will savor its taste and give thanks. I will maketh every hour count and each minute I will trade only for something of value. I will labor harder than ever before and push my muscles until they cry for relief, and then I will continue. I will make more calls than ever before. I will sell more goods than ever before. I will earn more gold than ever before. Each minute of today will be more fruitful than hours of yesterday. My last must be my best.

I will live this day as if it is my last.

And if it is not, I shall fall to my knees and give thanks.

SUCCESS RECORDER
The Sixteenth Week

✦✦✦

Monday   Date...................................   No. of times daily

1. I read The Scroll Marked V
          Review Paragraph for the Week
2. I greeted this morning with gratitude for the gift of an-   **Rating**
   other day; I mourned not yesterday's mistakes and de-
   feats; I wasted none of my precious time on foolishness;
   I treated everyone with tenderness as if I would see them
   no more and I truly lived this day as if it were my last.   **Total**
                              (Insert number in each box)

Tuesday   Date...................................   No. of times daily

1. I read The Scroll Marked V
2. I read the review paragraph above   **Rating**

                                                  Total

Wednesday   Date...................................   No. of times daily

1. I read The Scroll Marked V
2. I read the review paragraph above   **Rating**

                                                  Total

Thursday   Date...................................   No. of times daily

1. I read The Scroll Marked V
2. I read the review paragraph above   **Rating**

                                                  Total

Friday   Date...................................   No. of times daily

1. I read The Scroll Marked V
2. I read the review paragraph above   **Rating**

                                                  Total

                    Total points for the week

*Appointments for the week*_____

Monday_____
_____
_____
_____
_____

Tuesday_____
_____
_____
_____
_____

Wednesday_____
_____
_____
_____
_____

Thursday_____
_____
_____
_____
_____

Friday_____
_____
_____
_____
_____

*Achievements of the week*_____
_____
_____
_____
_____

Reflection For The Week

The life of every man is a diary in which he means to write one story, and writes another; and his humblest hour is when he compares the volume as it is with what he hoped to make it. —*James M. Barrie*

SUCCESS RECORDER
The Seventeenth Week

✦✦

Monday   Date............................   No. of times daily

1. I read The Scroll Marked V
            Review Paragraph for the Week   Rating
2. I greeted this morning with gratitude for the gift of another day; I mourned not yesterday's mistakes and defeats; I wasted none of my precious time on foolishness;
   I treated everyone with tenderness as if I would see them
   no more and I truly lived this day as if it were my last.   Total
                              (Insert number in each box)

Tuesday   Date............................   No. of times daily

1. I read The Scroll Marked V
2. I read the review paragraph above   Rating

                                                    Total

Wednesday   Date............................   No. of times daily

1. I read The Scroll Marked V
2. I read the review paragraph above   Rating

                                                    Total

Thursday   Date............................   No. of times daily

1. I read The Scroll Marked V
2. I read the review paragraph above   Rating

                                                    Total

Friday   Date............................   No. of times daily

1. I read The Scroll Marked V
2. I read the review paragraph above   Rating

                                                    Total

                              Total points for the week

*Appointments for the week*_____

Monday_____
_____
_____
_____
_____

Tuesday_____
_____
_____
_____
_____

Wednesday_____
_____
_____
_____

Thursday_____
_____
_____
_____
_____

Friday_____
_____
_____
_____

*Achievements of the week*_____
_____
_____
_____
_____

Reflection For The Week

There is no cure for birth and death save to enjoy the interval. The dark background which death supplies brings out the tender colors of life in all their purity.

—George Santayana

SUCCESS RECORDER
The Eighteenth Week

❖❖

Monday   **Date**........................... No. of times daily

1. I read The Scroll Marked V
   Review Paragraph for the Week
2. I greeted this morning with gratitude for the gift of an- **Rating**
  other day; I mourned not yesterday's mistakes and defeats; I wasted none of my precious time on foolishness;
  I treated everyone with tenderness as if I would see them
  no more and I truly lived this day as if it were my last. **Total**
           (Insert number in each box)

Tuesday   **Date**........................... No. of times daily

1. I read The Scroll Marked V
2. I read the review paragraph above **Rating**

               Total

Wednesday   **Date**........................... No. of times daily

1. I read The Scroll Marked V
2. I read the review paragraph above **Rating**

               Total

Thursday   **Date**........................... No. of times daily

1. I read The Scroll Marked V
2. I read the review paragraph above **Rating**

               Total

Friday   **Date**........................... No. of times daily

1. I read The Scroll Marked V
2. I read the review paragraph above **Rating**

               Total

        Total points for the week

*Appointments for the week*_____

Monday_____

_____

_____

_____

_____

Tuesday_____

_____

_____

_____

_____

Wednesday_____

_____

_____

_____

_____

Thursday_____

_____

_____

_____

_____

Friday_____

_____

_____

_____

_____

*Achievements of the week*_____

_____

_____

_____

✠✠

Reflection For The Week

When I reflect, as I frequently do, upon the felicity I have enjoyed, I sometimes say to myself, that were the offer made me, I would engage to run again, from beginning to end, the same career of life. All I would ask, should be the privilege of an author, to correct in a second edition, certain errors of the first.

—Benjamin Franklin

✠✠

SUCCESS RECORDER
The Nineteenth Week

✦✦

Monday   **Date**....................................   No. of times daily

1. I read The Scroll Marked V
          Review Paragraph for the Week
2. I greeted this morning with gratitude for the gift of an-   **Rating**
   other day; I mourned not yesterday's mistakes and de-
   feats; I wasted none of my precious time on foolishness;
   I treated everyone with tenderness as if I would see them
   no more and I truly lived this day as if it were my last.   **Total**
                         (Insert number in each box)

Tuesday   **Date**....................................   No. of times daily

1. I read The Scroll Marked V
2. I read the review paragraph above   **Rating**

                                              Total

Wednesday   **Date**....................................   No. of times daily

1. I read The Scroll Marked V
2. I read the review paragraph above   **Rating**

                                              Total

Thursday   **Date**....................................   No. of times daily

1. I read The Scroll Marked V
2. I read the review paragraph above   **Rating**

                                              Total

Friday   **Date**....................................   No. of times daily

1. I read The Scroll Marked V
2. I read the review paragraph above   **Rating**

                                              Total

                         Total points for the week

*Appointments for the week*_____

Monday_____
_____
_____
_____
_____

Tuesday_____
_____
_____
_____
_____

Wednesday_____
_____
_____
_____
_____

Thursday_____
_____
_____
_____
_____

Friday_____
_____
_____
_____
_____

*Achievements of the week*_____
_____
_____
_____
_____
_____

Reflection For The Week

I count all that part of my life lost which I spent not in communion with God, or in doing good.   —Donne

SUCCESS RECORDER
The Twentieth Week

✦✦✦

Monday   Date.............................   No. of times daily

1. I read The Scroll Marked V
                Review Paragraph for the Week
2. I greeted this morning with gratitude for the gift of an-   Rating
   other day; I mourned not yesterday's mistakes and defeats; I wasted none of my precious time on foolishness;
   I treated everyone with tenderness as if I would see them
   no more and I truly lived this day as if it were my last.   Total
                (Insert number in each box)

Tuesday   Date.............................   No. of times daily

1. I read The Scroll Marked V
2. I read the review paragraph above   Rating

                                                    Total

Wednesday   Date.............................   No. of times daily

1. I read The Scroll Marked V
2. I read the review paragraph above   Rating

                                                    Total

Thursday   Date.............................   No. of times daily

1. I read The Scroll Marked V
2. I read the review paragraph above   Rating

                                                    Total

Friday   Date.............................   No. of times daily

1. I read The Scroll Marked V
2. I read the review paragraph above   Rating

                                                    Total

                        Total points for the week

*Appointments for the week*_____

Monday_____
_____
_____
_____
_____

Tuesday_____
_____
_____
_____
_____

Wednesday_____
_____
_____
_____
_____

Thursday_____
_____
_____
_____
_____

Friday_____
_____
_____
_____
_____

*Achievements of the week*_____
_____
_____
_____
_____
_____

Reflection For The Week

Be such a man, and live such a life, that if every man were such as you, and every life like yours, this earth would be a God's Paradise. **—Phillips Brooks**

Chapter VIII

Do you get moody?

Of course you do. There are days when you'd like to crawl into a hole and just hide from the world. Everything you touch turns to sawdust. You just can't win. You can't make a sale. What's the sense to anything? Right?

And then there are other days when you can do nothing wrong. From the time you awake you're wearing rose colored glasses and enjoying every minute of it. Sales? Completed projects? You can't miss. Everything is going your way.

What causes these fluctuations in our emotional level? We don't know, but some time ago I was fortunate enough to work closely with Professor Edward R. Dewey, head of The Foundation for the Study of Cycles at the University of Pittsburgh. We co-authored a book entitled *"Cycles, The Mysterious Forces That Trigger Events"* (published by Hawthorn Books).

One of the many cycles we dealt with was the emotional cycle in human beings. Several years ago a scientific study was conducted by Professor Rex Hersey of the University of Pennsylvania. His conclusion was that the emotional cycle in man has an average length of about five weeks. This is the typical length of time it takes for a normal individual to move from one period of elation down the scale to a feeling of worry (the most destructive emotion according to Hersey) and back up again to the next period of elation.

Five weeks! Maybe your emotional cycle is longer or shorter but I'm sure you'll agree that it would be great to know your "high" and "low" periods. Here's a simple method to learn this important secret about yourself. Just prepare a chart similar to the one below:

		Month											
		1	2	3	4	5	6	7	8	9	10		
Elated	+3												
Happy	+2												
Pleasant feeling	+1												
Neutral	0												
Unpleasant feeling	−1												
Disgusted; sad	−2												
Worried; depressed	−3												

Set up graph for 30 days

Every evening take a moment to review your general mood of the day. Then place a dot in the box which seems to fit your state of mind for that day. Connect the dots as time goes on.

Soon you will see a pattern forming. This is your natural mood rhythm, and in most cases it will continue.

After a few months you will know, with amazing accuracy, when your next "high" is due and when you should prepare for your next "low." With this knowledge, this ability to predict your future behavior, you will be able to adjust your activities to suit your mood. When you are going through your high period of elation, you will think twice before making rash promises, impossible commitments, or misguided installment purchases. You will also be able to live through your low periods, when nothing is going right, because now you know that this will soon pass.

The Scroll Marked VI wisely reminds you of another fact . . . that your prospect or customer or supervisor or spouse is also going through a mood cycle. You may be "up" . . . but if that other person is "down" you've got a tough road ahead of you . . . yet this should not discourage you. In a few days that individual, now "up" in his mood will be completely receptive to you and your ideas.

Okay, now we know we have moods . . . but we just can't stay home during those "down" weeks or half a year's productivity goes out the window. So what do we do to remain productive even when we're "down?"

For centuries man believed that his thoughts controlled his actions. Then, along came that great psychologist William James who said that "your actions can control your thoughts . . . and your mood." In other words if you act happy you will feel happy . . . if you act enthusiastically you will feel enthusiastic . . . if you act healthy you will feel healthy. You can call it mind-control or any other name you wish . . . but I want to assure you that it works. Yet it remains a deep, dark secret to most salesmen or individuals in every walk of life. Now, you can make every day a great day as you will learn in:

The Scroll Marked VI

Today I will be master of my emotions.

The tides advance; the tides recede. Winter goes and summer comes. Summer wanes and the cold increases. The sun rises; the sun sets. The moon is full; the moon is black. The birds arrive; the birds depart. Flowers bloom; flowers fade. Seeds are sown; harvests are reaped. All nature is a circle of moods and I am a part of nature and so, like the tides, my moods will rise; my moods will fall.

Today I will be master of my emotions.

It is one of nature's tricks, little understood, that each day I awaken with moods that have changed from yesterday. Yesterday's joy will become today's sadness; yet today's sadness will grow into tomorrow's joy. Inside me is a wheel, constantly turning from sadness to joy, from exultation to depression, from happiness to melancholy. Like the flowers, today's full bloom of joy will fade and wither into despondency, yet I will remember that as today's dead flower carries the seed of tomorrow's bloom so, too, does today's sadness carry the seed of tomorrow's joy.

Today I will be master of my emotions.

And how will I master these emotions so that each day

will be productive? For unless my mood is right the day will be a failure. Trees and plants depend on the weather to flourish but I make my own weather, yea I transport it with me. If I bring rain and gloom and darkness and pessimism to my customers then they will react with rain and gloom and darkness and pessimism and they will purchase naught. If I bring my joy and enthusiasm and brightness and laughter to my customers they will react with joy and enthusiasm and brightness and laughter and my weather will produce a harvest of sales and a granary of gold for me.

Today I will be master of my emotions.

And how will I master my emotions so that every day is a happy day, and a productive one? I will learn this secret of the ages: *Weak is he who permits his thoughts to control his actions; strong is he who forces his actions to control his thoughts.* Each day, when I awake, I will follow this plan of battle before I am captured by the forces of sadness, self-pity and failure—

If I feel depressed I will sing.
If I feel sad I will laugh.
If I feel ill I will double my labor.
If I feel fear I will plunge ahead.
If I feel inferior I will wear new garments.
If I feel uncertain I will raise my voice.
If I feel poverty I will think of wealth to come.
If I feel incompetent I will remember past success.
If I feel insignificant I will remember my goals.

Today I will be master of my emotions.

Henceforth, I will know that only those with inferior ability can always be at their best, and I am not inferior. There will be days when I must constantly struggle against forces which would tear me down. Those such as despair and sadness are simple to recognize but there are others which approach with a smile and the hand of friendship and they can also destroy me. Against them, too, I must never relinquish control—

If I become overconfident I will recall my failures.

If I overindulge I will think of past hungers.

If I feel complacency I will remember my competition.

If I enjoy moments of greatness I will remember moments of shame.

If I feel all-powerful I will try to stop the wind.

If I attain great wealth I will remember one unfed mouth.

If I become overly proud I will remember a moment of weakness.

If I feel my skill is unmatched I will look at the stars.

Today I will be master of my emotions.

And with this new knowledge I will also understand and recognize the moods of he on whom I call. I will make allowances for his anger and irritation of today for he knows not the secret of controlling his mind. I can withstand his arrows and insults for now I know that tomorrow he will change and be a joy to approach.

No longer will I judge a man on one meeting; no longer will I fail to call again tomorrow on he who meets me with hate today. This day he will not buy gold chariots for a penny, yet tomorrow he would exchange his home for a tree. My knowledge of this secret will be my key to great wealth.

Today I will be master of my emotions.

Henceforth I will recognize and identify the mystery of moods in all mankind, and in me. From this moment I am prepared to control whatever personality awakes in me each day. I will master my moods through positive action and when I master my moods I will control my destiny.

Today I control my destiny, and my destiny is to become the greatest salesman in the world!

I will become master of myself.

I will become great.

SUCCESS RECORDER
The Twenty-first Week

++

Monday   Date......................................   No. of times daily

1. I read The Scroll Marked VI
         Review Paragraph for the Week
2. I avoided all negative thoughts of failure and despair by   Rating
   making my actions control my thoughts; I smiled often; I
   moved swiftly; I raised my voice to strengthen my confidence; I made allowances for the moods of others and
   I refused to allow any set-back or problem to discolor
   my day.   Total

                        (Insert number in each box)

Tuesday   Date......................................   No. of times daily

1. I read The Scroll Marked VI
2. I read the review paragraph above   Rating

                             Total

Wednesday   Date......................................   No. of times daily

1. I read The Scroll Marked VI
2. I read the review paragraph above   Rating

                             Total

Thursday   Date......................................   No. of times daily

1. I read The Scroll Marked VI
2. I read the review paragraph above   Rating

                             Total

Friday   Date......................................   No. of times daily

1. I read The Scroll Marked VI
2. I read the review paragraph above   Rating

                             Total

                 Total points for the week

*Appointments for the week*_____

Monday_____
_____
_____
_____
_____

Tuesday_____
_____
_____
_____
_____

Wednesday_____
_____
_____
_____
_____

Thursday_____
_____
_____
_____
_____

Friday_____
_____
_____
_____
_____

*Achievements of the week*_____
_____
_____
_____

Reflection For The Week

If you want to succeed in the world you must make your own opportunities as you go on. The man who waits for some seventh wave to toss him on dry land will find that the seventh wave is a long time a-coming. You can commit no greater folly than to sit by the roadside until someone comes along and invites you to ride with him to wealth or influence. —*John B. Gough*

SUCCESS RECORDER
The Twenty-second Week

❋❋❋

Monday   **Date**............................   No. of times daily

1. I read The Scroll Marked VI
      Review Paragraph for the Week

2. I avoided all negative thoughts of failure and despair by   **Rating**
   making my actions control my thoughts; I smiled often; I
   moved swiftly; I raised my voice to strengthen my confidence; I made allowances for the moods of others and
   I refused to allow any set-back or problem to discolor
   my day.   **Total**

                              (Insert number in each box)

Tuesday   **Date**............................   No. of times daily

1. I read The Scroll Marked VI
2. I read the review paragraph above   **Rating**

                                                          Total

---

Wednesday   **Date**............................   No. of times daily

1. I read The Scroll Marked VI
2. I read the review paragraph above   **Rating**

                                                          Total

---

Thursday   **Date**............................   No. of times daily

1. I read The Scroll Marked VI
2. I read the review paragraph above   **Rating**

                                                          Total

---

Friday   **Date**............................   No. of times daily

1. I read The Scroll Marked VI
2. I read the review paragraph above   **Rating**

                                                          Total

---

                              Total points for the week

*Appointments for the week*_____.

Monday_____
_____
_____
_____
_____

Tuesday_____
_____
_____
_____
_____

Wednesday_____
_____
_____
_____
_____

Thursday_____
_____
_____
_____
_____

Friday_____
_____
_____
_____
_____

*Achievements of the week*_____
_____
_____
_____
_____
_____

Reflection For The Week

The golden moments in the stream of life rush past
us, and we see nothing but sand; the angels come to
visit us, and we only know them when they are gone.
—George Eliot

SUCCESS RECORDER
The Twenty-third Week

✦✦✦

Monday   **Date**............................   No. of times daily

1. I read The Scroll Marked VI
   Review Paragraph for the Week
2. I avoided all negative thoughts of failure and despair by
   making my actions control my thoughts; I smiled often; I
   moved swiftly; I raised my voice to strengthen my confidence; I made allowances for the moods of others and
   I refused to allow any set-back or problem to discolor
   my day.

Rating

Total

(Insert number in each box)

Tuesday   **Date**............................   No. of times daily

1. I read The Scroll Marked VI
2. I read the review paragraph above

Rating

Total

Wednesday   **Date**............................   No. of times daily

1. I read The Scroll Marked VI
2. I read the review paragraph above

Rating

Total

Thursday   **Date**............................   No. of times daily

1. I read The Scroll Marked VI
2. I read the review paragraph above

Rating

Total

Friday   **Date**............................   No. of times daily

1. I read The Scroll Marked VI
2. I read the review paragraph above

Rating

Total

Total points for the week

*Appointments for the week*_____

Monday_____
_____
_____
_____
_____

Tuesday_____
_____
_____
_____
_____

Wednesday_____
_____
_____
_____
_____

Thursday_____
_____
_____
_____
_____

Friday_____
_____
_____
_____
_____

*Achievements of the week*_____
_____
_____
_____
_____
_____

Reflection For The Week

Everyone has a fair turn to be as great as he pleases.
—*Jeremy Collier*

SUCCESS RECORDER
The Twenty-fourth Week

✦✦✦

Monday   Date............................   No. of times daily

1. I read The Scroll Marked VI
        Review Paragraph for the Week
2. I avoided all negative thoughts of failure and despair by   **Rating**
   making my actions control my thoughts; I smiled often; I
   moved swiftly; I raised my voice to strengthen my confidence; I made allowances for the moods of others and
   I refused to allow any set-back or problem to discolor
   my day.   **Total**

                    (Insert number in each box)

Tuesday   Date............................   No. of times daily

1. I read The Scroll Marked VI
2. I read the review paragraph above   **Rating**

                                                        Total

---

Wednesday   Date............................   No. of times daily

1. I read The Scroll Marked VI
2. I read the review paragraph above   **Rating**

                                                        Total

---

Thursday   Date............................   No. of times daily

1. I read The Scroll Marked VI
2. I read the review paragraph above   **Rating**

                                                        Total

---

Friday   Date............................   No. of times daily

1. I read The Scroll Marked VI
2. I read the review paragraph above   **Rating**

                                                        Total

---

                    Total points for the week

*Appointments for the week*_____

Monday_____
_____
_____
_____
_____

Tuesday_____
_____
_____
_____
_____

Wednesday_____
_____
_____
_____
_____

Thursday_____
_____
_____
_____
_____

Friday_____
_____
_____
_____
_____

*Achievements of the week*_____
_____
_____
_____
_____
_____

Reflection For The Week

A wise man will make more opportunities than he finds. —*Bacon*

SUCCESS RECORDER
The Twenty-fifth Week

✦✦

Monday   **Date**................................   No. of times daily

1. I read The Scroll Marked VI
          Review Paragraph for the Week
2. I avoided all negative thoughts of failure and despair by   Rating
   making my actions control my thoughts; I smiled often; I
   moved swiftly; I raised my voice to strengthen my confidence; I made allowances for the moods of others and
   I refused to allow any set-back or problem to discolor
   my day.   Total
                    (Insert number in each box)

Tuesday   **Date**................................   No. of times daily

1. I read The Scroll Marked VI
2. I read the review paragraph above   Rating

          Total

Wednesday   **Date**................................   No. of times daily

1. I read The Scroll Marked VI
2. I read the review paragraph above   Rating

          Total

Thursday   **Date**................................   No. of times daily

1. I read The Scroll Marked VI
2. I read the review paragraph above   Rating

          Total

Friday   **Date**................................   No. of times daily

1. I read The Scroll Marked VI
2. I read the review paragraph above   Rating

          Total

                    Total points for the week

*Appointments for the week*_____

Monday_____
_____
_____
_____
_____

Tuesday_____
_____
_____
_____
_____

Wednesday_____
_____
_____
_____
_____

Thursday_____
_____
_____
_____
_____

Friday_____
_____
_____
_____
_____

*Achievements of the week*_____
_____
_____
_____
_____

Reflection For The Week

The best men are not those who have waited for
chances but who have taken them; besieged the
chance; conquered the chance; and made chance their
servant.   —*E. H. Chapin*

Chapter IX

Stand on any busy corner and look at faces.

How many are smiling? How many even seem pleased, or happy? We are becoming a nation of frowning robots, rushing like blind ants from place to place, worrying about, well, you name it. I wish we had some statistics on smiles and laughter for I wonder what percentage of us, on any particular day, never laugh or even smile, from the time we rise to the time we retire.

Aren't we foolish . . . as we stagger around with the weight of the world on our shoulders and that frown adding wrinkles where they're not needed? Our somber mood is even killing us. Dr. James Walsh of Fordham University says, "People who laugh actually live longer than those who don't laugh. Few people realize that health actually varies according to the amount of their laughter."

Not only have we forgotten how to laugh, we've forgotten how important it is. Our forefathers who could afford it trotted jesters and buffoons past their dinner table to make them laugh so that their digestion was improved.

Apparently there are a tremendous number of nonlaughers out there because, since *The Greatest Salesman In The World* was published I have probably received more mail concerning The Scroll Marked VII, which you are about to begin reading, than any other, with most of the remarks directed at the scroll's specific injunction to start laughing at yourself.

Sammy Davis was once asked to define success. I'll never forget his answer: "I don't know what success is, but I know what failure is. Failure is trying to please everybody."

If you're trying to please everybody, and you've forgotten how to laugh at others, *and yourself*, now is the time to learn how to say "to heck with it." Stop taking others, and yourself, too seriously. You are a miracle of nature but that doesn't mean you were put here to be a sourpuss, as you will discover in:

The Scroll Marked VII

I will laugh at the world.

No living creature can laugh except man. Trees may bleed when they are wounded, and beasts in the field will cry in pain and hunger, yet only I have the gift of laughter and it is mine to use whenever I choose. Henceforth I will cultivate the habit of laughter.

I will smile and my digestion will improve; I will chuckle and my burdens will be lightened; I will laugh and my life will be lengthened for this is the secret of long life and now it is mine.

I will laugh at the world.

And most of all, I will laugh at myself for man is most comical when he takes himself too seriously. Never will I fall into this trap of the mind. For though I be nature's greatest miracle am I not still a mere grain tossed about by the winds of time? Do I truly know whence I came or whither I am bound? Will my concern for this day not seem foolish ten years hence? Why should I permit the petty happenings of today to disturb me? What can take place before this sun sets which will not seem insignificant in the river of centuries?

I will laugh at the world.

And how can I laugh when confronted with man or deed which offends me so as to bring forth my tears or my curses? Four words I will train myself to say until they become a habit so strong that immediately they will appear in my mind whenever good humor threatens to depart from me. These words, passed down from the ancients, will carry me through every adversity and maintain my life in balance. These four words are: *This too shall pass.*

I will laugh at the world.

For all worldly things shall indeed pass. When I am heavy with heartache I shall console myself that this too shall pass; when I am puffed with success I shall warn myself that this too shall pass. When I am strangled in poverty I shall tell myself that this too shall pass; when I am burdened with wealth I shall tell myself that this too shall pass. Yea, verily, where is he who built the pyramid? Is he not buried within its stone? And will the pyramid, one day, not also be buried under sand? If all things shall pass why should I be of concern for today?

I will laugh at the world.

I will paint this day with laughter; I will frame this night in song. Never will I labor to be happy; rather will I remain too busy to be sad. I will enjoy today's happiness today. It is not grain to be stored in a box. It is not wine to be saved in a jar. It cannot be saved for the morrow. It must be sown and reaped on the same day and this I will do, henceforth.

I will laugh at the world.

And with my laughter all things will be reduced to their proper size. I will laugh at my failures and they will vanish in clouds of new dreams; I will laugh at my successes and they will shrink to their true value. I will laugh at evil and it will die untasted; I will laugh at goodness and it will thrive and abound. Each day will be triumphant only when my smiles bring forth smiles from others and this I do in selfishness, for those on whom I frown are those who purchase not my goods.

I will laugh at the world.

Henceforth will I shed only tears of sweat, for those of sadness or remorse or frustration are of no value in the market place whilst each smile can be exchanged for gold and each kind word, spoken from my heart, can build a castle.

Never will I allow myself to become so important, so wise, so dignified, so powerful, that I forget how to laugh at myself and my world. In this matter I will always remain as a child, for only as a child am I given the ability to look up to another. I will never grow too long for my cot.

I will laugh at the world.

And so long as I can laugh never will I be poor. This then, is one of nature's greatest gifts, and I will waste it no more. Only with laughter and happiness can I truly become a success. Only with laughter and happiness can I enjoy the fruits of my labor. Were it not so, far better would it be to fail, for happiness is the wine that sharpens the taste of the meal. To enjoy success I must have happiness, and laughter will be the maiden who serves me.

I will be happy.

I will be successful.

I will be the greatest salesman the world has ever known.

SUCCESS RECORDER
The Twenty-sixth Week

✠✠

Monday   **Date**.............................   No. of times daily

1. I read The Scroll Marked VII
       Review Paragraph for the Week
2. I laughed at the world, and at myself, refusing to take too
   seriously my petty undertakings; I laughed at my problems, my heartaches, my failures . . . even my successes
   and I maintained my perspective by telling myself
   throughout this day, "this too shall pass."

Rating

Total

(Insert number in each box)

Tuesday   **Date**.............................   No. of times daily

1. I read The Scroll Marked VII
2. I read the review paragraph above

Rating

Total

Wednesday   **Date**.............................   No. of times daily

1. I read The Scroll Marked VII
2. I read the review paragraph above

Rating

Total

Thursday   **Date**.............................   No. of times daily

1. I read The Scroll Marked VII
2. I read the review paragraph above

Rating

Total

Friday   **Date**.............................   No. of times daily

1. I read The Scroll Marked VII
2. I read the review paragraph above

Rating

Total

Total points for the week

*Appointments for the week*_____

Monday_____

_____

_____

_____

_____

Tuesday_____

_____

_____

_____

_____

Wednesday_____

_____

_____

_____

_____

Thursday_____

_____

_____

_____

_____

Friday_____

_____

_____

_____

_____

*Achievements of the week*_____

_____

_____

_____

_____

_____

Reflection For The Week

A laugh is worth a hundred groans in any market.

—Lamb

SUCCESS RECORDER
The Twenty-seventh Week

****

Monday   Date....................   No. of times daily

1. I read The Scroll Marked VII
         Review Paragraph for the Week
2. I laughed at the world, and at myself, refusing to take too   **Rating**
   seriously my petty undertakings; I laughed at my prob-
   lems, my heartaches, my failures . . . even my successes
   and I maintained my perspective by telling myself
   throughout this day, "this too shall pass."   **Total**

(Insert number in each box)

Tuesday   Date....................   No. of times daily

1. I read The Scroll Marked VII
2. I read the review paragraph above   **Rating**

                               Total

Wednesday   Date....................   No. of times daily

1. I read The Scroll Marked VII
2. I read the review paragraph above   **Rating**

                               Total

Thursday   Date....................   No. of times daily

1. I read The Scroll Marked VII
2. I read the review paragraph above   **Rating**

                               Total

Friday   Date....................   No. of times daily

1. I read The Scroll Marked VII
2. I read the review paragraph above   **Rating**

                               Total

                         Total points for the week

Appointments for the week _____

Monday _____
_____
_____
_____
_____

Tuesday _____
_____
_____
_____
_____

Wednesday _____
_____
_____
_____
_____

Thursday _____
_____
_____
_____
_____

Friday _____
_____
_____
_____
_____

Achievements of the week _____
_____
_____
_____
_____

Reflection For The Week

If we consider the frequent reliefs we receive from laughter, and how often it breaks the gloom which is apt to depress the mind, one would take care not to grow too wise for so great a pleasure of life.   —*Addison*

SUCCESS RECORDER
The Twenty-eighth Week

✦✦✦

Monday   Date.................................   No. of times daily

1. I read The Scroll Marked VII
              Review Paragraph for the Week
2. I laughed at the world, and at myself, refusing to take too   **Rating**
   seriously my petty undertakings; I laughed at my prob-
   lems, my heartaches, my failures . . . even my successes
   and I maintained my perspective by telling myself
   throughout this day, "this too shall pass."   **Total**
                            (Insert number in each box)

Tuesday   Date.................................   No. of times daily

1. I read The Scroll Marked VII
2. I read the review paragraph above   **Rating**

                                               Total

Wednesday   Date.................................   No. of times daily

1. I read The Scroll Marked VII
2. I read the review paragraph above   **Rating**

                                               Total

Thursday   Date.................................   No. of times daily

1. I read The Scroll Marked VII
2. I read the review paragraph above   **Rating**

                                               Total

Friday   Date.................................   No. of times daily

1. I read The Scroll Marked VII
2. I read the review paragraph above   **Rating**

                                               Total

                    Total points for the week

*Appointments for the week*_____

Monday_____
_____
_____
_____
_____

Tuesday_____
_____
_____
_____
_____

Wednesday_____
_____
_____
_____
_____

Thursday_____
_____
_____
_____
_____

Friday_____
_____
_____
_____
_____

*Achievements of the week*_____
_____
_____
_____
_____
_____

Reflection For The Week

The most utterly lost of all days is that in which you
have not once laughed.   —*Chamfort*

SUCCESS RECORDER
The Twenty-ninth Week

Monday   **Date**................................   No. of times daily

1. I read The Scroll Marked VII
      Review Paragraph for the Week
2. I laughed at the world, and at myself, refusing to take too   Rating
   seriously my petty undertakings; I laughed at my problems, my heartaches, my failures . . . even my successes
   and I maintained my perspective by telling myself
   throughout this day, "this too shall pass."   Total

   (Insert number in each box)

Tuesday   **Date**................................   No. of times daily

1. I read The Scroll Marked VII
2. I read the review paragraph above   Rating

                             Total

Wednesday   **Date**................................   No. of times daily

1. I read The Scroll Marked VII
2. I read the review paragraph above   Rating

                             Total

Thursday   **Date**................................   No. of times daily

1. I read The Scroll Marked VII
2. I read the review paragraph above   Rating

                             Total

Friday   **Date**................................   No. of times daily

1. I read The Scroll Marked VII
2. I read the review paragraph above   Rating

                             Total

                    Total points for the week

*Appointments for the week*_____

Monday_____
_____
_____
_____
_____

Tuesday_____
_____
_____
_____
_____

Wednesday_____
_____
_____
_____
_____

Thursday_____
_____
_____
_____
_____

Friday_____
_____
_____
_____
_____

*Achievements of the week*_____
_____
_____
_____
_____

Reflection For The Week

I had rather have a fool make me merry, than experience make me sad. —*Shakespeare*

SUCCESS RECORDER
The Thirtieth Week

✢✢

Monday   Date...........................   No. of times daily

1. I read The Scroll Marked VII
   Review Paragraph for the Week
2. I laughed at the world, and at myself, refusing to take too   Rating
   seriously my petty undertakings; I laughed at my problems, my heartaches, my failures . . . even my successes
   and I maintained my perspective by telling myself
   throughout this day, "this too shall pass."   Total

                          (Insert number in each box)

Tuesday   Date...........................   No. of times daily

1. I read The Scroll Marked VII
2. I read the review paragraph above   Rating

                              Total

Wednesday   Date...........................   No. of times daily

1. I read The Scroll Marked VII
2. I read the review paragraph above   Rating

                              Total

Thursday   Date...........................   No. of times daily

1. I read The Scroll Marked VII
2. I read the review paragraph above   Rating

                              Total

Friday   Date...........................   No. of times daily

1. I read The Scroll Marked VII
2. I read the review paragraph above   Rating

                              Total

                    Total points for the week

*Appointments for the week*_____

Monday_____
_____
_____
_____
_____

Tuesday_____
_____
_____
_____
_____

Wednesday_____
_____
_____
_____
_____

Thursday_____
_____
_____
_____
_____

Friday_____
_____
_____
_____
_____

*Achievements of the week*_____
_____
_____
_____
_____

Reflection For The Week

Be cheerful always. There is no path but will be easier traveled, no load but will be lighter, no shadow on the heart and brain but will lift sooner for a person of determined cheerfulness.　　　　—*Willitts*

Chapter X

You've hung on so well, and you're looking so great! I'm proud of you.

I'm so proud of you that I'm going to let you in on the greatest secret in the world. The president of your company knows it . . . and so does every other individual who ever made it to the top in his own particular career. It really shouldn't be classified as a secret because successful people constantly talk about it openly . . . *but nobody is listening!*

Including you.

Maybe you'll pay attention, now.

The greatest secret in the world is that you only have to be a small, measurable amount better than mediocrity . . . and you've got it made.

Read that again. Burn it into your mind and never forget it.

We live in a world of mediocrity . . . and mediocre individuals. You know it, without taking my word for it. Think of that last new car you bought and how sloppily it was assembled by people who just did their job well enough to get by. And how many things were unfinished in that new house you bought? Remember that jacket with the pockets still sewn together . . . and that magazine you bought with sixteen pages missing?

Charles H. Brower, one of our century's most able and brilliant business executives, put his finger on it all when he said, "We, in America, are living in the high tide of the mediocre, the great era of the goof-off, the age of the job half-done. The land from coast to coast has been enjoying a stampede away from responsibility. It is populated with laundrymen who won't iron shirts, with waiters who won't serve, with carpenters who will come around some day maybe, with executives whose minds are on the golf course, with teachers who demand a single salary schedule so that achievement cannot be rewarded nor poor work punished, with students who take cinch courses because the hard ones make them think, with spiritual delinquents of all kinds who have been triumphantly determined to enjoy what was known until the present crisis as the 'new leisure.'"

You don't have to move ahead to be a success! Just stand fast where you are, doing the best you can, and without your advancing one inch forward you'll be ahead of the pack. Why? Because the others will have all retreated! The struggle was too rough for them. They quit . . . and ran . . . and there you are because there's no one remaining. Mr. Success!

For, as Mr. Brower concluded, "I am a man of great faith. Here and there you see bright minds who are not interested in clockwatching and goofing off. And I would like to say to them, do not be discouraged when you find yourself afloat in a sea of mediocrity. Do not be downhearted when the tides of foolishness are running high. It is the earnest and devoted few who can turn that tide."

I purposely waited until we were this far along in the book before sharing this secret with you. And I have purposely "buried" it, in the text, so that the casual browser won't find it. Those whom we have lost, along the way, only help to prove the secret they'll never know.

You . . . are something special, and you are worth a fortune to yourself and those you love, if you will only heed the words in:

The Scroll Marked VIII

Today I will multiply my value a hundredfold.

A mulberry leaf touched with the genius of man becomes silk.

A field of clay touched with the genius of man becomes a castle.

A cyprus tree touched with the genius of man becomes a shrine.

A cut of sheep's hair touched with the genius of man becomes raiment for a king.

If it is possible for leaves and clay and wood and hair to have their value multiplied a hundred, yea a thousandfold by man, cannot I do the same with clay which bears my name?

Today I will multiply my value a hundredfold.

I am liken to a grain of wheat which faces one of three futures. The wheat can be placed in a sack and dumped in a stall until it is fed to swine. Or it can be ground to flour and made into bread. Or it can be placed in the earth and allowed to grow until its golden head divides and produces a thousand grains from the one.

I am liken to a grain of wheat with one difference. The wheat cannot choose whether it be fed to swine, ground for bread, or planted to multiply. I have a choice and I will not let my life be fed to swine nor will I let it be ground under the rocks of failure and despair to be broken open and devoured by the will of others.

Today I will multiply my value a hundredfold.

To grow and multiply it is necessary to plant the wheat grain in the darkness of the earth and my failures, my despairs, my ignorance, and my inabilities are the darkness in which I have been planted in order to ripen. Now, like the wheat grain which will sprout and blossom only if it is nurtured with rain and sun and warm winds, I too must nurture my body and mind to fulfill my dreams. But to grow to full stature the wheat must wait on the whims of nature. I need not wait for I have the power to choose my own destiny.

Today I will multiply my value a hundredfold.

And how will I accomplish this? First I will set goals for the day, the week, the month, the year, and my life. Just as the rain must fall before the wheat will crack its shell and sprout, so must I have objectives before my life will crystallize. In setting my goals I will consider my best performance of the past and multiply it a hundredfold. This will be the standard by which I will live in the future. Never will I be of concern that my goals are too high for is it not better to aim my spear at the moon and strike only an eagle than to aim my spear at the eagle and strike only a rock?

Today I will multiply my value a hundredfold.

The height of my goals will not hold me in awe though I may stumble often before they are reached. If I stumble I will rise and my falls will not concern me for all men must stumble often to reach the hearth. Only a worm is free from the worry of stumbling. I am not a worm. I am not an onion plant. I am not a sheep. I am a man. Let others build a cave with their clay. I will build a castle with mine.

Today I will multiply my value a hundredfold.

And just as the sun must warm the earth to bring forth the seedling of wheat so, too, will the words on these scrolls warm my life and turn my dreams into reality. Today I will surpass every action which I performed yesterday. I will climb today's mountain to the utmost of my ability yet tomorrow I will climb higher than today, and the next will be higher than tomorrow. To surpass the deeds of others is unimportant; to surpass my own deeds is all.

Today I will multiply my value a hundredfold.

And just as the warm wind guides the wheat to maturity, the same winds will carry my voice to those who will listen and my words will announce my goals. Once spoken I dare not recall them lest I lose face. I will be as my own prophet and though all may laugh at my utterances they will hear my plans, they will know my dreams; and thus there will be no escape for me until my words become accomplished deeds.

Today I will multiply my value a hundredfold.

I will commit not the terrible crime of aiming too low.

I will do the work that a failure will not do.

I will always let my reach exceed my grasp.

I will never be content with my performance in the market.

I will always raise my goals as soon as they are attained.

I will always strive to make the next hour better than this one.

I will always announce my goals to the world.

Yet, never will I proclaim my accomplishments. Let the world, instead, approach me with praise and may I have the wisdom to receive it in humility.

Today I will multiply my value a hundredfold.

One grain of wheat when multiplied a hundredfold will produce a hundred stalks. Multiply these a hundredfold, ten times, and they will feed all the cities of the earth. Am I not more than a grain of wheat?

Today I will multiply my value a hundredfold.

And when it is done I will do it again, and again, and there will be astonishment and wonder at my greatness as the words of these scrolls are fulfilled in me.

SUCCESS RECORDER
The Thirty-first Week

✦✦✦

Monday   Date........................   No. of times daily

1. I read The Scroll Marked VIII
            Review Paragraph for the Week

2. I set goals for today that were double my productivity of   Rating
   yesterday; I put myself "on the spot" by announcing
   those goals to all; I attempted at least one task which I
   would have avoided like the plague yesterday and I am
   still not content with this day's performance.   Total
                           (Insert number in each box)

Tuesday   Date........................   No. of times daily

1. I read The Scroll Marked VIII
2. I read the review paragraph above   Rating

                                                    Total

Wednesday   Date........................   No. of times daily

1. I read The Scroll Marked VIII
2. I read the review paragraph above   Rating

                                                    Total

Thursday   Date........................   No. of times daily

1. I read The Scroll Marked VIII
2. I read the review paragraph above   Rating

                                                    Total

Friday   Date........................   No. of times daily

1. I read The Scroll Marked VIII
2. I read the review paragraph above   Rating

                                                    Total

                                        Total points for the week

*Appointments for the week*_____

Monday_____
_____
_____
_____
_____

Tuesday_____
_____
_____
_____
_____

Wednesday_____
_____
_____
_____
_____

Thursday_____
_____
_____
_____
_____

Friday_____
_____
_____
_____
_____

*Achievements of the week*_____
_____
_____
_____
_____
_____

Reflection For The Week

Mediocrity is excellent to the eyes of mediocre people. —*Joubert*

SUCCESS RECORDER
The Thirty-second Week

❖❖

Monday   Date.............................   No. of times daily

1. I read The Scroll Marked VIII
              Review Paragraph for the Week
2. I set goals for today that were double my productivity of   Rating
    yesterday; I put myself "on the spot" by announcing
    those goals to all; I attempted at least one task which I
    would have avoided like the plague yesterday and I am
    still not content with this day's performance.   Total

                 (Insert number in each box)

Tuesday   Date.............................   No. of times daily

1. I read The Scroll Marked VIII
2. I read the review paragraph above   Rating

                                      Total

Wednesday   Date.............................   No. of times daily

1. I read The Scroll Marked VIII
2. I read the review paragraph above   Rating

                                      Total

Thursday   Date.............................   No. of times daily

1. I read The Scroll Marked VIII
2. I read the review paragraph above   Rating

                                      Total

Friday   Date.............................   No. of times daily

1. I read The Scroll Marked VIII
2. I read the review paragraph above   Rating

                                      Total

                           Total points for the week

*Appointments for the week*_____

Monday_____
_____
_____
_____
_____

Tuesday_____
_____
_____
_____

Wednesday_____
_____
_____
_____

Thursday_____
_____
_____
_____

Friday_____
_____
_____
_____

*Achievements of the week*_____
_____
_____
_____

Reflection For The Week

The highest order of mind is accused of folly, as well as the lowest. Nothing is thoroughly approved but mediocrity. The majority has established this, and it fixes its fangs on whatever gets beyond it either way.

—*Pascal*

SUCCESS RECORDER
The Thirty-third Week

❖❖

Monday   **Date**................................   No. of times daily

1. I read The Scroll Marked VIII
                Review Paragraph for the Week
2. I set goals for today that were double my productivity of   Rating
   yesterday; I put myself "on the spot" by announcing
   those goals to all; I attempted at least one task which I
   would have avoided like the plague yesterday and I am
   still not content with this day's performance.   Total
                        (Insert number in each box)

Tuesday   **Date**................................   No. of times daily

1. I read The Scroll Marked VIII
2. I read the review paragraph above   Rating

                                          Total

Wednesday   **Date**................................   No. of times daily

1. I read The Scroll Marked VIII
2. I read the review paragraph above   Rating

                                          Total

Thursday   **Date**................................   No. of times daily

1. I read The Scroll Marked VIII
2. I read the review paragraph above   Rating

                                          Total

Friday   **Date**................................   No. of times daily

1. I read The Scroll Marked VIII
2. I read the review paragraph above   Rating

                                          Total

                        Total points for the week

*Appointments for the week*_____

Monday_____
_____
_____
_____
_____

Tuesday_____
_____
_____
_____
_____

Wednesday_____
_____
_____
_____
_____

Thursday_____
_____
_____
_____
_____

Friday_____
_____
_____
_____
_____

*Achievements of the week*_____
_____
_____
_____
_____
_____

Reflection For The Week

Folks who never do any more than they get paid for,
never get paid for any more than they do. —*Elbert Hubbard*

SUCCESS RECORDER
The Thirty-fourth Week

✦✦✦

Monday   **Date**..   No. of times daily

1. I read The Scroll Marked VIII
          Review Paragraph for the Week   ☐
2. I set goals for today that were double my productivity of   **Rating**
    yesterday; I put myself "on the spot" by announcing   ☐
    those goals to all; I attempted at least one task which I
    would have avoided like the plague yesterday and I am
    still not content with this day's performance.   **Total**
                          (Insert number in each box)   ☐

_____

Tuesday   **Date**..   No. of times daily

1. I read The Scroll Marked VIII   ☐
2. I read the review paragraph above   **Rating**
                                                                 ☐
                                           Total ☐

_____

Wednesday   **Date**..   No. of times daily

1. I read The Scroll Marked VIII   ☐
2. I read the review paragraph above   **Rating**
                                                                 ☐
                                           Total ☐

_____

Thursday   **Date**..   No. of times daily

1. I read The Scroll Marked VIII   ☐
2. I read the review paragraph above   **Rating**
                                                                 ☐
                                           Total ☐

_____

Friday   **Date**..   No. of times daily

1. I read The Scroll Marked VIII   ☐
2. I read the review paragraph above   **Rating**
                                                                 ☐
                                           Total ☐

                              Total points for the week   ☐

*Appointments for the week*_____

Monday_____
_____
_____
_____
_____

Tuesday_____
_____
_____
_____
_____

Wednesday_____
_____
_____
_____
_____

Thursday_____
_____
_____
_____

Friday_____
_____
_____
_____

*Achievements of the week*_____
_____
_____
_____
_____
_____

Reflection For The Week

Those who attain to any excellence commonly spend life in some one single pursuit, for excellence is not often gained upon easier terms. —*Johnson*

SUCCESS RECORDER
The Thirty-fifth Week

❖❖

Monday   **Date**...........................   **No. of times daily**

1. I read The Scroll Marked VIII
              Review Paragraph for the Week
2. I set goals for today that were double my productivity of   Rating
   yesterday; I put myself "on the spot" by announcing
   those goals to all; I attempted at least one task which I
   would have avoided like the plague yesterday and I am
   still not content with this day's performance.   Total
                        (Insert number in each box)

Tuesday   **Date**...........................   **No. of times daily**

1. I read The Scroll Marked VIII
2. I read the review paragraph above   Rating

                                                    Total

Wednesday   **Date**...........................   **No. of times daily**

1. I read The Scroll Marked VIII
2. I read the review paragraph above   Rating

                                                    Total

Thursday   **Date**...........................   **No. of times daily**

1. I read The Scroll Marked VIII
2. I read the review paragraph above   Rating

                                                    Total

Friday   **Date**...........................   **No. of times daily**

1. I read The Scroll Marked VIII
2. I read the review paragraph above   Rating

                                                    Total

                            Total points for the week

*Appointments for the week*_____

Monday_____
_____
_____
_____
_____

Tuesday_____
_____
_____
_____
_____

Wednesday_____
_____
_____
_____
_____

Thursday_____
_____
_____
_____
_____

Friday_____
_____
_____
_____
_____

*Achievements of the week*_____
_____
_____
_____
_____
_____

Reflection For The Week

Great souls have wills; feeble ones have only wishes.
—Chinese Proverb

Chapter XI

Some very brilliant individuals at our National Bureau of Standards have been telling us that this still beautiful earth on which we all perform is slowing down in its daily rotation. Eventually, they claim, this will produce a twenty-five hour day . . . 1,800,000 *centuries* from now!

But you can't wait until then for that extra bonus hour to sell or produce more goods for a higher income . . . and in truth, how much of this day's 23 hours, 56 minutes, 4.09 seconds do you use wisely?

George Severance, who represents the Ohio National Life Insurance Company, is one of the most outstanding and productive salesmen in the entire insurance industry . . . now. But there were leaner and almost desperate days before he took stock of himself, as he disclosed to W. Clement Stone in an article for Success Unlimited:

"One day the total amount of my debts struck me like a bolt of lightning. I was faced with a real financial crisis. Then I recalled a statement I had read somewhere, 'Don't expect what you don't expect.'"

George decided to keep a record of how he spent his time, every salesman's greatest asset. "I found that I had been spending as much as 32 hours in a single month drinking coffee with my friends. I was amazed, for I realized that this was equivalent to four working days. And then I realized that my lunch hours were sometimes a full hour longer than they should have been."

Just as you are using your Success Recorder as a means of self-examining how you perform daily regarding one specific success principle, George developed what he called a Social Time Recorder so that he could account, to himself, for his productive and non-productive time each day.

"When I looked back, I found that in many respects I was a social success during business hours. But when I developed my Social Time Recorder, I realized:

'If a business day is a social success, it has been a business failure.'"

The italics in the above statement are mine. If I could convince my publisher to print that statement in 32-point Day-Glo letters I'd do it . . . for I want you never to forget what you have just read:

"If a business day is a social success, it has been a business failure."

Why is it easier to make any day a social success than a business success? You know the answer . . . because you've been there. I've been there. Socializing is easy, it's fun. Selling, working, doing the things that are difficult to do, is rough and not fun. So, like the rest of nature which also follows the line of least resistance we procrastinate, we stall, we make innumerable excuses to avoid what we *know* should be done.

We avoid getting into action, productive action, as long as possible, and if there is any single identifying characteristic of those 95% who have settled for a life of mediocrity it is this trait of inactivity.

But that's not for you. You've come too far to let this bad habit defeat you. Procrastination can be driven from your personality through the simple technique of constantly commanding yourself to get into action . . . and then obeying that command immediately. You begin your basic training on this bad habit with little acts such as:

You walk across your living room rug. On the rug is a piece of torn paper. The "old you" would leave it for your wife to attend to when she cleans the room. The "new you" picks it up, *now*.

You pull your automobile out of the garage in the morning. The city's rubbish pick-up service has already come by and emptied your two containers. The "old you" would leave them in the driveway until you returned from work that evening before putting them back in the garage. The "new you" puts them back, *now*.

The "old you" reviews his morning mail and then answers only those memos and letters which absolutely must be handled and puts the rest aside for later. The "new you," knowing how much time can be saved by handling every piece of correspondence only once, answers every piece, *now*.

The "old you" gets a pain, of one sort or another, in your chest, and resolves to go to a doctor, some day when you're not so "busy." The "new you" goes, *now*.

(That "some day" for the "old you" might never come!)

I'm reasonably certain that you could fill many pages with the things you do that fit into this "put-off" category. Yet, if you cannot overcome this vice then all the time you have put into your Success Recorder has been wasted and we've both got too much invested in you to let that happen.

So let's get into action! Let's begin reading!

The Scroll Marked IX

My dreams are worthless, my plans are dust, my goals are impossible.

All are of no value unless they are followed by action. I will act now.

Never has there been a map, however carefully executed to detail and scale, which carried its owner over even one inch of ground. Never has there been a parchment of law, however fair, which prevented one crime. Never has there been a scroll, even such as the one I hold, which earned so much as a penny or produced a single word of acclamation. Action, alone, is the tinder which ignites the map, the parchment, this scroll, my dreams, my plans, my goals, into a living force. Action is the food and drink which will nourish my success.

I will act now.

My procrastination which has held me back was born of fear and now I recognize this secret mined from the depths of all courageous hearts. Now I know that to conquer fear I must always act without hesitation and the flutters in my heart will vanish. Now I know that action reduces the lion of terror to an ant of equanimity.

I will act now.

Henceforth, I will remember the lesson of the firefly who gives off its light only when it is on the wing, only when it is in action. I will become a firefly and even in the day my glow will be seen in spite of the sun. Let others be as butterflies who preen their wings yet depend on the charity of a flower for life. I will be as the firefly and my light will brighten the world.

I will act now.

I will not avoid the tasks of today and charge them to tomorrow for I know that tomorrow never comes. Let me act now even though my actions may not bring happiness or success for it is better to act and fail than not to act and flounder. Happiness, in truth, may not be the fruit plucked by my action yet without action all fruit will die on the vine.

I will act now.

I will act now. I will act now. I will act now. Henceforth, I will repeat these words again and again and again, each hour, each day, every day, until the words became as much a habit as my breathing and the actions which follow become as instinctive as the blinking of my eyelids. With these words I can condition my mind to perform every act necessary for my success. With these words I can condition my mind to meet every challenge which the failure avoids.

I will act now.

I will repeat these words again and again and again.

When I awake I will say them and leap from my cot while the failure sleeps yet another hour.

I will act now.

When I enter the market place I will say them and immediately confront my first prospect while the failure ponders yet his possibility of rebuff.

I will act now.

When I face a closed door I will say them and knock while the failure waits outside with fear and trepidation.

I will act now.

When I face the temptation I will say them and immediately act to remove myself from evil.

I will act now.

When I am tempted to quit and begin again tomorrow I will say them and immediately act to consummate another sale.

I will act now.

Only action determines my value in the market place and to multiply my value I will multiply my actions. I will walk where the failure fears to walk. I will work when the failure seeks rest. I will talk when the failure remains silent. I will call on ten who can buy my goods while the failure makes grand plans to call on one. I will say it is done before the failure says it is too late.

I will act now.

For now is all I have. Tomorrow is the day reserved for the labor of the lazy. I am not lazy. Tomorrow is the day when the evil become good. I am not evil. Tomorrow is the day when the weak become strong. I am not weak. Tomorrow is the day when the failure will succeed. I am not a failure.

I will act now.

When the lion is hungry he eats. When the eagle has thirst he drinks. Lest they act, both will perish.

I hunger for success. I thirst for happiness and peace of mind. Lest I act I will perish in a life of failure, misery, and sleepless nights.

I will command, and I will obey mine own command.

I will act now.

Success will not wait. If I delay she will become betrothed to another and lost to me forever.

This is the time. This is the place. I am the man.

I will act now.

SUCCESS RECORDER
The Thirty-sixth Week

✦✦

Monday   Date...........................   No. of times daily

1. I read The Scroll Marked IX
   Review Paragraph for the Week
2. I got into action from the time I awoke; I leaped quickly   Rating
   from my bed; I repeated to myself throughout the day,
   "Act now, now, now!"; I overcame my fears through action; I put off no distasteful chore for another time; I
   moved swiftly from prospect to prospect or from project
   to project and I moved fast to avoid temptations. Today
   I was in action!   Total

                   (Insert number in each box)

Tuesday   Date...........................   No. of times daily

1. I read The Scroll Marked IX
2. I read the review paragraph above   Rating

                   Total

Wednesday   Date...........................   No. of times daily

1. I read The Scroll Marked IX
2. I read the review paragraph above   Rating

                   Total

Thursday   Date...........................   No. of times daily

1. I read The Scroll Marked IX
2. I read the review paragraph above   Rating

                   Total

Friday   Date...........................   No. of times daily

1. I read The Scroll Marked IX
2. I read the review paragraph above   Rating

                   Total

             Total points for the week

*Appointments for the week*_____

Monday_____
_____
_____
_____
_____

Tuesday_____
_____
_____
_____
_____

Wednesday_____
_____
_____
_____
_____

Thursday_____
_____
_____
_____
_____

Friday_____
_____
_____
_____
_____

*Achievements of the week*_____
_____
_____
_____
_____
_____

Reflection For The Week

Heaven never helps the man who will not act.
—*Sophocles*

SUCCESS RECORDER
The Thirty-seventh Week

✦✦

Monday   **Date**............................   No. of times daily

1. I read The Scroll Marked IX
        Review Paragraph for the Week
2. I got into action from the time I awoke; I leaped quickly   Rating
   from my bed; I repeated to myself throughout the day,
   "Act now, now, now!"; I overcame my fears through action; I put off no distasteful chore for another time; I
   moved swiftly from prospect to prospect or from project
   to project and I moved fast to avoid temptations. Today
   I was in action!   Total

(Insert number in each box)

Tuesday   **Date**............................   No. of times daily

1. I read The Scroll Marked IX
2. I read the review paragraph above   Rating

Total

Wednesday   **Date**............................   No. of times daily

1. I read The Scroll Marked IX
2. I read the review paragraph above   Rating

Total

Thursday   **Date**............................   No. of times daily

1. I read The Scroll Marked IX
2. I read the review paragraph above   Rating

Total

Friday   **Date**............................   No. of times daily

1. I read The Scroll Marked IX
2. I read the review paragraph above   Rating

Total

Total points for the week

*Appointments for the week*_____

Monday_____
_____
_____
_____
_____

Tuesday_____
_____
_____
_____
_____

Wednesday_____
_____
_____
_____
_____

Thursday_____
_____
_____
_____
_____

Friday_____
_____
_____
_____
_____

*Achievements of the week*_____
_____
_____
_____
_____
_____

Reflection For The Week

I have never heard anything about the resolutions of
the apostles, but a good deal about their acts.

—Horace Mann

SUCCESS RECORDER
The Thirty-eighth Week

✦✦

Monday   Date ....   No. of times daily

1. I read The Scroll Marked IX
    Review Paragraph for the Week

2. I got into action from the time I awoke; I leaped quickly   Rating
    from my bed; I repeated to myself throughout the day,
    "Act now, now, now!"; I overcame my fears through ac-
    tion; I put off no distasteful chore for another time; I
    moved swiftly from prospect to prospect or from project
    to project and I moved fast to avoid temptations. Today
    I was in action!   Total

                        (Insert number in each box)

Tuesday   Date ....   No. of times daily

1. I read The Scroll Marked IX
2. I read the review paragraph above   Rating

                                            Total

Wednesday   Date ....   No. of times daily

1. I read The Scroll Marked IX
2. I read the review paragraph above   Rating

                                            Total

Thursday   Date ....   No. of times daily

1. I read The Scroll Marked IX
2. I read the review paragraph above   Rating

                                            Total

Friday   Date ....   No. of times daily

1. I read The Scroll Marked IX
2. I read the review paragraph above   Rating

                                            Total

                        Total points for the week

*Appointments for the week*_____

Monday_____
_____
_____
_____
_____

Tuesday_____
_____
_____
_____
_____

Wednesday_____
_____
_____
_____
_____

Thursday_____
_____
_____
_____
_____

Friday_____
_____
_____
_____
_____

*Achievements of the week*_____
_____
_____
_____
_____
_____
_____

Reflection For The Week

Good thoughts, though God accept them, yet toward men are little better than good dreams except they be put in action.　　　　　　　　　　**—Bacon**

SUCCESS RECORDER
The Thirty-ninth Week

✦✦✦

Monday   Date ....   No. of times daily

1. I read The Scroll Marked IX
           Review Paragraph for the Week
2. I got into action from the time I awoke; I leaped quickly   Rating
   from my bed; I repeated to myself throughout the day,
   "Act now, now, now!"; I overcame my fears through action; I put off no distasteful chore for another time; I
   moved swiftly from prospect to prospect or from project
   to project and I moved fast to avoid temptations. Today
   I was in action!   Total

                              (Insert number in each box)

Tuesday   Date ....   No. of times daily

1. I read The Scroll Marked IX
2. I read the review paragraph above   Rating

                                                                Total

Wednesday   Date ....   No. of times daily

1. I read The Scroll Marked IX
2. I read the review paragraph above   Rating

                                                                Total

Thursday   Date ....   No. of times daily

1. I read The Scroll Marked IX
2. I read the review paragraph above   Rating

                                                                Total

Friday   Date ....   No. of times daily

1. I read The Scroll Marked IX
2. I read the review paragraph above   Rating

                                                                Total

                              Total points for the week

*Appointments for the week*_____

Monday_____
_____
_____
_____
_____

Tuesday_____
_____
_____
_____
_____

Wednesday_____
_____
_____
_____
_____

Thursday_____
_____
_____
_____
_____

Friday_____
_____
_____
_____
_____

*Achievements of the week*_____
_____
_____
_____
_____
_____

Reflection For The Week

Life was not given for indolent contemplation and study of self; nor for brooding over emotions of piety; actions and actions only determine the worth.   —*Fichte*

SUCCESS RECORDER
The Fortieth Week

❖❖❖

Monday   **Date** ....   No. of times daily

1. I read The Scroll Marked IX
          Review Paragraph for the Week
2. I got into action from the time I awoke; I leaped quickly   **Rating**
   from my bed; I repeated to myself throughout the day,
   "Act now, now, now!"; I overcame my fears through action; I put off no distasteful chore for another time; I
   moved swiftly from prospect to prospect or from project
   to project and I moved fast to avoid temptations. Today
   I was in action!   **Total**
                          (Insert number in each box)

Tuesday   **Date** ....   No. of times daily

1. I read The Scroll Marked IX
2. I read the review paragraph above   **Rating**

                                              Total

Wednesday   **Date** ....   No. of times daily

1. I read The Scroll Marked IX
2. I read the review paragraph above   **Rating**

                                              Total

Thursday   **Date** ....   No. of times daily

1. I read The Scroll Marked IX
2. I read the review paragraph above   **Rating**

                                              Total

Friday   **Date** ....   No. of times daily

1. I read The Scroll Marked IX
2. I read the review paragraph above   **Rating**

                                              Total

                          Total points for the week

*Appointments for the week*_____

Monday_____
_____
_____
_____
_____
_____

Tuesday_____
_____
_____
_____
_____
_____

Wednesday_____
_____
_____
_____
_____
_____

Thursday_____
_____
_____
_____
_____
_____

Friday_____
_____
_____
_____
_____
_____

*Achievements of the week*_____
_____
_____
_____
_____
_____

Reflection For The Week

Our grand business is not to see what lies dimly at a
distance, but to do what lies clearly at hand. —*Carlyle*

Chapter XII

Does God exist?

If you're positive he does not . . . then you can skip these last five weeks of your Success Recorder . . . because The Scroll Marked X deals with a prayer and there's not much sense praying if you don't believe that anyone is listening.

In 1958, as their contribution to honor the International Geophysical Year, G. P. Putnam's Sons published a book entitled *The Evidence of God in an Expanding Universe*. For anyone who has doubted, at one time or another, that there is a Power beyond any we know (and who of us have perfect faith?) I strongly urge you to find a copy and read it.

In its pages you will meet not one religious leader or Biblical expert. Instead, forty men of science, each with his own long record of accomplishments and honors, present their scientific reasons for believing that there is a God.

I was amazed then, and still am today, that this learned group of men would expose their personal beliefs to ridicule from so many of their scientific peers whose philosophy is usually one of atheistic materialism and whose only god is modern technical achievement.

Yet, there they were, men like biophysicist Frank Allen, zoologist Edward Luther Kessel, physiologist Walter Oscar Lundberg, mathematician and physicist Donald Henry Porter, geneticist John William Klotz, geochemist Donald Robert Carr, astronomer Peter W. Stoner, chemical engineer Olin Carroll Karkalits, medical internist Malcolm Duncan Winter, Jr., biologist Cecil Boyce Hamann, research chemist Edmund Carl Kornfield, soil scientist Lester John Zimmerman and twenty-eight other creative scientists. And each presented logic and reason for the existence of God from his own field of science which did more to buttress my wavering faith than all the sermons I had ever heard.

I'm going to assume, although assuming anything is a good way to get into trouble, that you do believe in a power or force which does have some control over your life and although you might have done very little to maintain "lines of communication" in recent years you still believe that there is "something there." That's all I ask.

I will not dare hope that I can touch you as much as a famous surgeon once was affected by a little girl on whom he was about to operate. As he was about to place her on the operating table he said, "Before we can make you well we must put you to sleep."

She smiled up at him and said, "If you are going to put me to sleep I must say my prayers first." And with that she jumped from the table, knelt on the marble floor and prayed, "Now I lay me down to sleep . . ."

Later, the surgeon said that he prayed that night for the first time since he was a child.

During the next five weeks (and hopefully forever after) you are not going to pray for help or personal gain of any sort . . . only for guidance. Did you know that in Washington, D.C., hundreds of our lawmakers meet each week in private prayer breakfasts which end with these powerful individuals on their knees seeking divine guidance?

Can you picture generals, admirals, cabinet members, senators, representatives, White House staff members, individuals with the most powerful positions in the most powerful country in the world . . . on their knees . . . in a spirit of helpless humility . . . praying?

Can you picture that two-hundred pound, six feet three, rugged and handsome Senator Harold Hughes of Iowa, wearing a wrist watch containing the twelve letters JUST FOR TODAY instead of numbers, fall to his knees after conducting a seminar for visiting foreign dignitaries and educators . . . and leading them in prayer?

Do they know something we don't know?

Perhaps. And what they know is that they can't "hack it" alone. But they never ask for favors or petty victories . . . only for the guidance which will enable them to make their own choice to resolve their problems and challenges of the day.

It is my belief that prayers uttered for personal gain or to resolve some crisis in your life fall on deaf ears like the man and his son who were plowing their field in Georgia when a terrible lightning storm erupted. The man ran for the farmhouse, looked back and saw his son staring skyward.

"Hey," he yelled, "what in tarnation you doin'?"

"I'm prayin', Dad."

"Prayin'! A scared prayer ain't worth a damn, Son—run!"

The Salesman's Prayer, in the final scroll, is an ideal finale for all the weeks you have labored so long to keep your Success Recorder. In its text you will find a review of all the success principles which you have concentrated on, individually, to improve your life.

And through it, you, I know, will find the strength and the inspiration to continue moving forward no matter what fate has in store for you.

Remember, *"Failure will never overtake you if your determination to succeed is strong enough."*

Have a happy and beautiful five weeks with:

The Scroll Marked X

Who is of so little faith that in a moment of great disaster or heartbreak has not called to his God? Who has not cried out when confronted with danger, death, or mystery beyond his normal experience or comprehension? From where has this deep instinct come which escapes from the mouth of all living creatures in moments of peril?

Move your hand in haste before another's eyes and his eyelids will blink. Tap another on his knee and his leg will jump. Confront another with dark horror and his mouth will say, "My God" from the same deep impulse.

My life need not be filled with religion in order for me to recognize this greatest mystery of nature. All creatures that walk the earth, including man, possess the instinct to cry for help. Why do we possess this instinct, this gift?

Are not our cries a form of prayer? Is it not incomprehensible in a world governed by nature's law to give a lamb, or a mule, or a bird, or man the instinct to cry out for help lest some great mind has also provided that the cry should be heard by some superior power having the ability to hear and to answer our cry? Henceforth I will pray, but my cries for help will only be cries for guidance.

Never will I pray for the material things of the world. I am not calling to a servant to bring me food. I am not ordering an innkeeper to provide me with room. Never will I seek delivery of gold, love, good health, petty victories, fame, success, or happiness. Only for guidance will I pray, that I may be shown the way to acquire these things, and my prayer will always be answered.

The guidance I seek may come, or the guidance I seek may not come, but are not both of these an answer? If a child seeks bread from his father and it is not forthcoming has not the father answered?

I will pray for guidance, and I will pray as a salesman, in this manner—

Oh creator of all things, help me. For this day I go out into the world naked and alone, and without your hand to guide me I will wander far from the path which leads to success and happiness.

I ask not for gold or garments or even opportunities equal to my ability; instead, guide me so that I may acquire ability equal to my opportunities.

You have taught the lion and the eagle how to hunt and prosper with teeth and claw. Teach me how to hunt with words and prosper with love so that I may be a lion among men and an eagle in the market place.

Help me to remain humble through obstacles and failures; yet hide not from mine eyes the prize that will come with victory.

Assign me tasks to which others have failed; yet guide me to pluck the seeds of success from their failures. Confront me with fears that will temper my spirit; yet endow me with courage to laugh at my misgivings.

Spare me sufficient days to reach my goals; yet help me to live this day as though it be my last.

Guide me in my words that they may bear fruit; yet silence me from gossip that none be maligned.

Discipline me in the habit of trying and trying again; yet show me the way to make use of the law of averages. Favor me with alertness to recognize opportunity; yet endow me with patience which will concentrate my strength.

Bathe me in good habits that the bad ones may drown; yet

grant me compassion for weaknesses in others. Suffer me to know that all things shall pass; yet help me to count my blessings of today.

Expose me to hate so it not be a stranger; yet fill my cup with love to turn strangers into friends.

But all these things be only if thy will. I am a small and a lonely grape clutching the vine yet thou hast made me different from all others. Verily, there must be a special place for me. Guide me. Help me. Show me the way.

Let me become all you planned for me when my seed was planted and selected by you to sprout in the vineyard of the world.

Help this humble salesman.
Guide me, God.

SUCCESS RECORDER
The Forty-first Week

✦✦

Monday   **Date**............................   No. of times daily

1. I read The Scroll Marked X
            Review Paragraph for the Week
2. I prayed today; I repeated The Salesman's Prayer as part   Rating
   of the scroll but I also spoke a few words of my own, asking for guidance in my personal and business problems
   and thanking my Creator for giving me the privilege of
   making something of this day . . . and my life.   Total
                        (Insert number in each box)

_____

Tuesday   **Date**............................   No. of times daily

1. I read The Scroll Marked X
2. I read the review paragraph above   Rating

                                                        Total

_____

Wednesday   **Date**............................   No. of times daily

1. I read The Scroll Marked X
2. I read the review paragraph above   Rating

                                                        Total

_____

Thursday   **Date**............................   No. of times daily

1. I read The Scroll Marked X
2. I read the review paragraph above   Rating

                                                        Total

_____

Friday   **Date**............................   No. of times daily

1. I read The Scroll Marked X
2. I read the review paragraph above   Rating

                                                        Total

_____

                        Total points for the week

*Appointments for the week*_____

Monday_____
_____
_____
_____
_____

Tuesday_____
_____
_____
_____
_____

Wednesday_____
_____
_____
_____
_____

Thursday_____
_____
_____
_____
_____

Friday_____
_____
_____
_____
_____

*Achievements of the week*_____
_____
_____
_____
_____

Reflection For The Week

I have been driven many times to my knees by the
overwhelming conviction that I had nowhere to go. My
own wisdom, and that of all about me, seemed insuf-
ficient for the day.　　　　**—Abraham Lincoln**

SUCCESS RECORDER
The Forty-second Week

❖❖❖

Monday   Date ....   No. of times daily

1. I read The Scroll Marked X
            Review Paragraph for the Week
2. I prayed today; I repeated The Salesman's Prayer as part   **Rating**
   of the scroll but I also spoke a few words of my own, ask-
   ing for guidance in my personal and business problems
   and thanking my Creator for giving me the privilege of
   making something of this day . . . and my life.   **Total**

                              (Insert number in each box)

Tuesday   Date ....   No. of times daily

1. I read The Scroll Marked X
2. I read the review paragraph above   **Rating**

                                        Total

Wednesday   Date ....   No. of times daily

1. I read The Scroll Marked X
2. I read the review paragraph above   **Rating**

                                        Total

Thursday   Date ....   No. of times daily

1. I read The Scroll Marked X
2. I read the review paragraph above   **Rating**

                                        Total

Friday   Date ....   No. of times daily

1. I read The Scroll Marked X
2. I read the review paragraph above   **Rating**

                                        Total

                    Total points for the week

*Appointments for the week*_____

Monday_____
_____
_____
_____
_____

Tuesday_____
_____
_____
_____
_____

Wednesday_____
_____
_____
_____
_____

Thursday_____
_____
_____
_____
_____

Friday_____
_____
_____
_____
_____

*Achievements of the week*_____
_____
_____
_____
_____
_____
_____

Reflection For The Week

It is good for us to keep some account of our prayers,
that we may not unsay them in our practice.   —M. Hentry

SUCCESS RECORDER
The Forty-third Week

✦✦

Monday   **Date**............................   No. of times daily

1. I read The Scroll Marked X
          Review Paragraph for the Week
2. I prayed today; I repeated The Salesman's Prayer as part   Rating
   of the scroll but I also spoke a few words of my own, asking for guidance in my personal and business problems
   and thanking my Creator for giving me the privilege of
   making something of this day . . . and my life.   Total

          (Insert number in each box)

Tuesday   **Date**............................   No. of times daily

1. I read The Scroll Marked X
2. I read the review paragraph above   Rating

          Total

Wednesday   **Date**............................   No. of times daily

1. I read The Scroll Marked X
2. I read the review paragraph above   Rating

          Total

Thursday   **Date**............................   No. of times daily

1. I read The Scroll Marked X
2. I read the review paragraph above   Rating

          Total

Friday   **Date**............................   No. of times daily

1. I read The Scroll Marked X
2. I read the review paragraph above   Rating

          Total

          Total points for the week

*Appointments for the week*_____

Monday_____
_____
_____
_____
_____

Tuesday_____
_____
_____
_____
_____

Wednesday_____
_____
_____
_____
_____

Thursday_____
_____
_____
_____
_____

Friday_____
_____
_____
_____

*Achievements of the week*_____
_____
_____
_____
_____
_____

Reflection For The Week

True prayer never comes weeping home. I am sure
that I shall get either what I ask, or what I ought to
have asked.   **—Leighton**

SUCCESS RECORDER
The Forty-fourth Week

✦✦✦

Monday   **Date**............................   **No. of times daily**

1. I read The Scroll Marked X
              Review Paragraph for the Week
2. I prayed today; I repeated The Salesman's Prayer as part   Rating
   of the scroll but I also spoke a few words of my own, asking for guidance in my personal and business problems
   and thanking my Creator for giving me the privilege of
   making something of this day . . . and my life.   Total
                          (Insert number in each box)

Tuesday   **Date**............................   **No. of times daily**

1. I read The Scroll Marked X
2. I read the review paragraph above   Rating

                                                      Total

Wednesday   **Date**............................   **No. of times daily**

1. I read The Scroll Marked X
2. I read the review paragraph above   Rating

                                                      Total

Thursday   **Date**............................   **No. of times daily**

1. I read The Scroll Marked X
2. I read the review paragraph above   Rating

                                                      Total

Friday   **Date**............................   **No. of times daily**

1. I read The Scroll Marked X
2. I read the review paragraph above   Rating

                                                      Total

                              Total points for the week

*Appointments for the week*_____

Monday_____
_____
_____
_____
_____

Tuesday_____
_____
_____
_____
_____

Wednesday_____
_____
_____
_____
_____

Thursday_____
_____
_____
_____

Friday_____
_____
_____
_____
_____

*Achievements of the week*_____
_____
_____
_____
_____
_____

Reflection For The Week

Pray to God, at the beginning of all thy works, so
that thou mayest bring them all to a good ending.

—Xenophon

SUCCESS RECORDER
The Forty-fifth Week

✦✦

Monday   Date........................   No. of times daily

1. I read The Scroll Marked X
             Review Paragraph for the Week
2. I prayed today; I repeated The Salesman's Prayer as part   **Rating**
    of the scroll but I also spoke a few words of my own, ask-
    ing for guidance in my personal and business problems
    and thanking my Creator for giving me the privilege of
    making something of this day . . . and my life.   Total
                        (Insert number in each box)

Tuesday   Date........................   No. of times daily

1. I read The Scroll Marked X
2. I read the review paragraph above   **Rating**

                                              Total

Wednesday   Date........................   No. of times daily

1. I read The Scroll Marked X
2. I read the review paragraph above   **Rating**

                                              Total

Thursday   Date........................   No. of times daily

1. I read The Scroll Marked X
2. I read the review paragraph above   **Rating**

                                              Total

Friday   Date........................   No. of times daily

1. I read The Scroll Marked X
2. I read the review paragraph above   **Rating**

                                              Total

                              Total points for the week

*Appointments for the week*_____

Monday_____
_____
_____
_____
_____

Tuesday_____
_____
_____
_____
_____

Wednesday_____
_____
_____
_____
_____

Thursday_____
_____
_____
_____
_____

Friday_____
_____
_____
_____
_____

*Achievements of the week*_____
_____
_____
_____
_____
_____

Reflection For The Week

More things are wrought by prayer than this world
dreams of.   **—Alfred Tennyson**

The End . . . or the Beginning

Commencement days are always fun . . . until the keynote speaker arises to remind you that commencement is "the time of beginning" and so far as duties and responsibilities are concerned you haven't really lived at all, yet, and all the marvelous challenges and opportunities are still before you.

After working so hard and so long, for that diploma, the last thing in the world you want to hear anybody tell you is that the road is going to get rougher, up ahead!

And after working and persisting with your Success Recorder all these weeks the last thing you want to hear from me is that I've got you scheduled for more work, more reading, more self-examination.

But that's exactly what I'm telling you!

Now that you have completed your Success Recorder the first thing I want you to do is dig up that memo you sent yourself before you began this program. On that memo you had indicated what you wanted to be earning in weekly income and what you wanted your title to be when you completed this program.

Like those push-ups, I'll wager you did a lot better than you thought you'd do. *Now, do it again.* Send yourself a similar memo spelling out specifically what you want to be earning in income and what you want your title to be one year from the date of your memo. If you like, also include some other 12-month objectives as material rewards for your courage and hard work . . . a vacation in Acapulco, a new Datsun 240-Z, that mink coat you've been telling "Mama" she was going to get, some day.

But what force will continue to motivate and spur you onward for another year now that you have completed *The Greatest Secret In The World?* What have I got up my sleeve for you, now?

In the next twelve months I want you to read as many as you can of the twelve greatest self-help, self-knowledge, and self-inspirational books ever written. Admittedly, naming any twelve books as the "greatest" in any category is an exercise in impudence on my part and my judgment is purely subjective. However, in nearly a decade of editing self-help material it is reasonably safe to say that nearly every so-called self-help "classic" has crossed my desk. From Franklin's "Autobiography," Great Britain's Samuel Smiles and his "Self-Help," Marden's "Pushing To The Front" down through the Shermans, Bristols, Carnegies, Hills, Peales, and Stones to some of the present and unfortunately different group of "motivators" who write books with exotic titles like, "How To Invigorate The Psychic Power Of Your Liver To Dynamically Master Others" . . . hundreds of books have been read by me and considered for possible excerption in *Success Unlimited Magazine.* What I hope to do for you, with the list I am about to suggest, is to save you many hours of non-profitable reading by helping you avoid the considerable amount of tripe that is being hustled today under the guise of "self-help literature." Just remember that every book which begins with "How to . . ." won't make you a millionaire or a saint.

Although some of this list may be out of print I'm sure you will find many of them at your local library. Regular visits to your library is a habit you should develop, anyway, if you're not already doing it.

Here are my selections, not in any preferential order. for they're all great:

The Twelve Greatest Self-Help Books

The Autobiography of Benjamin Franklin	by Benjamin Franklin
Think And Grow Rich	by Napoleon Hill
Success Through A Positive Mental Attitude	by W. Clement Stone and Napoleon Hill
The Power Of Faith	by Louis Binstock
Your Greatest Power	by J. Martin Kohe
I Dare You	by William Danforth
Acres Of Diamonds	by Russell H. Conwell
The Ability To Love	by Dr. Allan Fromme
How I Raised Myself From Failure To Success In Selling	by Frank Bettger
The Magic Power Of Emotional Appeal	by Roy Garn
As A Man Thinketh	by James E. Allen

But that's only eleven, you say. Well . . . the odds are excellent that you already have the twelfth one in your home. Perhaps you haven't opened it for years but it's there, waiting patiently to serve you . . . and it is the unlimited reservoir which has been used, and will be used, for nearly every self-help book . . . the Holy Bible.

I would also hope, if you haven't already, that somewhere along the way you manage to read the book, *The Greatest Salesman In The World*, for a deeper insight into the ten scrolls with which you have lived for so long.

Before our final parting let me give you a word of warning so that you will be armed to defend yourself against those who put down all self-help literature as the destroyer of moral values and voice of the materialistic "establishment." Every few years some writer, usually an associate professor with a foundation grant, puts together a volume which rips into every self-help author and inspirational book ever written. The private life of Horatio Alger is gleefully exposed, Benjamin Franklin is painted as a snob with a phony "homespun" exterior, Andrew Carnegie with a schizo-type personality, Norman Vincent Peale as a materialistic businessman masquerading as a preacher, Orison Swett Marden as a bumbling editor, and Dale Carnegie as a seducer of man's ego.

These anti-self-help books follow a common course whose logic is as follows: America is not, and never was, a great country except in the materialistic sense and since the self-help writings of the past hundred years have been credited with creating much of the motivation which produced our tremendous materialistic success then the self-help writings must accept a considerable portion of the blame for the "terrible" condition our country is in, today.

To supply you with a biographical sketch of every American whose success story and contributions to mankind are a rebuttal to this warped logic would fill your living room with books.

But what is most interesting to me is that this small group of "anti" writers have been blinded by their own prejudices so that they fail to realize that in order to complete their *own* book they needed to apply nearly all the virtues such as persistence, hard work, faith, courage, industry, resolution, order, sincerity, concentration, and action which they condemn others for suggesting we use.

The "anti" writers, in the final reckoning, are perfect examples that what they say won't work *does work!* Oh, ye of little faith. . . .

I must leave you, now, and I can think of no better way than with the words of Dr. Reinhold Niebuhr at another commencement exercise, many years ago:

"Nothing that is worth doing can be accomplished in your lifetime; therefore you will have to be saved by hope. Nothing that is beautiful will make sense in the immediate instance; therefore, you must be saved by faith. Nothing that is worth doing can be done alone, but has to be done with others; therefore you must be saved by love."

Peace!

The Greatest Miracle
in the World

Also I heard the voice of the Lord saying, Whom shall I send, and who will go for us? Then said I, Here am I; send me.

Isaiah 6:8

Now go, write it before them in a table and note it in a book, that it may be for the time to come for ever and ever.

Isaiah 30:8

To that beautiful redhead whom I have missed for many,
many years . . .
my mother, Margaret.

Chapter I

The first time I saw him?

He was feeding pigeons.

By itself, this simple act of charity is not an unusual sight. One can find old people, who themselves look as if they could use a good meal, dropping crumbs for birds on the wharves of San Francisco, the Common in Boston, the sidewalks of Times Square, and points of interest in every city.

But this old man was doing it at the peak of a brutal snowstorm that, according to the "all-news" station on my car radio, had already dumped a record-breaking twenty-six inches of white misery on Chicago and suburbs.

With rear wheels spinning, I had finally inched my car up the slight sidewalk incline to the gate of the self-park lot, a block behind my office, when I first noticed him. He was standing in the ebb of a monstrous snowdrift, obvious of the elements, rhythmically removing what appeared to be bread crumbs from a brown paper bag and dropping them carefully into a cluster of birds that swirled and swooped around the folds of his nearly ankle-length army-style overcoat.

I watched him through the metronomic sweeps of my hissing windshield wipers as I rested my chin on the steering wheel, trying to generate sufficient will power to open my car door, step out into the blizzard, and walk to the gate release box. He reminded me of those Saint Francis garden statues that one sees in plant and shrubbery stores. Snow almost completely covered his shoulder-length hair and had sprinkled itself through his beard. Flakes had even attached themselves to his heavy eyebrows, further accenting his dark high-cheekboned features. Around his neck hung a leather cord and attached to it was a wooden cross which swayed from side to side as he dispensed tiny bits of the staff of life. Tied to his left wrist was a piece of clothesline which led down to where it was wrapped around the neck of an old multicolored basset hound whose ears dragged deeply into the accumulation of whiteness that had been falling since yesterday afternoon. As I watched the old man, his face broke into a smile and he began talking to the birds. I shook my head in silent sympathy and reached for the door handle.

The twenty-six mile trip from home to office had consumed more than three hours, half a tank of gas, and nearly all of my patience. My faithful 240-Z, its transmission whining a constant and monotonous complaint in low gear, had run a broken-field course past countless stalled trucks and cars along Willow Road, down Edens Expressway, along Touhy Avenue, across Ridge, east on Devon and past the Broadway intersection to the parking lot on Winthrop Street.

It had been insanity on my part to even make the attempt to get to work that morning. But for the previous three weeks I had been touring the United States promoting my book, *The Greatest Salesman In The World*, and after I had told forty-nine radio and television audiences, plus more than two dozen newspaper reporters, that perseverance was one of the most important secrets of success, I didn't dare let myself be defeated even by that angry witch Mother Nature.

Furthermore, there was a board of directors meeting scheduled for the coming Friday. As *Success Unlimited Magazine*'s president, I needed this Monday, and every other day this week, to review our past year's performance and next year's projections with each department head. I wanted to be prepared, as I always had been, for any unexpected questions that might be tossed my way once I was on my feet at the head of that long boardroom table.

The parking lot, situated as it was in the midst of a decaying neighborhood, changed its character twice each twenty-four hours. During the evening and night-time hours it was occupied by vehicles that would have been sold for junk by any self-respecting used-car dealer. These were the cars owned by local apartment dwellers who had been unable to find a parking spot on the narrow street that bisected their soot-streaked buildings. Then, each morning, they all departed in a mass exodus to local and suburban factories and the lot replenished itself with a collection of Mercedes, Cadillacs, Corvettes, and BMW's as attorneys, doctors, and the Loyola University students came into the city from the suburban world to do their thing.

At any other time of the year the lot was a scabby blemish, a back-of-the-hand slap to every resident of the area. In all the years I had parked there I had yet to see its downtown owners make any attempt to remove the litter, soggy newspapers, tin cans and empty wine bottles that accumulated in their own mountains of disease against the rusty chain link fencing. The only thing the lot had going for it was that there was no other available public parking for ten blocks.

Today, however, with all the lot's sins buried under nearly three feet of snow, it reminded me of a stretch of California's Pacific Grove beach, even to its white mounds which only yesterday had been automobiles. Apparently there had been no exits by the locals this morning. They had probably taken one look at their buried machines, now igloos, and either bussed it or gone back to bed.

Entrance to the parking lot was through two posts, buried in concrete, set approximately nine feet apart, upon which rested a large hollow-iron-bar gate. To raise the gate, to get into the lot and park, you deposited two quarters in the slot of a chipped white metal box, waited for the gate to rise after it was tripped electronically by the coins, and then drove through. Then the car wheels depressed some sort of mechanism in the asphalt, automatically lowering the gate behind you. To leave the lot you needed two more quarters to bail yourself out . . . unless you had a special key which you could rent for twenty dollars a month. Keys were inserted into a special yellow box to activate the gate, both entering and leaving.

After turning my attention from the bird-feeding Samaritan, I found my gate-key in the glove compartment, pushed against the accumulated snow which was considerably higher than the bottom of my car door, and stepped gingerly outside. Immediately I became aware of the incompetency of a grown man dumb enough to wear low-cut rubbers on a day like this.

The old man ceased his feeding operation long enough to glance my way and wave. The dog barked once and then was silenced by some unintelligible words from his master. I nodded toward him and forced a weary smile. My "good morning" sounded strange and muffled in the noise-deadening snowfall.

His response, in the deepest voice I had ever heard, seemed to reverberate off the surrounding buildings. Once, when Danny Thomas met radio commentator Paul Harvey, Danny had said, "You had better be God because you sure sound like Him." This voice made my friend Paul sound like a timid choir boy.

"I bid you greetings on this beautiful day!"

I had neither the strength nor the desire to dispute his words. I turned my key in the yellow box until I heard the mechanism activate, then half-sliding, half walking, I returned to my car. Behind me, as I had heard it respond for several thousand mornings, the gate creaked as it raised itself for my entrance.

But . . . no sooner was I back in my car, ready to shift into "drive" and ease my way through the deep snow into the lot, then the gate crashed back down to its original horizontal position with a loud metallic clang.

I sighed in frustration, shifted back into "park," reopened the car door, stepped back into the cold snow, slid up to the yellow box, and turned my key again. The gate rose once more, pointed its rusted tip toward the snow-filled heavens, and then fell back. Bong! Impatiently I turned the key again, almost hard enough to snap it this time. Same thing. A short in the wiring, perhaps, from all this moisture? No matter. There was no way I was going to get my car into that parking lot. And if I left it on the street it was certain to be towed away. I just stood there, knee deep in snow, cursing the idiocy of this aborted journey while I rubbed snowflakes out of my eyes.

Just as I was beginning to doubt everything I had ever written or said about the value of perseverance the bird-feeding stranger interrupted my self-pity. "Let me help you."

That voice was truly something and there was a hint

of command as well as an offer of aid in the resonant tone. He had moved close to me and I found myself looking up into an amazing face, gaunt, heavily lined, set with large brown eyes. He had to be nearly seven feet tall because I'm no pygmy. I smiled and shrugged my shoulders at this Abraham Lincoln 'look alike' and said, "Thanks, but I don't think there's much we can do."

The deep furrows around his eyes and mouth arched into the warmest and most gentle smile I had ever seen on a human as he gestured toward the recalcitrant gate. "It will not be difficult. Turn your key in the box again. When the gate rises I shall step under it, grasp it with my outstretched hands, and hold it until your car passes through. Then I'll let it fall."

"That's a heavy gate."

His laugh boomed through the lot. "I am old but I am quite strong. And most certainly it is worth our efforts to relieve you of your problem. Carlyle wrote that every noble work seems at first impossible.

"Carlyle?"

"Yes, Carlyle. Thomas. Nineteenth-century English essayist."

I didn't believe this. I was standing in a snowdrift with an icy wind lacerating my face, my feet were soaked and freezing, and I was turning into a snow-man . . . while a long-haired seventy-year-old hippie was giving me a mini-course in English Lit.

What else could I do? I'm a great believer in considering one's options, but I've also learned there are times and situations when you don't have any. I mumbled my thanks and waited while the old man gently tugged his basset toward the fence, where he removed the rope from his wrist and tied it through two links. Then he returned to my side and nodded. Almost hypnotically I obeyed his silent command and turned my key in the box. Up groaned the gate bar. Then the old man stepped under it and grasped the cold metal bar firmly just as it began its descent.

I'm not too clear about the next several minutes although I've thought about it often. Perhaps the light-and-hurried breakfast and long drive had finally taken their toll. I felt dizzy and my vision seemed to shift out of focus . . . as if someone had smeared vaseline on my reading glasses. Everything seemed diffused. A strange tremor shook my body as I tried to fix on the apparition before me.

Through the falling snow I could see the wooden cross on his chest and perhaps that's what triggered the illusion . . . long hair, beard, hands extended at a forty-five-degree angle over his head . . . the gate bar . . . the cross bar . . . the *patibulum* carried by the condemned man on the way to Golgotha for his crucifixion. . . .

His voice, now touched with urgency, broke through my fantasy. "Hurry. Drive in! Drive in!"

I scrambled back into my car, shifted into low gear, gradually applied pressure to the accelerator, the tires grabbed, and I moved slowly past the stranger, under the bar and through the gate.

I eased the car gently into a low spot among the drifts and cut the ignition. My hands were trembling. My head was throbbing. My legs felt weak. Then I reached behind my seat, pulled out my attaché case, opened the door, and fell headfirst into the snow. I arose, brushed myself off, and locked the car.

I turned toward the gate to thank the old man.

My parking lot savior was nowhere in sight.

Chapter II

I didn't see him again until late spring.

It had been one of those Fridays that never seem to end. Problems concerning routine matters involved with publishing a monthly magazine had increased in velocity and number during the day, and by the time all the brush fires were extinguished I was alone and beat, both physically and mentally.

I sat at my desk listening to the gentle tick of my desk clock and dreading that long drive home in traffic. Even at this hour Edens Expressway would be jammed. Once more those nagging and recurring questions popped into my mind.

"Why are you working so damn hard?"

"Did you think it would be easier once you got to be Number One?"

"Why don't you resign? Your book royalties are already four times larger than your salary."

"What are you trying to prove now that the magazine is a success?"

"Why don't you go somewhere where it's peaceful and quiet and write all those books you've still got burning inside of you?"

Habit, and my own pride, seemed to be the only logical answer to these questions. I had taken *Success Unlimited Magazine* from a monthly circulation of only 4,000, with three employees, to its present 200,000 and a staff of thirty-four. Yet, I knew there were still 120,000,000 potential subscribers in our country and it was a challenge going after them. Then I tried to remember who had written, "The beginning of pride is in heaven. The continuance of pride is on earth. The end of pride is in hell." No luck. Bad memory.

I tossed my reading glasses into my attaché case, grabbed my jacket and topcoat, turned off the lights and locked the office. Except for the street lamp on the corner of Broadway and Devon, it was dark as I walked slowly past the window of Root Photographers, across the alley mouth behind our building, under the overhead train bridge, and through the small opening into the parking lot with its garish and cracked orange-and-yellow sign flashing, "Park Yourself, Only 50¢."

I was halfway across the shadowy lot, now nearly filled with neighborhood cars, before I saw him. His tall silhouette moved silently from behind a parked panel truck, and even in the blackness I recognized him before

I saw his dog trailing behind. I turned and walked toward him.

"Good evening."

That basso-profundo voice replied, "I bid you greetings on this most beautiful of evenings, sir."

"I never had the opportunity to thank you for helping me in the snow that day."

"It was nothing. We are all here to help one another."

I reached down to pat the basset, who had been nuzzling at my pant leg then I extended my hand toward the old man. "My name is Mandino . . . Og Mandino."

His giant fingers wrapped themselves around mine. "I am honored to meet you, Mister Mandino. My name is Simon Potter . . . and this four-legged ally of mine is called Lazarus."

"Lazarus?"

"Yes. He sleeps so much of the time that I never know whether he's dead or alive."

I laughed.

"You will forgive me, Mister Mandino, but your first name—it is very distinctive. Og, Og . . . how do you spell it?"

"O–G."

"That was your given name?"

I chuckled. "No, my real name is Augustine. Back in high school I wrote a column for our school paper, and one month I signed my piece AUG. After I had written it I decided to be different and spell it phonetically . . . OG. It stuck."

"That is a rare name. There cannot be many Ogs in the world."

"I've been told that one is too many."

"Do you still write?"

"Yes."

"What sort of writing?"

"Books, articles."

"Your books have been published?"

"Yes, five of them."

"That is marvelous. Who would expect to meet an author here among the empty wine bottles?"

"I'm afraid that's where you're liable to meet a lot of authors, Simon."

"Yes. Sad, but true. I, too, write a little . . . but only to pass the time and to satisfy myself."

The old man moved closer as if to study my face. "You look tired, Mister Mandino . . . or rather, I think I shall call you Mister Og."

"I am tired. Long day . . . long week."

"You have far to journey before you reach home?"

"About twenty-six miles."

Simon Potter turned and pointed his long arm toward the drab four-story brown-brick apartment house facing the parking lot. "I live there. On the second floor. Before you begin your long drive come have a glass of sherry with me. It will relax you."

I began to shake my head but, as in the snow that day, I found myself wanting to obey him. I unlocked my car door, tossed in my topcoat and case, closed and locked the door and fell into step behind Lazarus.

We passed through the unswept lobby, past the pock-marked brass mail boxes with their yellowed plastic nameholders, and climbed the worn and pitted concrete stairway. Simon removed a key from his pocket, turned it in the lock of a pine-stained door on which number '21' had been stencilled in red, pushed it open and made a sweeping gesture for me to enter. He flipped the light switch and said, "Forgive my humble retreat. I live alone, except for Lazarus, and housework was never one of my better skills."

His apologies were unnecessary. The tiny living room was immaculate, from the lint-free braided oval rug to the cobwebless ceiling. Almost immediately I spotted the books, hundreds of them, spilling from the two large bookcases and stacked up in neat piles as tall as their owner.

I looked at Simon quizzically. He shrugged his shoulders and warmed the room with his smile, "What else can an old man do but read . . . and think? Please make yourself comfortable and I shall pour our sherry."

When Simon went off to the kitchen I walked over to his books and began reading titles, hoping they would tell me something about this fascinating giant. I cocked my head and ran my eyes along some of the book spines—Will Durant's *Caesar And Christ*, Gibran's *The Prophet*, Plutarch's *Lives Of Great Men*, Fulton's *Physiology Of The Nervous System*, Goldstein's *The Organ-*

ism, Eiseley's *The Unexpected Universe*, Cervantes' *Don Quixote*, Aristotle's *Works*, Franklin's *Autobiography*, Menninger's *The Human Mind*, Kempis' *The Imitation Of Christ, The Talmud,* several Bibles . . .

My host walked toward me holding out my glass of wine. I took it and placed it gently against his glass. The rims touched with a soft lovely note in that silent room. Simon spoke, "To our friendship. May it be long and filled with good."

"Amen," I replied.

He pointed his glass toward the books. "What do you think of my library?"

"It's a great collection. I wish I had them. You have wide interests."

"Not really. They are an accumulation from many years of pleasant hours in second-hand book stores. Still they have a common theme which makes each volume very special."

"Special?"

"Yes. Each in its own way deals with and explains some aspect of the greatest miracle in the world and so I call them 'hand of God' books."

"Hand of God?"

"It is difficult for me to put into words . . . yet I am positive that certain pieces of music, certain works of art, and certain books and plays were created, not by the composer, artist, author, or playwright but by God, and those whom we have acknowledged as the creators of these works were only the instruments employed by

God to communicate with us. What's the matter, Mister Og?"

Apparently I had jumped at his words. Only two weeks earlier, in New York City, Barry Farber, a popular radio host, had used those exact words, 'the hand of God' when praising my book to his audience during my appearance on his program.

"You mean you believe that God still communicates with us as He did during the days of the ancient Jewish prophets?"

"I am positive. For thousands of years this world witnessed a countless parade of prophets pronouncing and explaining the will of God: Elijah, Amos, Moses, Ezekiel, Isaiah, Jeremiah, Samuel, and all the other marvelous messengers until Jesus and Paul. And then . . . no more? I cannot believe that. No matter how many of His prophets were ridiculed, chastised, tortured, and even murdered, I cannot conceive that God finally gave up on us and turned His back on our needs, causing some of us to finally assume that He must be dead since we hadn't heard from Him in so long a time. Instead, I truly believe that He has sent, to every generation, special people, talented people, brilliant people . . . all bearing the same message in one form or another . . . that every human is capable of performing the greatest miracle in the world. And, it is man's most grievous fault that he has not comprehended the message, blinded as he is by the trivia of each succeeding civilization."

"What's this greatest miracle in the world that we can all perform?"

"First, Mister Og, can you define a miracle for me?"

"I think so. It's something that happens contrary to the laws of nature or science . . . a temporary suspension of one of these laws?"

"That is very concise and accurate, Mister Og. Now tell me, do you believe you are capable of performing miracles . . . of suspending any laws of nature or science?"

I laughed nervously and shook my head. The old man rose, picked up a small glass paperweight from the coffee table and held it across to me. "If I release this weight it will fall to the floor, is that not true?"

I nodded.

"What law decrees that it will fall to the floor?"

"The law of gravity?"

"Exactly." Then, without warning, he let the paperweight fall from his hands. Instinctively I reached for it and caught it before it hit the floor.

Simon folded his hands and looked down at me with a self-satisfied grin. "Do you realize what you have just done, Mister Og?"

"I caught your paperweight."

"More than that. Your action temporarily suspended the law of gravity. By any definition of a miracle you have just performed one. Now what would you judge has been the greatest miracle ever performed on this earth?"

I thought for several minutes. "Probably those cases where the dead have supposedly come back to life."

"I agree, as would a consensus of world opinion I am sure."

"But how does all this connect to those books you've got piled up. Certainly they don't contain any secret methods on how to come back from the dead."

"Ah, but they do, Mister Og. Most humans, in varying degrees, are already dead. In one way or another they have lost their dreams, their ambitions, their desire for a better life. They have surrendered their fight for self-esteem and they have compromised their great potential. They have settled for a life of mediocrity, days of despair and nights of tears. They are no more than living deaths confined to cemeteries of their choice. Yet they need not remain in that state. They can be resurrected from their sorry condition. They can each perform the greatest miracle in the world. They can each come back from the dead . . . and in those books are the simple secrets, techniques, and methods which they can still apply to their own lives to become anything they wish to be and to attain all the true riches of life."

I didn't know what to say or how to respond. I sat, staring at him, until he broke the silence. "Do you accept the possibility of individuals performing such a miracle with their own life, Mister Og?"

"Yes I do."

"Do you ever write about such miracles in your books?"

302

"Sometimes."

"I would like to read what you have written."

"I'll bring you a copy of my first book."

"There are miracles in it?"

"Yes, many."

"When you wrote it did you feel the hand of God upon you?"

"I don't know, Simon. I don't think so."

"Perhaps I shall be able to tell you after I have read it, Mister Og."

We sat, after that exchange, in a stillness interrupted only by an occasional rumble from a truck or bus bouncing along the ruts of Devon Avenue. I sipped the sherry and felt more relaxed and at peace with the world than I had in many months. Finally I placed my glass on the small polished end table next to my chair and found myself staring at two small photographs, each enclosed in a small bronze frame. One was of a lovely brunette woman and the other of a blond male child in military uniform. I glanced at Simon and he sensed my silent question.

"My wife. My son."

I nodded. His voice, now so soft that I could scarcely hear him, seemed to float across the small room to me. "Both are dead."

I closed my eyes and nodded again. His next words were barely a whisper, "Dachau, nineteen-thirty-nine."

When I opened my eyes the old man had his head bowed and his two giant hands were clenched together, tightly against his forehead. Then, as if embarrassed that he had momentarily exposed his grief to a stranger, he sat up and forced a smile.

I changed the subject. "What do you do, Simon? Do you have a job?"

The old man hesitated for several moments. Then he smiled again, spread his hands in a self-effacing gesture and said, "I am a ragpicker, Mister Og."

"I thought ragpickers disappeared with the soup kitchens and hunger marches of the early nineteen-thirties."

Simon reached across, placed his hand on my shoulder and squeezed it gently. "By definition, Mister Og, a ragpicker is one who picks up rags and other waste materials from the streets and junk heaps to earn a livelihood. I would imagine that sort of ragpicker has almost disappeared from the American scene during these years of nearly full employment, but we could see them again if conditions change."

"I doubt it. Our crime rate seems to be telling us that we've discovered faster and easier ways of laying our hands on a buck—like mugging, armed robbery, and burglary."

"I'm afraid that what you say is true, Mister Og. Still, in this day of soaring prices for paper and metals, I would imagine that a ragpicker or junk man could do quite well for himself. However, I am not that sort of ragpicker. I seek more valuable materials than old newspapers and aluminum beer cans. I search out waste materials of the human kind, people who have been discarded by others, or even themselves, people who still have great potential but have lost their self-esteem and their desire for a better life. When I find them I try to change their lives for the better, give them a new sense of hope and direction, and help them return from their living death . . . which to me is the greatest miracle in the world. And of course the wisdom I have received from my 'hand of God' books has helped me immensely in my—what shall I call it—profession.

"See this wooden cross that I often wear. It was carved by a young man who once was a shipping clerk. I ran into him one night on Wilson Avenue . . . or rather I should say he ran into me. He was intoxicated. I brought him here. After several pots of black coffee, a cold shower, and some food, we talked. He was truly a lost soul, nearly crushed by his inability to properly support his wife and two young children. He had been working at two jobs, more than seventeen hours a day, for almost three years and he had reached the breaking point. He had begun to hide in the bottle when I found him . . . trying not to face his living death and a conscience that was telling him he didn't deserve his wonderful young family. I managed to convince him that his situation was common and far from hopeless and he began to visit me, nearly every day, before he went to his night job. Together we explored and discussed many of the ancient and modern secrets of happiness and success. I imagine I touched on every wise man from Solomon to Emerson to Gibran. And he listened carefully."

"What happened to him?"

"When he had a thousand dollars saved he quit both jobs, packed his family in their old Plymouth, and headed for Arizona. Now they have a tiny roadside stand, just outside of Scottsdale, and he's beginning to command fairly large prices for his wood carvings. Now and then he writes, always thanking me for giving him the courage he needed to change his life. This cross was one of his first carvings. He's now a happy and fulfilled man . . . not any richer, mind you, just happier. You see, Mister Og, most of us build prisons for ourselves and after we occupy them for a period of time we become accustomed to their walls and accept the false premise that we are incarcerated for life. As soon as that belief takes hold of us we abandon hope of ever doing more with our lives and of ever giving our dreams a chance to be fulfilled. We become puppets and begin to suffer living deaths. It may be praiseworthy and noble to sacrifice your life to a cause or a business or the happiness of others, but if you are miserable and unfulfilled in that lifestyle, and know it, then to remain in it is a hypocrisy, a lie, and a rejection of the faith placed in you by your creator."

"Simon, forgive me, but does it ever occur to you that perhaps you should not interfere in the lives of people or that you have no right to do so? After all, they're not out there looking for you. You must find them and then convince them that they can have a new life if they are willing to try. Aren't you trying to play God?"

The old man's face softened in a look of sympathy and compassion for my apparent lack of perception and understanding. Yet his reply was brief . . . and forgiving.

"Mister Og, I am not playing God. What you will learn, sooner or later, is that God very often plays man. God will do nothing without man and whenever He works a miracle it is always done through man."

He rose as if to bring our visit to an abrupt end, a technique I have used frequently at the office if it was in my best interest to terminate an interview.

I shook his hand as I stepped into the hallway. "Thanks for the hospitality and the sherry."

"It was my pleasure, Mister Og. And please bring me a copy of your book when you have a chance."

During that long drive home, one question continued to intrude itself into my thoughts.

If that wise old ragpicker specialized in rescuing human refuse why was he wasting his time on me, an affluent and successful company president in the fifty-percent tax bracket who had just written a national best-seller?

Chapter III

Several days later, as I was getting out of my car in the parking lot, I heard my name being called with a volume of sound only slightly lower in decibel count than the public address system at Wrigley Field. I looked around but couldn't see him.

"Mister Og, Mister Og . . . up here!"

Simon was leaning out of his second-floor apartment window, over a plant-filled window box, waving a small blue watering can to attract my attention.

I waved.

"Mister Og, Mister Og . . . your book, your book. Don't forget your promise."

I nodded.

He pointed inside his apartment. "This evening . . . before you go home?"

I nodded again.

He smiled and shouted, "I'll have your sherry ready."

I threw him a circled thumb and forefinger, locked the car, and headed for the problems of the day.

"Simon Potter, *who* are you?

"Simon Potter, *what* are you?

"Simon Potter, *why* are you?"

Like some simple almost forgotten roundelay from my youth, I found myself silently repeating these three questions in time with my steps as I hurried toward the office.

I had been unable to get a handle on my feelings about the old man and it bothered me. He fascinated me . . . and, for some inexplicable reason, he frightened me. Both his appearance and his demeanor fit all my preconceived notions of how the Biblical prophets and mystics must have looked and acted, and I would think about him at the strangest times, in the middle of a budget meeting, while reading submitted articles, when writing a book review. His face, his voice, his charismatic manner would intrude themselves into whatever I was thinking and momentarily wipe out my concentration. Who was he? Where did he come from? What was this latter-day Isaiah doing in my life? Maybe I'd get some answers this evening. For my own peace of mind I hoped so.

Toward closing time I asked Pat Smith, my secretary, to requisition a copy of my book, *The Greatest Salesman In The World*, from our inventory. She paused in the doorway after placing the book in my hands. "Anything else, Og?"

"No thanks, Pat, see you in the morning. Good night."

"Good night . . . and don't forget to turn off the coffee machine."

"I won't."

"You said that the last time you worked late . . . and ruined two pots."

I heard her lock the outside door while I sat holding the book, my book, my creation that was now being acclaimed by *Publishers Weekly* as "the bestseller that nobody knows." In four years it had never made the big city "bestseller lists" and yet, with a phenomenal sale of four hundred thousand hardcover copies, it had already outsold every hardcover edition of every book written by Harold Robbins, Irving Wallace, or Jacqueline Susann.

Now there were rumors that several paperback houses were interested in acquiring the reprint rights, and they were talking big money . . . six digit money. Home run! What if it all happened? Could I handle it? Could I cope with all that sudden wealth and the national publicity that would surely follow a promotional campaign conducted by any of the large paperback houses? What kind of a personal price would I end up paying for all this? Would I regret it later? I remembered what Simon had said about the lifetime prisons we build around ourselves. Would this kind of success be a key to release myself . . . or a key to lock myself in? What more did I want from life, anyway? Would I change my lifestyle if I had that kind of financial freedom? Who can really ever have an answer to these questions before the fact?

I tried to put all the "what-if" thoughts out of my mind

and opened the book to autograph it for Simon. What could I inscribe on the flyleaf that would be appropriate for this saintlike man? Somehow the proper words were important to me. And what would an expert on Gibran, Plutarch, Plato, Seneca, and Eiseley think of my little book after he had read it? That was important. To me.

I began to write . . .

> *For Simon Potter*
> *God's Finest Ragpicker*
> *With love*
> *Og Mandino*

I remembered to turn off the coffee machine, turned on the burglar alarm, flicked off the lights, locked up, and walked across the shadowy parking lot to his apartment building. I found #21 scrawled in yellow crayon above one of the lobby mail boxes, hit the bell button twice, and climbed the stairs. Simon was waiting for me in the hall.

"You remembered!"

"You reminded me!"

"Ah, yes. Like most old men I am both rude and presumptuous. Forgive me my trespasses, Mister Og. Come in, come in."

While we were still standing we conducted our exchange. I handed him my book and he gave me a glass of sherry. He frowned when he read the title.

"*The Greatest Salesman In The World?* Very interesting. May I guess who that might be?"

311

"You'll never guess, Simon. It's not who you think it is."

Then he opened the cover and read my inscription. His face seemed to soften and when he looked at me his big brown eyes were moist. "Thank you. I know I shall enjoy it. But why did you inscribe it in such a manner? Ragpicker, yes . . . but God's Finest?"

I pointed toward his stacks of books. "When I was here, before, you were telling me about your theory that some books were written and guided by the hand of God. I just figured that if you could recognize when a writer had been touched by God's hand you must be a special friend of His."

He studied my face intently, staring at me for interminably uncomfortable minutes until I broke our eye contact.

"And you would like me to read your book and decide whether or not I think it belongs in the same category as the others . . . assisted by the hand of God, as it were?"

"I don't know whether I want you to do that or not, Simon. Maybe subconsciously I do but I hadn't thought about it. All I know, for sure, is that I get the strangest premonitions when I'm with you. You are in my mind a good deal and I don't know why."

The old man leaned his head back on his overstuffed chair and closed his eyes. "A premonition is a forewarning, a foreboding of something about to happen. Is that how you feel when you are with me or when you think about me?"

"I'm not quite sure that explains the sensation."

"Perhaps it is a feeling that we have met before or shared some experience in the past? What do the French call it? Ah yes . . . déjà vu."

"That's closer to it. Have you ever had a dream and then when you awoke you tried and tried to remember it and all that remained in your memory were shadows and unrecognizable voices with no meaning and no relationship to your life?"

The old man nodded, "Many times."

"Well, that's how I feel when I'm with you or think about you. I guess the kids would call it 'vibes,' only I can't characterize it because I've never experienced it before."

"The mind is a very strange mechanism, Mister Og."

"Simon, I couldn't even begin to guess how many books and magazine articles I've read about the mind in the past ten years, for possible use in my magazine. Yet, the more I read the more I have come to realize how very little we know about that mystery within us . . . or even where it's located."

The old man rubbed his hand across his cheek and said, "Dr. Karl Menninger wrote that the human mind is far more than the brain's little bag of tricks. It is, instead, the entire personality made up of a human's instincts, habits, memories, organs, muscles, and sensations, all going through a constantly changing process."

"I know Dr. Menninger."

"Personally? Really?"

"Yes."

"What kind of man is he?"

"He's a giant of a man, almost your size, a beautiful man, like you . . . and he always has a twinkle in his eyes when he speaks."

"Is there, what do you call it, a 'twinkle,' in my eyes, Mister Og?"

"Sometimes, Simon. Sometimes."

He smiled sadly. "I like, best, what Milton wrote about the mind. 'The mind is its own place, and in itself can make a heaven of hell, and a hell of heaven.' Mister Og, our mind is the greatest creation on earth and it can generate the most sublime happiness for its owner—or it can destroy him. Yet, although we have been given the secret of how to control it, for our happiness and benefit, we still function completely ignorant of its potential, like the most stupid of animals."

"The secret of how to control our mind for our benefit . . . ?"

Simon pointed toward the book stacks. "It's all there. One has only to study the treasures that lie, exposed, all around us. For countless centuries man compared his mind to a garden. Seneca said that soil, no matter how rich, could not be productive without cultivation and neither could our minds. Sir Joshua Reynolds wrote that our mind was only barren soil, soon exhausted and unproductive unless it was continually fertilized with new ideas. And James Allen, in his monumental classic, *As A Man Thinketh*, wrote that a man's mind was like a garden which may be intelligently cultivated or allowed to run wild, but whether cultivated or neglected, it would produce. If no useful seeds were planted, then an abundance of useless weed-seeds would fall into the land, and the results would be wrong, useless, harmful, and impure plants. In other words, whatever we allow to enter our minds will always bear fruit."

I lit a cigarette and hung on his every word.

"Now, man is comparing his mind to a computer but his conclusions are the same as Seneca's and the others. The computer people have a phrase, actually an acronym, 'GIGO' . . . 'garbage in, garbage out.' If one puts faulty information into a computer, out will come faulty answers. So it is with our minds . . . whether one is thinking in terms of a garden or an IBM Three-Sixty. Put negative material in . . . and that's what you'll reap. On the other hand, if you program in, or plant, beautiful, positive, correct thoughts and ideas, that's what you'll harvest. So it's simple, you see. You can actually become whatever you are thinking. As a man thinketh in his heart, so is he. Allen wrote, 'Man is made or unmade by himself; in the armory of thought he forges the weapons by which he destroys himself; he also fashions the tools with which he builds for himself heavenly mansions of joy and strength and peace. By the right choice and true application of thought man ascends to the divine perfection.' Mister Og, note those words, 'by the right choice.' They are the cornerstone of a happy life and perhaps, at some other time, you will let me elaborate."

"In other words, Simon, you're saying that we can program our mind. But how?"

"Very simple. We can do it for ourselves or others will do it for us. Merely by hearing or reading a thought or an affirmation, whether it be truthful or the vilest of lies, over and over, our mind will eventually imprint that thought and it will become a permanent part of our personality, so strong that we will even act on it without consideration or reflection in the future. Hitler, you may recall, did this to an entire country, and 'brainwashing' is a phrase with which we are all too familiar after many sad experiences by our captured troops in the Orient."

"We become what we think?"

"Always!"

This seemed like a good opportunity to do some probing and so I took it. "Simon, tell me about yourself. Do you mind?"

He shook his head, placed the wine glass on the lamp table, folded his hands in his lap, and looked down at them as he spoke. "I do not mind. This opportunity has not come to me in many years, and I also realize that you are hoping I might touch upon some fact, some clue, that will clarify whatever seems to concern you about our relationship. First, I am seventy-eight years old and in good health. I have been in this country since nineteen-forty-six."

"You came here right after the war?"

"Yes."

"What did you do before the war?"

He smiled. "I realize it will require a good deal of blind faith on your part to believe me, but I headed the largest export-import firm in Germany that dealt exclusively with goods from the Middle East. My home was in Frankfort but the firm's main office was in . . ."

I interrupted . . . "Damascus?"

He glanced at me strangely. "Yes, Mister Og, Damascus."

I rubbed my hand across my face and downed the rest of the sherry. How in the name of God did I know that? For some inexplicable reason I had the sudden urge to get up and run out of his apartment. Instead I just sat there, with two absolutely immobile legs, paralyzed by an unknown dilemma. I didn't want to hear anymore and yet I wanted to hear it all. The reporter in me finally won and I began firing questions at him like some ambitious county prosecutor. He responded to each of my questions at his own pace.

"Simon, did you have any branch offices?"

"Ten, in cities such as Jerusalem, Baghdad, Alexandria, Cairo, Beirut, Aleppo . . ."

"Ten?"

"Ten."

"What kind of merchandise did you export and import?"

"Mostly goods with some degree of rarity and value. Finished wools and linens, fine glassware, precious stones, the finest rugs, some leather goods, coated papers . . ."

317

"Your firm, you said, was large?"

"We were the largest of its kind in the world. Our annual sales volume, even in the midst of the depression, in nineteen-thirty-six, exceeded more than two hundred million dollars in American currency."

"And you were company president?"

Simon cocked his head, shyly. "It is not difficult to be company president when one is sole owner and founder and . . ." he held up my book, pointing to the title, "also the company's top salesman."

My host rose and refilled my glass. I downed half of it as I studied him carefully. Was he putting me on? Finally I grasped his arm and turned him gently toward me so that I was staring directly into his eyes, "Simon, in truth, you have already read my book?"

"Forgive me, Mister Og, but I have never seen a copy of your book until this evening. Why?"

"*The Greatest Salesman In The World* is set in the time of Christ. It tells the story of a young camel boy, Hafid, who had ambitions to become a salesman in order to earn his share of the gold that he saw were the fruits of the efforts of the other salesmen in the caravan. Finally, after many rebuffs, Hafid is given one robe by the caravan master and dispatched to a nearby village, called Bethlehem, to prove that he can sell. Instead, the youth after failing to sell the robe for three humiliating days, presents it to warm a newborn baby sleeping in a manger in a cave. Then he returns to the caravan, believing he had failed as a salesman, never noticing the bright star that followed him. But the caravan master interprets the star as a sign that had been prophesied many years before and he gives our young man ten scrolls of success which the youth eventually applies to his life to become . . . The Greatest Salesman In The World."

"That is a very touching plot, Mister Og."

"There's more, Simon. When the youth, Hafid, becomes wealthy and powerful, he establishes his main warehouse in a certain city. Would you care to guess the city?"

"Damascus?"

"Yes. And in time he opens other warehouses and branches throughout the Middle East. How many, Simon?"

"Ten?"

"Yes, again. And the goods he sold, as described in my book, were the same goods you sold!"

The old man turned his head away from me and spoke very slowly. "Those . . . are . . . exceedingly . . . strange . . . coincidences . . . Mister Og."

I pressed on. "Tell me about your family, Simon."

He hesitated for several minutes before speaking again. "Well, as I have mentioned, my home was in Frankfort. Actually we lived in a suburb, Sachsenhausen, on a lovely estate in sight of the River Main. Yet, my time there was limited. It seemed as if I was always saying goodby to my family at the airport. More and more I came to hate the days and weeks when I was apart from my wife and young son. Finally, in nineteen thirty-five, I decided to do something about my life. I made very careful plans for the future. I decided to work very hard, until nineteen-forty, and then I would take, from the business, sufficient assets for my family and me to live comfortably for the rest of our lives. Then I would transfer controlling interest in the company to those in my employ who had been so loyal to me through the years. . . ."

I interrupted him again . . . and this time my voice broke. "Simon, when you read my book you will learn that my great salesman, Hafid, finally gave his business and most of his wealth to those who had helped him build it."

The old man was frowning and shaking his head at me. "That cannot be! That cannot be!"

"You will read it for yourself. And what of your family?"

"By this time, Hitler had come to power. Yet I, like most business people, had no idea of the monster we had blindly allowed to take control of our country. My wife was a Jew, and while I was on one of my many trips to Damascus I was visited, one day, by one of Hitler's agents. He calmly notified me that both my wife and son were in what he called protective custody and they would be released to me only upon my signing over, to the National Socialist Party, my entire company and all its assets. I signed without hesitation. Then I immediately flew back to Frankfort and was arrested, by the secret police, at the airport gate. I spent the entire war years being trucked from one concentration camp to another. Not being a Jew, I guess, saved my life."

"And your wife and son?"

"I never saw them again."

I started to say 'I'm sorry' but didn't.

"And your business?"

"Gone. Everything confiscated by the Nazis. After the war I spent nearly four years trying to find any clue concerning my family. Both the Americans and British were most cooperative and sympathetic. Finally I learned, through American intelligence, that both my wife and son had been murdered and cremated at Dachau almost immediately after they had been taken captive."

It was tough to continue. I felt like some cruel inquisitor forcing the old man to relive memories that he had long ago probably pushed into the background of his mind in order to maintain his sanity. Still I continued. "How did you get to this country?"

"In my affluent days I had made many fine friends in Washington. One of them interceded with the proper immigration authorities, who waived my lack of passport. Another loaned me money for passage. I had visited Chicago in nineten-thirty-one and liked its vitality, so I came here."

"What have you been doing all these years?"

He shrugged his shoulders and stared up at the ceiling. "What can an ex-millionaire company president, whose ambitions all died in a gas chamber, do? I worked at a hundred odd jobs, only to survive . . . night club janitor, cook, city sanitation work, construction work . . . anything. I knew I had all the necessary knowledge, experience, and ability to start a new business of my own, but I had no stomach for it anymore. There was no reason to succeed or to acquire wealth, and so I made no effort. Finally I passed the city examinations and became a school janitor on Foster Avenue. That was very good for me. I was around laughing children all day. Very good. And now and then I would see a lad that reminded me of my Eric. It was a fine, decent job. I retired when I was sixty-five, and the city began paying me a small pension, enough to live . . . and read."

"Whatever made you decide to become what you call a ragpicker?"

Simon smiled and leaned back in his chair, staring up at the ceiling again as if trying to remember details of an event that had been long undisturbed among his memories.

"I moved into this small apartment soon after I retired. Lazarus, myself, and my books. Each morning it became a ritual for Lazarus and me to walk completely around this block. One morning, as I was leaving the building, I happened to look across at the gate to the parking lot, where I first met you, and there was a young lady who appeared to be in some sort of difficulty. Her automobile was parked at the approach to the gate, which was down, and she was angrily pounding on the metal box which accepts the coins that activate the gate. I went over to her and asked if I could be of assistance. She was crying, and between her sobs she told me that she had put her last two quarters in the coin box and the gate had not risen. Furthermore she was due in class, at Loyola, in less than ten minutes, for a final exam. I did what anyone else would have done. I removed two quarters from my pants pocket, dropped them into the coin slot, and this time the gate went up. Then I continued my walk with Lazarus."

By now the old man was pacing the room.

"We had not gone very far when I heard footsteps hurrying up behind me and I turned to see the lovely young lady coming toward me, still with tears in her eyes, but smiling. Before I realized what she was doing, she had reached up, thrown her arms around me, pulled me down to her, and kissed me on the cheek . . . the first time a woman had embraced me since my wife. The young lady said nothing . . . there was just the hug and a kiss . . . and then she scampered off. That trivial incident was what gave my life a new meaning and direction, Mister Og. I resolved to stop hiding in my small apartment, to stop feeling sorry for what life had given me, and to begin giving some of myself to others after all the years of self-pity. Actually, you see, it was a selfish decision because the feeling that went through me, when that grateful girl kissed me, was one I had not known for many years. It was the feeling that only comes when one has helped another with no thought of personal gain. I have been a ragpicker ever since."

I felt drained. The questions and answers had exhausted me. Still, there was one thing more I had to know.

"Simon, you mentioned that your son's name was Eric. What was your wife's name?"

"Mister Og, my wife had a name as lovely as her soul . . . Lisha."

All I could do was sigh and whisper, "Simon, please hand me my book."

The old gentleman placed the book in my lap. I turned hurriedly through the first few pages and stopped on page fourteen. "Simon, look! Here . . . where I am pointing, halfway down the page—is the name I gave to the wife of Hafid, the greatest salesman in the world. Read it!"

A half-sob, half-cry of anguish, escaped from the old man's lips as he focused on the printed page. Then he looked up at me, unbelieving, large tears forming in those unforgettable eyes.

"It cannot be, it cannot be!"

He took the book in his giant hands, staring intently at the page. Finally he raised it to his cheek, caressed it gently against his beard, and murmured softly, over and over, "Lisha . . . Lisha . . . Lisha."

Chapter IV

A month passed before I saw him again.

It was well past closing time and I was alone in my office trying to make some dent in the correspondence that had accumulated during my absence. I heard the outer office door click, and stiffened. Whoever had been last out had neglected to lock up, and robberies were becoming a way of life in that neighborhood.

Then Lazarus appeared in my office doorway in a flurry of uncoordinated movements, tail wagging, ears rising and falling, sad eyes weeping, tongue flashing— pulling on the rope which led back to his master.

The old man hugged me. "Mister Og, it is good to see you. Lazarus and I, we were both worried about you."

"I've been away on book business, Simon. I think someone is trying to change my life."

"For the better?"

"I'm not sure. Maybe you'll be able to tell me."

"I knew you weren't here, Mister Og. Each day I

would look out my window for your little brown car. No car . . . no Mister Og. And then this morning, there it was. I was so happy. I wanted to see you and yet I didn't want to bother you. It took all day to get up the courage to come here."

"I'm glad you did. I'd have come over to see you, anyway, to tell you the news about the book."

"Good news?"

"I'm still not sure it's happening to me."

The old man nodded and patted my shoulder proudly. Then he led Lazarus to my coat rack and tied a loose knot around its base with the rope. The dog buried his nose in the heavy carpet and closed his eyes.

"You look great, Simon. I've never seen you in a suit and tie before."

My visitor shyly rubbed his long fingers on his wrinkled jacket lapel and shrugged. "I could not come to visit a company president looking like a bum, could I?"

"Why not? I imagine you ragpickers work in all sorts of disguises and have probably infiltrated more walks of life than the CIA. Angels without portfolio."

The beginning of a smile evaporated suddenly when I said "angels." Then he collected himself and forced a wry grin. "Only a writer would coin such a poignant description. Still we ragpickers are very short-handed. There is also a population explosion on humanity's junk piles, and not enough of us to do the job properly. I wonder if your magazine's publisher, W. Clement Stone, is a ragpicker."

We both turned our heads toward a portrait of my boss staring warmly at me from the paneled wall at the right side of my desk. "I think he must be, Simon. He picked me off the junk pile, sixteen years ago, when I was broke, alone, and taking frequent dives into the bottle. Funny, but you ragpickers also seem to have a policy of secrecy about your good deeds. Since I'm so close to him I happen to know about some of the people that Mister Stone has helped and yet very few of his Good Samaritan activities ever get into the papers."

Simon nodded. "That is because we ragpickers all try to follow the Biblical command which Lloyd Douglas popularized in his book *Magnificent Obsession*."

"You mean to do good . . . and shut up."

His booming laugh filled my office. "That's what I mean although I've never heard it put exactly that way. I think I still prefer the original injunction from Jesus, as Matthew wrote it."

"Simon, did you know that when the book *Magnificent Obsession* was published, Bible sales skyrocketed throughout the world?"

"Why was that, Mister Og?"

"Because everyone began to search for the biblical passage that formed the theme of the book, and Douglas, with a stroke of genius, never specifically pointed it out in the book. Looking for that passage almost became the most popular pastime in this country for a year or more and made *Magnificent Obsession* a bestseller. And those who found the injunction would keep the specific gospel,

THE GREATEST MIRACLE IN THE WORLD

chapter, and verse to themselves, as if it were a privileged secret that one could only become a part of through one's own discovery."

"We could use that sort of game today, Mister Og."

"Yes we could. Do you know the passage, Simon?"

The old man smiled, rose to his full height, faced me across the desk, cupped his right hand so that only his index finger was pointed toward me . . . and proceeded to send shivers through me.

" 'Take heed that ye do not your alms before men, to be seen of them; otherwise ye have no reward of your Father which is in heaven.

" 'Therefore, when thou doest thine alms, do not sound a trumpet before thee, as the hypocrites do, in the synagogues, and in the streets, that they may have glory of men. Verily I say unto you, they have their reward.

" 'But when thou doest alms, let not thy left hand know what thy right hand doeth; that thine alms may be in secret; and thy Father which seeth in secret, himself shall reward thee openly.' "

I'm positive that it was never delivered better . . . except on that mountain . . . two thousand years ago.

I poured my friend a cup of terrible coffee and we made small talk as he strolled, cup in hand, slowly around my office. He paused at the wall studded with autographed photographs and read the names aloud, his voice rising gradually in pitch with each additional name, as if to signify that he was impressed. The old fox was teasing me and I loved it.

"Rudy Vallee, Art Linkletter, John F. Kennedy, Charles Percy, Harland Sanders, Joey Bishop, Senator Harold Hughes, Frank Gifford, James Stewart, Robert Cummings, Robert Redford, Barbra Streisand, Ben Hogan, Norman Vincent Peale . . . these are your friends?"

"Some are . . . and the others thought they'd show their gratitude for an article we did on them at one time or another."

"I like James Stewart. All his movies . . . good movies. You know him?"

"I knew him many years ago. I was a bombardier in his B-24 group in World War II."

"He was brave?"

"Very brave. He completed his combat tour long before there was much fighter escort to protect our bombers. And he could outdrink all of us."

"Good. Good."

Simon continued his casual inventory of my office, probably comparing it to his long-ago presidential trappings in Damascus. A faint smell of camphor seeped from his severely cut pinstriped suit and yet he wore it with a dignity and style that made it easy to picture him behind a large mahogany desk, dispensing advice when necessary and also giving hell when someone deserved it.

Finally he put down his coffee cup and said, "I can wait no longer. Tell me of your good news, Mister Og."

"You brought me good luck, Simon, I'm sure of it.

There must be a lot of leprechaun beneath that rag-picker facade of yours. Remember that last night, at your place, when we discovered all those amazing co-incidences between my book hero and you?"

"How can I ever forget?"

"Well, when I got home there was a message to call my publisher, Frederick Fell. He told me that a large paperback house wanted to meet with him, his vice-president, Charles Nurnberg, and myself on Monday to discuss their possible purchase of the reprint rights to the book. So, that Sunday night I was on my way to New York."

"Were you nervous, worried?"

"Not very much . . . at least not that night. But the next morning, in New York, I was up at six and I smoked a lot and drank a ton of coffee waiting for our one-o'clock meeting. Even so, I arrived at the publisher's building on Fifth Avenue an hour early. So . . . I did something I haven't done for a long, long time. Right next door was a church. I don't even remember its name but it was open and I went in."

"And what did you do?"

"I prayed. I actually walked up to the altar, knelt at the rail, and prayed."

"How did you pray?"

"The only way I know. I didn't ask for anything, just that God would give me the guidance and courage to handle whatever came up. Funny, Simon, but I could almost hear a voice asking, 'Where have you been, Og?'

Then, before I knew what was happening, I was bawling
. . . and I couldn't stop. Luckily no one was around
but I felt like a damned fool anyway."

"Why were you crying? Do you know?"

"I guess being in that church reminded me of all the
Sundays I had gone to mass with my mother when I
was young. My world almost stopped when she died of
a heart attack right after I graduated from high school.
She was something special and had me convinced that I
was going to be a writer even when I was in grade
school. I still remember how she would review my com-
positions or the other written work I brought home, and
we had such a great relationship that she could criticize
my work, constructively, and I'd always accept it and
resolve to try harder. She was so proud when I became
news editor of our high school paper you'd have thought
I'd just been tapped by *The New York Times.* She wanted
me to go to college, but we were having a tough time
just surviving in nineteen-forty. Then she died . . . and
I joined the Army Air Force."

"You never attended college, Mister Og."

"No."

The old man looked around my office again and
shook his head. "Amazing. What else took place in that
church?"

"Nothing else. I finally got control of myself, and by
then it was nearly time for our appointment, so I left
the church, walked across the street and into the publisher's lobby. When I got off the elevator on the twenty-

sixth floor I found myself walking down this long hall, flanked by giant posters of some of the most famous writers in the world, published by this firm. All I could think was, 'Mom, we made it. We're here with the best!' "

"And your meeting with the publishing executives?"

"It went sensationally. Large boardroom table, large room, many names, many faces. As we were told later, they had already decided to purchase the paperback rights. What they wanted to learn was whether I was marketable and promotable along with the book."

"Balzac, Dickens, Tolstoy . . . they would have failed that test."

"You're probably right. Anyway, I spoke to them for about ten minutes, told them how the book came to be written, and I guess I made the proper impression."

The old man was now vicariously reliving every minute of my command performance. He leaned forward excitedly and pointed both hands at me, motioning me to continue.

"Finally, their chairman of the board looked at my publisher, Fred Fell, and asked what we wanted for the paperback rights. Mister Fell, in his best poker-playing voice replied that he wanted one dollar for every hardcover copy we had sold . . . and we had, at that point, sold three hundred and fifty thousand copies. There was a little gasping and groaning around the table and the chairman said that he hadn't expected to go that high. Then he excused himself, beckoned to one of his vice-presidents, and left the room. I guess they were only gone for a few minutes, Simon, but so help me it seemed like a year. When they came back the chairman went over to Mister Fell, put out his hand and they shook. That was it!"

"It was that simple?"

"Yes."

"They are paying you three hundred and fifty thousand dollars?"

"Yes."

"Mister Og, you are wealthy!"

"Not as wealthy as you think. Mister Fell gets half of that and then we both must share with Uncle Sam."

"But, Mister Og, you have already earned a considerable sum of money in royalties from all those hardcover sales, have you not?"

"Yes."

"Did you know that F. Scott Fitzgerald, three years after *The Great Gatsby* was published, received only five dollars and fifteen cents in royalties and by the time he died that marvelous book was already out of print?"

"No, I didn't know that, Simon. And don't misunderstand. I'm not ungrateful. I can't believe it's happened to me yet. Maybe it was that prayer in church."

"And maybe it was your mother's prayers, my friend. Now where have you been for the rest of the month?"

"Well, since the paperback won't be out until next spring, Fell decided to promote the hardcover book heavily through this summer and fall and so I agreed to go on a radio, television, and newspaper promotion tour for three weeks. I've been in fourteen cities, been interviewed more than ninety times . . . and I'm getting to like it . . . even the book-store autographing sessions."

"I'm very proud and happy for you, Mister Og."

We sat for awhile, two comrades, sharing a victory. There was more small talk before I finally got up enough courage to ask, "Simon, did you ever get around to reading my book?"

"Of course. The very same night you left it with me. It is a beautiful thing. The paperback people will sell millions of copies. The world needs your book, Mister Og."

That was good enough for me. They could have all the other rave book reviews I had been saving. Simon rose and said, "Come. We must celebrate. One sherry for your good fortune."

I went.

After we were seated in our usual chairs and Simon had poured, he resumed our office conversation. "Mister Og, the haunting similarities between your great salesman and my own life have caused me many sleepless nights. And the probable odds, after all the other coincidences, that Hafid's wife and mine would both be named Lisha must be beyond the ability of any computer to calculate."

"I've tried to put it out of my mind, Simon. I think the extrasensory perception people call that sort of thing precognition. Or maybe not. I did write the book before I knew about you but you lived those events before I wrote the book. I don't know what they'd call that, but it's still scary as hell to think about. Do you believe it's all just coincidence, chance?"

The old man sighed and shook his head. "Coleridge wrote that chance is but the pseudonym of God for those particular cases which He does not choose to subscribe too openly with His own signature."

"I like that. And if it is one of God's secrets there isn't much we can do about it . . . and so I'm not going to dwell on it. I haven't even discussed it with anyone else. Who'd believe me?"

"It is fortunate that we have each other, Mister Og."

We sipped our sherry in a peaceful stillness that can only be experienced by two people who truly relate to each other, a quiet that neither felt necessary to disturb with words merely to reinforce friendship. I didn't know what Simon was thinking, but I was trying to muster up enough courage to spring a suggestion on him, one that had occurred to me while flying back from my New York meeting with the paperback publishers.

One thing I had learned in New York was that good self-help and inspirational writing was at a premium. Whether it was the state of the nation, or just another publishing cycle, every publishing house, it seemed, was on the lookout for another *Wake Up And Live* or *The Power Of Positive Thinking* or *How To Win Friends And Influence People*. Whenever our country gets down on itself it seems that self-help books rise to the top of the sales charts and most publishers, trying to anticipate the future, were apparently figuring the country was in another "down." I thought Simon would be a natural. I took the plunge.

"Simon, how many people do you figure you have helped turn their lives around in your role as ragpicker?"

There was no hesitation. "In the past thirteen years . . . one hundred."

"Exactly?"

"Yes."

"How do you know? Have you kept a diary of some sort?"

"No. When I first began this adventure my intentions were good but my methods of trying to help were trial and error . . . mostly error. I'm afraid I did more harm than good to those early cases I discovered, for I brought them partly out of their living death and then, through my ignorance, let them fall back. You see I was trying to deal with each in a different way consistent with the individual personality involved. Only gradually did I come to realize that while we are all different, each unique in his or her own way, our lack of self-esteem which produced our failure is a universal sickness always originating from the complex of either anxiety, guilt, or inferiority . . . the three standard emotional problems recognized by most students of psychiatry. Not being learned in this area I had to be taught the hard way . . . in the gutters and junk piles, and then from my books."

"And when you found this common denominator you

did something to standardize your system of assistance?"

"Yes. Man has been trying to solve the challenge of his elusive self-esteem since he first walked upright, and wise men have been writing of the disease and its cure for thousands of years . . . each giving us similar solutions which, of course, we continue to ignore. When this truth became clear to me I spent several months in this apartment with my books, extracting and distilling the true secrets of success and happiness into words that were as simple as the truths they proclaimed . . . so simple that most individuals searching for answers to their problems scarcely would recognize them, much less pay the price to follow such unexotic rules for a happy and meaningful life."

"How many rules are there?"

"Only four . . . and after months of labor and a mountain of notes, the few pages which contained the essence of the simple secrets of success seemed hardly worthy of all the research I had done. Then I reminded myself that it took many tons of rock to produce an ounce of gold. Subsequently I took my findings out into the world and used them in my own manner . . . and they have never failed!"

"You have this material in writing, now?"

"When I had completed my work, in longhand, I brought it to a small printing establishment on Broadway. They typed it, in the format that I requested, and used that master copy to reproduce one hundred sets. Then I numbered each copy one to a hundred."

"How did you distribute the material? You didn't just hand the thing to every downtrodden soul you met?"

"Oh no. Man usually does not throw himself on the junk pile until after the realization comes to him that no one in the world truly cares about him. When I find someone who needs help I first try to convince him, or her, that there are still two who care: God . . . and me. One in heaven . . . and one on earth."

"Then what?"

"Once I have convinced them that we truly care and wish to help, once I know they have confidence in me, I tell them that I am going to give them a very special document which contains a message from God. I tell them that all I want from them is twenty minutes of their time each day, to read their message from God . . . just before they go to sleep. And this is to continue for one hundred consecutive evenings. In exchange for these few daily minutes, a small price to pay, especially for people where time no longer has much value, they will learn how to pick themselves off the junk pile and perform the greatest miracle in the world. They will resurrect themselves from living deaths, literally, and eventually achieve all the true riches of life that they dreamed about. In other words, the message from God, absorbed day by day into their deep subconscious mind that never sleeps, enables them to become their own ragpicker. Self-help at its best!"

"A message from God. Doesn't that terrify them? Especially since you already look and sound as most of us picture God. Your beard, your figure, your manner, your height, your voice . . ."

"Mister Og, you are already forgetting one fact. I pull these people from their own living hells. They have already deserted this life in their minds. They are positive that they can do nothing to help themselves and so they are willing to grasp at any hand that reaches out to help them. It is a hand of hope."

"Hope?"

"Yes. Do you know that story about the famous perfume manufacturer who at his retirement dinner was asked to explain his secret of success? He reminded his audience that his success had not come because of the fine fragrances or packaging or merchandising methods he had used so brilliantly. He had succeeded because he was the only perfume manufacturer who realized that what he was selling to women was not exotic odors or glamor or sexual magnetism. What he was selling them was . . . hope!"

"That's wonderful. Now, back to this message from God. . . ."

"Actually, Mister Og, when I hand the document to them they see that it is not just a message . . . it is a memorandum from God. I had the document typed and printed in the format of a general office memorandum."

I started to laugh. "A memorandum from God? Simon . . . !"

"Why not? Long ago God communicated with us by chiseling ten commandments on two tablets which He delivered to Moses on Mount Sinai. Later, He wrote a warning on the wall of King Belshazzar's palace. How would He communicate with us, today, if He decided to do it in writing? What is the most modern form of written communication?"

"Memorandums?"

"Exactly. They are concise, have a universal form, are practical, and can be found in nearly every country in the world. Our nation runs on memorandums . . . or perhaps despite them. How many workers begin each day with instructions they receive in the form of memorandums from their supervisors . . . memorandums tacked on bulletin boards . . . taped to punch presses . . . at the end of assembly lines . . . throughout the armed forces . . . and passing from desk to desk in millions of offices? A memorandum is most relative to this generation . . . and so what more effective format, in this hurried world, could one give to those who need help than four secrets of happiness and success compressed into a brief memorandum from God?"

His disclosure shook me up so much that I had almost forgotten my reason for bringing the whole thing up. Half to myself I muttered, "A memorandum from God?"

Simon heard me and pointed toward his stacks of books. "Why not? You've heard me expound, enough times, on my theories that God was involved in the writing of so many books. I've merely distilled their essence, eliminated the middle men, and written a consensus message directly from God."

"Dear friend, I'm certainly no expert on such matters but wouldn't many people call that sort of thing blasphemy?"

The old man shook his head in that patronizing way one does when dealing with a child who is obviously having great difficulty trying to grasp what seems so simple to the adult. "Why is it blasphemy? Blasphemy involves dealing with matters of God in a mocking or profane way. What I have done has been consummated with love and respect and with no thought of personal gain. And . . . it works!"

"How does it work, Simon? You're not telling me that merely by reading a twenty-minute memorandum, from God or anyone else, that one can change one's life for the better. Can reading anything have much influence on one . . . for either good or bad? I remember recently reading some crime-commission report where one of its members had said that there was no direct traceable relationship between pornography and crime and that, so far as he knew, no one had ever yet gotten pregnant or diseased by reading a dirty book."

"Mister Og, the individual who made that remark must be a very stupid and unworldly person. Remember what I told you about the thoughts that a man thinks and how they affect his actions and his life. I agree that reading any twenty-minute message by itself, once, will do little good. But, reading that same message each night, before you go to sleep, opens many hidden passages in your mind . . . and throughout the night those

341

ideas seep into all levels of your being. Next day, when you awake, unconsciously you begin to react, almost imperceptibly at first, to the message you imprinted on your brain the previous evening. Slowly, day by day, you change . . . as the message transforms itself from words and ideas into action and reaction on your part. It cannot fail, providing you read and imprint each night."

"But Simon, we've had the Ten Commandments for several thousand years and look at the mess this world is in."

"Mister Og, do not blame the Commandments. How many read them? How many know them? Can you, for example, recite all ten?"

I shook my head, and by this time I had almost abandoned my original idea that had triggered this conversation. Still I probed for an opening. "Simon, you mentioned that you have helped one hundred people. You also said that when you printed 'The God Memorandum' you ordered one hundred copies and numbered them. Does that mean you are now out of copies?"

"Yes, except for the master copy, from which the others were reproduced."

"Are you going to have more printed?"

"Mister Og, I am old and my days are numbered on this earth and, as I have already told you, ragpickers are in short supply. It is time that I make the supreme effort to multiply myself so that my work will continue after I am no longer here."

"How, Simon?"

"I would like you to consider a proposition. I would like to see that the master copy of 'The God Memorandum' fulfills what must be its certain fate . . . its pre-ordained destiny."

"How?"

"At the end of your book you have the greatest salesman in the world, now an old man like me, pass on his ten scrolls of success to a very special person. Would it not be fitting if, after all the other mysterious coincidences between your book's hero and myself, we have one more . . . the ultimate coincidence?"

"I'm sorry . . . I don't follow you, Simon."

"If you are willing, if you accept . . . I would like to pass the master copy of 'The God Memorandum' on to a very special person . . . you! If it pleases you, if you become convinced that it can help others as I assure you it can, you have my permission to include it in one of your future books, if you wish, and then it will go out into the world and benefit thousands—perhaps millions—with your following. How better could one old ragpicker ever hope to multiply himself than that?"

Had he read my mind? Or was it just another impossible coincidence that he should offer his writings to me on this day, of all days, when I had been planning to ask about them?

"I don't know what to say, Simon. I'm honored that you would even consider me to be your instrument of transmittal."

"You would be perfect. But make no hasty decision on this. Sleep on my offer for many nights. There is time yet. And of course, if you accept 'The God Memorandum' I must ask a small payment for my work as would any self-respecting author."

"Payment? Okay."

"No, no . . . you do not understand. I am not talking of money. If 'The God Memorandum' passes to you it is necessary, first, that you promise me that you will use it personally, as I have instructed, before you present it to the world. You are a wonderful and sensitive person, Mister Og. Yet there is a look in your eyes that tells me you have not found peace or contentment or fulfillment even with all your success. The world praises you, yet you do not praise yourself. There is that familiar, to me, sense of quiet desperation in your demeanor. Something is undone in you and sooner or later I am fearful that you will explode unless you reshape your world. If you explode they will toss you on the junk pile and this old ragpicker will not be around to save you. That must not happen. An ounce of prevention is still worth a pound of cure. So, when you receive 'The God Memorandum' you must agree that you will first employ it to strengthen and guide you in your own quest for happiness and peace of mind. Then, and only then, are you to pass it on to others who are ready . . . to those who have eyes to see and ears to hear . . . and the desire to help themselves."

"All right, Simon . . . !"

"Mister Og, you have great potential. You are a rare talent. You must not be wasted. I shall see that you are not!"

"Simon, your words make me feel very humble, very small."

"You are far from small, dear friend. Look! Look where I have placed your book."

I turned my head and followed the direction of his open hand toward the tallest pile of "hand of God" books in his living room.

There, on the top of the pile, was mine!

Chapter V

"The God Memorandum" was not discussed again during that entire summer and fall while our friendship gradually ripened into a bond of love. Stopping off at Simon's place nearly every evening, and soon during the lunch hour too, were the highlights of my week. Simon's frugal quarters became my oasis of peace and equanimity during each working day, and the weekends seemed tortuously endless away from him. Yet, for reasons I still do not understand, I never discussed him, never even mentioned him to my family or anyone at Success Unlimited.

Simon became my adopted father, my teacher, my business consultant, my comrade, my rabbi, my priest, my minister, my guru . . . my Delphic oracle. I canceled business invitations and skipped social functions to spend my time with him, and I literally began to sit at his feet to listen to him lecture to his classroom of one, me, on any subject.

Displaying an amazing range of knowledge and experience he would expound, for all too seemingly brief periods, on love, politics, religion, literature, psychiatry, nature, and even more exotic matters such as extrasensory perception, astrology, and even exorcism. Occasionally I would prod him on with a question or statement that was calculated to keep him talking or I might introduce a new subject on which I wanted his opinion. The depth of his knowledge, especially in philosophy and the behavior of man, never ceased to amaze me.

Once he interrupted himself, while deep in a violent condemnation of the attitude of complacency, lack of pride, and standard of mediocrity that he was convinced had become our world's way of life, to ask me if I realized that by listening to him I was taking a "pre-rag-picker" course . . . just as others took "pre-med" or "pre-law." Then he hastened to show his approval of my presence by reminding me that those who eventually became the best ragpickers were individuals, like myself, who had done time on junk heaps and walked away from their own cemetery for the living.

For five months I attended the finest university in the country.

Professor Simon Potter taught.

I listened . . . and learned . . . as he skillfully introduced his favorite people to me, both living and dead, through fascinating, little-known anecdotes and quotes to help him dramatize his most pressing theme . . . that we all had more than enough ability to change our lives for the better . . . and that God had never placed any of us in a hole from which we could not grow. And, if we had locked ourselves in a prison of failure and self-pity, we were the only jailers . . . we had the only key to our freedom.

He spoke of our fear to take chances, to venture into unfamiliar enterprises and territories, and how even those few who risked their future in order to advance still found it necessary to constantly fight that compelling urge to flee back to their previous familiar womb of security no matter how bleak their old existence had been. Simon pointed out that Abraham Maslow, one of America's greatest psychologists, had called this the "Jonah" complex, the innate desire to hide from the possibility of failure.

He was a great believer in making decisions and then burning your bridges behind you so that you had to make good, and he told how Alexander the Great once handled such a situation. It seems that the great general was about to lead his army against a powerful foe whose men greatly outnumbered his own. Because of the odds against them, his army had shown little enthusiasm for the upcoming battle as they set sail for what they feared would be their end. When Alexander finally unloaded his men and equipment on enemy shores he issued an order for all his ships to be burned. As their means of retreat slowly sank in flames behind them Alexander rose to address his men and said, "See your crafts going up in smoke, their ashes floating on the sea? That is our assurance that we shall be victorious for none of us can leave this despicable land unless we are victorious in battle. Men, when we go home we are going home in their ships!"

Simon did not believe that one should continue to work at a job which made him or her unhappy or miserable. He quoted Faulkner to reinforce his argument, trying to imitate the great writer's southern drawl: "One of the saddest things in life is that the only thing we can do for eight hours a day, day after day, is work. We can't eat for eight hours a day, nor drink for eight hours a day, nor make love for eight hours a day . . . all we can do for eight hours is work. Which is the reason why man makes himself and everybody else so miserable and unhappy." Then, to summarize that particular lecture, he would once again state his point that a job that made one unhappy should be abandoned. "It is not true, Mister Og, that a rolling stone gathers no moss. A rolling stone can gather moss and a good deal more!"

He presented Mark Twain to illustrate his belief that experience was usually an overrated quality. I could almost picture old Samuel L. Clemens, in his wrinkled white suit, saying, "We should be careful to get out of an experience all the wisdom that is in it . . . not like the cat that sits down on a hot stove lid. She will never sit down on a hot stove lid again . . . and that is well . . . but also, she will never sit down on a cold one, anymore."

He had little sympathy for those who blamed their plight or poor fortune on a handicap, either physical or environmental. He reminded me of Milton's blindness, Beethoven's deafness, Roosevelt's polio, Lincoln's poverty, Tchaikovsky's tragic marriage, Isaac Hayes' frightening early years of poverty, Helen Keller's lack of hearing and sight, and even Archie Moore's climb out of the ghetto. He relived for me John Bunyan writing *Pilgrim's Progress* while in prison, Charles Dickens pasting labels on blacking pots, Robert Burns and Ulysses S. Grant fighting the hell of alcoholism, and Benjamin Franklin dropping out of school when he was only ten.

Then I was afloat with Eddie Rickenbacker, who was asked, after he was rescued, what the biggest lesson was that he had learned while drifting about with his buddies in life rafts for twenty-one days when lost in the Pacific during World War II. Rickenbacker had replied, "The biggest lesson I learned was that if you have all the fresh water you want to drink and all the food you want to eat, you ought never to complain about anything."

Simon's point was that no person ever had a defect that was not really a potential benefit rather than an adversity . . . and once he told me a short fable. It seemed that a handsome stag admired his horns and hated his ugly feet. But one day, a hunter came and the stag's ugly feet enabled him to flee to safety. Later, his beautiful horns became caught in the thicket and before he could escape he was shot.

Simon would stare at me and say, "Mister Og, when you begin feeling sorry for yourself, remember this tiny couplet, 'I had the blues . . . because I had no shoes . . . until upon the street, . . . I met a man who had no feet.' "

He was always defining abstract words with colorful analogies. Once, when I asked him to describe love he said, "A few years ago, at your Indianapolis race, a fine driver named Al Unser skidded and hit the wall. He lay slumped in his burning car for only a few seconds before another racing vehicle skidded and stopped alongside his wrecked automobile. Then, while the other cars roared past, some coming dangerously close to the second car, out clambered a young man named Gary Bettenhausen, who rushed over to Unser's car and began pulling him from the flames. Mr. Bettenhausen had completely put out of his mind that he was in a race for which he had expended a fortune and months of preparation." That act, to Simon, was what love was all about.

Simon had another favorite in the auto racing world, Stirling Moss. After quoting Thoreau's axiom that men were born to succeed, not fail, the old man would beautifully mimic Moss's precise British accent to make the point that man could accomplish any goal if he were willing to pay the price. He would repeat Moss's famous quote, "I was taught that everything is attainable if you're prepared to give up, to sacrifice, to get it. Whatever you want to do, you can do it, if you want to do it badly enough . . . and I do believe that. I believe that if I wanted to run a mile in four minutes I could do it. I would have to give up everything else in life, but I could run a mile in four minutes. I believe that if a man wanted to walk on water and was prepared to give up everything else in life, he could do that."

And, of course, Simon was always saying that most humans quit too soon in life. "Mister Og, in Sonoma, California, there is a marvelous driving school for aspiring race drivers or anyone who really wants to learn the fine art of driving. It is called the Bob Bondurant School, I believe. Their instructors say that most drivers on our nation's roads abandon their car too soon when they see an accident coming. As the collision looms they stop trying to save either the automobile or themselves by proper steering and braking, when a good deal could have been done up to the moment of impact to lessen the seriousness of the crash. They give up . . . and they pay for it. So do most humans . . . in most of their daily activities." Then he would rise, scowl at me, extend two fingers upward in a V, and deliver what he said Winston Churchill had claimed was the greatest secret of success ever formulated, and it only was six words long.

"Never, never, never, never give up!"

While his discussions often wandered far afield, they always eventually returned to his concern about the growing lack of self-esteem in man and its usual end-product, a living death. What frustrated him most were the living deaths that finally became actual suicides, lives he had been unable to save because, as he put it, he just "couldn't be everywhere" and there never seemed to be enough ragpickers to go around.

"Mister Og, look at your watch. Fix the time in your mind and then remember this. By this same hour, tomorrow night, more than nine hundred and fifty individuals will try to kill themselves in this country! Think of that! And do you know what? More than one hundred will succeed!"

He would pound the arm of his chair and continue, "That is not all. We will add forty new heroin addicts in the next twenty-four hours. Thirty-seven will die of alcoholism . . . and nearly four thousand unfortunate individuals will have their first mental collapse by this time tomorrow. Then think of the other ways that we show how little we appreciate the amazing creation that we are. In the next twenty-four hours nearly six thousand sick and confused individuals will be arrested for being drunk and disorderly, and more than one hundred and fifty will show how little they value their precious lives by driving too fast, causing their own deaths or the deaths of others. Mister Og, do you know why this condition exists and is growing in tempo, here and throughout the world?"

I would merely shake my head and wait.

"Because all of us know that we can be better than we are. Oh, it is true that most humans cannot translate this hidden feeling into words, but there has been something implanted within each human being that removes him or her, completely, from the animal kingdom. And that something, almost a second conscience, continues to remind us at the most unexpected moments of our dull lives that we are not living up to our potential. It is only logical, therefore, that if we know we can do better and we are not doing better, if we know we can be earning more worldly goods and we are not, if we know we can handle a more difficult and better-paying job and we are not . . . then we do not think very much of this failure who walks around with our name. Gradually we grow to hate that person. Do you know of Maslow, Mister Og?"

"I've never been able to understand too much that he wrote, Simon."

"Maslow is not difficult if you read slowly and think . . . two out-of-style activities in this country, I know. Maslow once wrote that either people do things which are fine and good, and thus respect themselves, or they do contemptible things and feel despicable, worthless, and unlovable. To my way of thinking, Maslow did not go far enough. I believe that most humans feel despicable, worthless, and unlovable without doing contemptible things. Just being sloppy in their work, or not caring about their appearance, or not studying or working a little longer to improve their position in life, or taking that unnecessary drink, or doing a thousand other stupid, small acts that tarnish their already bruised self-image is enough to increase their self-hatred. Most of us not only have a will to die . . . we also have a will to fail!"

Sometimes Simon would even quote one writer quoting another writer. "We are all unhappy, Mister Og. Henry Miller was always haunted by Tolstoy's sentence,

'If you are unhappy . . . and I *know* that you are un-happy.'"

"But Simon, most of us are unhappy only because we have problems. I can take you, right now, to a hospital in this city, where they have ward after ward of tremen-dously happy people . . . they're laughing all the time . . . they no longer face their problems . . . and there are bars on their windows."

"I am not suggesting an impossible, euphoric state of permanent happiness as a lifetime shield from our prob-lems. That is impossible. Problems, big and small, will be with every one of us so long as we live. Norman Vin-cent Peale once said that the only time he found people with no problems was when he walked through a ceme-tery. No, happiness is not a cure-all, it is an antidote . . . something that will enable us to handle and deal with our problems and still maintain our self-esteem so that we do not resign from the human race . . . and the ultimate form of resignation, of course, is suicide."

"Why in the hell do we do such a poor job of dealing with our problems, Simon? Why are we all so unhappy when the ingredients for happiness are all around us? Is that another curse, like original sin, only worse?"

"Why are we unhappy? I will repeat it for you. We are unhappy because we no longer have our self-esteem. We are unhappy because we no longer believe we are a special miracle, a special creation of God. We have become cattle, numbers, punch cards, slaves, ghetto resi-dents all. We look in our mirrors and no longer see the godlike qualities that once were so evident. We have lost faith in ourselves. We have really evolved into the naked apes that Desmond Morris wrote about."

"When did all this happen?"

"I don't know for a certainty, but of course I have a hypothesis. I believe it may have begun with Copernicus."

"Copernicus? The Polish astronomer?"

"Yes. Actually he was a medical man. Astronomy was only a hobby with him. Still, before Copernicus, man actually believed that he lived in the absolute center of God's universe, here on earth, and that all those tiny lights above merely hung there for his pleasure, entertainment, and illumination. Then Copernicus proved that our planet was not the center of anything and that we were just another tiny ball of dirt and stone moving around in space and held captive by an immense globe of fire many times our size. This was a tremendous jolt to our ego. We refused to accept this brilliant man's discoveries for centuries. To pay that price, to acknowledge that we were less than God's special children, was too terrible to contemplate. So, we postponed payment. We refused to listen."

"And then . . . ?"

"Four hundred years later our self-esteem was seriously wounded again. Great Britain produced a brilliant naturalist, Darwin, and he told us that we were not special creatures of God but had our roots in an evolving animal kingdom. He even rubbed salt in our self-esteem by telling us that we were descended from the animal kingdom. This was an exceedingly distasteful pill for man to swallow. In many quarters, as you know, he still has not gulped it down. Still it was a great boon to many, for here was science now recognizing and condoning mankind's bestial behavior. After all, if we were only animals, what could you expect from us? Thus, our self-image, our self-esteem, our self-love, slipped a few more rungs down the ladder to misery and hell. Darwin gave us our animal permits."

"After Darwin, what . . . ?"

"After Darwin? Freud! And more broken windows in the house of self-esteem. Freud told us that we were unable to control many of our actions and thoughts nor could we even understand them since they had originated from very early childhood experiences involving love and hate and repression, now buried deeply within our subconscious mind. That's just what we needed. Now we had a license from one of the world's most brilliant medical authorities to do anything we wished, to ourselves . . . and to others. We no longer needed a rational explanation for our activities. Just act . . . and blame the consequences on our father or our mother."

"Simon, let me be sure if I comprehend what you're saying. Your position is that man, at one time, perhaps through a closer communion with his God, believed that he was truly a marvelous creation, a superior being made in the image of God. Then he began to make discoveries that gradually chipped away at the high opinion he had of himself, until he eventually was thinking, 'If we're not godlike people, if we do not live in the center of God's world, if we are really only animals, and if we cannot control and explain many of our actions, then we are not of any more consequence than the weeds in our garden. If we are not, in truth, very much of anything, then how can we be proud of ourselves? And if we are not proud of what we are, how can we like ourselves? And if we don't like ourselves, who wants to live with that sort of person . . . so . . . let's get rid of ourselves. Let's drive too fast, or drink too much, or eat too much, or purposely foul-up so that we can get ourselves fired from our jobs so that we can sit in the corner and suck our thumbs and tell ourselves that we're worthless anyway, so what the hell.' Is that it?"

"Exactly."

Now it was my turn. "Let me add what may be another nail in the coffin of self-esteem, Simon, when and if it is eventually proven correct. Are you familiar with Professor Edward Dewey and his Foundation for the Study of Cycles at the University of Pittsburg?"

"Yes. Many years ago I purchased a large collection of back-number copies of his foundation's monthly magazine, *Cycles.* I have them packed away here, somewhere. What of him, Mister Og?"

"Professor Dewey has spent more than forty years of his life studying cycles, rhythmic fluctuations that repeat with regularity in everything from earthquakes to abundance of grain crops to stock market prices to sun spot eruptions, and several hundred other disciplines."

"I know."

"Professor Dewey visited me, three years ago, and said that he had been impressed by my writings in *Success Unlimited*. He asked if I'd be willing to work with him in writing a book about cycles that the layman could understand. I was so honored by his request that I jumped at the chance. I spent more than a year digging through his files and notes and charts and we finally brought forth a book called *Cycles, Mysterious Forces That Trigger Coming Events*."

"Mister Og, the longer I know you the more you amaze me."

"That's mutual, Simon. Anyway, Professor Dewey believes that there may be another factor affecting our activities and attitudes. He thinks there is a strong possibility that several planetary positions, when they occur, may exert some sort of immeasurable force that effects our actions in groups, so that sometime they make us fight, sometime they make us love, sometime they make us write and paint and compose . . . and all the while we think we are doing these and other things solely for rational reasons. He says that we may all be puppets on a string and that we must learn what controls that string, out there, and then cut it, otherwise we will never reach our full potential nor will we ever regain our self-esteem."

"I like your professor, Mister Og. Now, if you have been raised and educated with these possibilities that you are only a grain of sand with little or no control over your fate, and then you are exposed, each day, to events that drain all your individuality, and you are immersed constantly in the negative garbage that spews upon you from newspapers, radio, television, movies, and the theatre, and combine all that with concern for your personal security, your life's savings, your family's well-being, your own future, and then add to that the fear that the world is becoming a cesspool of pollution or may blow itself up some bright spring day, how can you really maintain any degree of self-esteem when you must spend most of your time and effort merely trying to survive? Why should you think very highly of yourself? How can you be happy? What is there to like in you? What's so great about this life? Who called this heaven on earth?"

"Somehow, old friend, I suspect you're asking me rhetorical questions."

Simon frowned and his shoulders slumped in momentary weariness from his long discourse. Then a full smile transfigured his face, his eyes opened wide, and he raised his voice. "The paradoxical reply, Mister Og, is that despite all the forces arrayed against us we still want, very much, to be proud of our lives. We still desire, with all our heart, to reach our full potential, and it is only because this small flame of hope still burns inside all of us that we weep in shame at our failures,

at our gradual descent into the common pit of mediocrity. We are like those figures in so many Renaissance
paintings portraying souls condemned to hell and slid-
ing down into the molten fire while their hands still reach
out, still reach up, still seek help, help that usually never
comes."

"Is there any hope, Simon? Does it really do much
good to light one tiny candle in all this darkness?"

"There is always hope. When all hope has gone the
world will end. And do not think of only one candle
when you seek to overcome the blackness of despair. If
everyone lit a candle we could turn the darkest night
into the brightest day."

I tried playing the devil's advocate. "But hasn't the
human race been scarred and maimed beyond the point
of repair? The world is moving too fast for the average
person. He steps off the road, early in life, and forfeits
his place to the swift, the unscrupulous, and the mean.
For every so-called success story in this world there are
a thousand miserable failures and that ratio doesn't seem
to change for the better as the population increases."

"Mister Og, I am surprised to hear you talk that way.
You seem to be measuring success and failure like everyone else. You cannot mean what you are asking. You
could not have written your book believing that success
is measured solely by bank balances."

"I don't Simon. Yet, I can't tell you how many pro-
grams I've been on where this kind of question has been
asked of me by some interviewer who has not read my

book and therefore assumes that I've written another rah, rah book telling the reader how to be successful, which is always equated with how to get rich. Let's face it, 'rich' and 'success' are synonymous in this country."

"I know. It is sad but true."

"Then when you try to explain, while the television camera is staring at you with its little red light shining, that your book has little to do with financial gain and everything to do with peace of mind or happiness, you usually get a sarcastic chuckle and a series of questions fired at you that are damn tough to handle."

"For instance, Mister Og?"

"Okay. It's all very well for you to talk about happiness and peace of mind, they say, but how do you bring a smile to the face of a man who is out of work, with five hungry mouths to feed and nothing in the refrigerator? How do you calm the mind and soul of a young ghetto mother who has been ground up by her environment while she struggles to support her three fatherless children? How do you convince a dying person that he can still enjoy what's remaining of his life? What do you tell a housewife who is certain that she is doomed to a life of dirty dishes and unmade beds?"

"None of those problems you pose are easy, Mister Og, and yet let me remind you, once again, that each of these individuals and everyone else in the world still have their own pilot light burning inside them. It may be very diminished, in some, but this I tell you . . . it never, never goes out! So long as there is a breath of life remaining there is still hope . . . and that's what we rag-pickers count on. Just give us a chance and we can provide the fuel that will be ignited by any pilot light, no matter how diminished it may be. A human being, my friend, is an amazing and complex and resilient organism capable of resuscitating itself from its own living death, many times, if it is given the opportunity and shown the way."

"And that's where you ragpickers operate? Among the living dead . . . the losers of humanity?"

"Usually. I have discovered that most individuals are neither willing nor ready to accept help until they have hit bottom. At that point they figure that they have nothing to lose, and so they are far more receptive to my simple technique to help them try to begin a new life . . . to perform the greatest miracle in the world . . . to resurrect themselves from their living death. Do you read Emerson, Mister Og?"

"I haven't read Emerson since my senior year in high school."

"What a shame. Emerson should be read by thirty- and forty- and fifty-year-olds, not teenagers. Emerson wrote, 'Our strength grows out of our weakness. The indignation which arms itself with secret forces does not awaken until we are pricked and stung and sorely assailed. When man is pushed, tormented, defeated, he has a chance to learn something; he has been put on his wits, on his manhood, he has gained facts, learns his ignorance, is cured of the insanity of conceit, has got moderation and real skill.' "

"But isn't your ultimate goal an impossible dream? Aren't you, like Don Quixote, trying to escape from the reality of this life, and aren't you concerned that you are doomed to the same fate? The old values, the old principles, just don't work today. What you must do in order for them to be meaningful again, is change the entire environment. Simon, you're talking about changing the world. That's been tried again and again. We've got a Who's Who Of Martyrs who have tried and failed."

"They have not failed. While mighty Rome collapsed around him, a wise man named Paulinus continued to care for one small shrine in order to maintain his sanity and equanimity. You can still find his words of wisdom in any library . . . this old and wise ragpicker. Martyrs do not fail when their hearts cease to pump. If they did you and I would not be sitting here discussing the possibility of carrying on their common goal of making this world a better place for all of God's creatures!"

The old man returned to his seat, reached across and placed a hand on my knee.

"Mister Og, why not try to change the world? Why not teach others that they can perform a miracle with their lives? Of what importance is it to man that he does not live in the center of the universe so long as he can create his own beautiful world? Why should man care that he has descended from the animal kingdom once he realizes that he has powers possessed by no other animal? And why should it concern him that some of his actions are triggered by youthful impressions buried in his subconscious mind when he still has the power to control his mind and thus ordain his ultimate destiny? Only man, each in his own way, has the ultimate decision on how his life is lived."

He had said so much that was deep and meaningful that I had to call a halt to our discussion, or at least lighten the mood, in order to have time to digest his remarks. So, I lit a cigarette and tried to bait him. "Simon, the astrologers wouldn't think much of your remarks about man having the ability to control his own destiny."

He nodded his head, sadly, and smiled. "Seers, astrologers, medicine men, palmists, numerologists, psychics . . . each age has many security blankets."

The old man tousled my gray hair. "You know Shakespeare, Mister Og?"

"A little."

" 'The fault, dear Brutus, is not in our stars, but in ourselves. . . .' "

Chapter VI

I surprised him with a gift on his seventy-ninth birthday.

The shock that I had remembered the exact date, November thirteenth, from one of our very first conversations together almost did the old boy in.

I detest shopping but I had spent two torturous Saturdays searching for something unique and relevant to buy Simon. I finally found it in Marshall Field's at Woodfield . . . an Italian cast-glass geranium plant. It stood nearly two feet tall with coloring and leafing so natural that unless one touched it there was no way to know that it hadn't been grown and pampered in the fussiest of greenhouses.

Simon owned a window box, the only one hanging outside any apartment window on the entire blighted block. He said he had built and hung it soon after he had moved in, and each year he would haul it in and carefully paint it with fresh green paint. Also, each spring, he would plant countless seedling geranium plants, his favorite flower, in that box, and they would always struggle their way skywards, then turn ugly shades of yellow and lavender and finally wither and die. Last year, he told me, he tried to change his luck by waiting until early summer and buying plants already full-grown and in bloom. Two weeks later they were brown and dead. Still he never gave up. He already had a new strain picked out in a seed catalog that he looked forward to trying next spring.

The old man insisted he had never lost a geranium in either his Damascus or his Sachsenhausen gardens. Once he went into a long description of how he would dig his favorite plants before frost came, hang them in his basements to dry, and then replant them in the spring . . . one of his earliest successes at helping living things to start new lives, he chuckled. Some of his geraniums had been more than twenty years old. But not in Chicago. Simon blamed it on the pollution.

"How can anything survive in this rain of death from above and from the gasoline monsters on the street? Look outside, Mister Og. It is a full moon, tonight. Can you see it? No! We are engulfed in our own refuse. We bathe in it. We breathe it. We eat it. Even the water that I pour on my plants contains chemicals that would kill a cockroach. Today, only the plants and birds die. Tomorrow, who knows? Still I have faith that eventually

I shall grow a geranium and that the human race will awake in time to prevent their world from becoming a giant junk pile."

"It's going to take an army of ragpickers to accomplish that, Simon."

"In order for this planet to survive, each human must eventually become his own ragpicker. He must not depend on his neighbor for salvation. Believe me, Mister Og, this will come to pass."

They had gift-wrapped the glass plant for me at Field's with one of their most extravagant papers, and when he opened the door I placed the large gold box in his hands and just said, "Happy birthday, old friend."

He took the box, mouth open, speechless. Then large tears popped from the corner of each eye and ran down deep wrinkles on both cheeks. He placed the box carefully on the floor and hugged me. Finally he placed one giant hand on each side of my face and kissed me on the forehead.

"Mister Og, this is the first birthday present I have received in thirty-five years. How did you know the day?"

"Oh, you let it slip one night. Open the box."

"I cannot. It is too magnificent to open. The paper, it is so lovely. It should not be torn."

"It's only paper. Go ahead. Open it."

Simon lowered his huge frame onto the rug and drew the large box toward him so that one long leg was on each side of it. First he carefully untied the ribbon and gently removed it. Then he slid his fingers under the paper, wherever he came in contact with sealing tape, and slowly peeled away the wrapping to eventually uncover a large brown cardboard box. Then he took out his pocket knife, cut the glued strip across the top, and moved back the cover flaps. He looked inside and frowned. Then he began to remove the yards of tissue paper which had been packed tightly around the plant, savoring each moment with the kind of childish excitement and anticipation that one usually sees only at Christmas. At last he reached in and tenderly removed his gift of glass from the carton.

"A geranium! I cannot believe it. A pelargonium of the highest class! A show flower, a blue-ribbon aristocrat if ever I have seen one. And it's not real. God! It's made of glass! Mister Og, where did you find such an incredible work of art? And look . . . look at the crimson of its blooms! Once, in Jerusalem, I saw a geranium with this same iridescent glow. I tried to purchase it from its owner but did not succeed. Such a gift. Such an expensive gift, Mister Og. What can I say?"

"Don't say anything, Simon. I'm happy that it pleases you. It's only a small token of love and thanks for all the hours of wisdom and hope you have shared with me. Happy birthday . . . and may you have seventy-nine more."

By now he was on his feet, carrying the plant from place to place, searching for the ideal spot to display it. He set it on the coffee table, stepped back, studied it for several minutes, shook his head and removed it. Then he tried it on top of the television set. No. Then the end table behind the pictures of his family. Better. But still no.

Watching him fuss and move his gift from place to place I suddenly had an inspiration. "Simon, there is really only one perfect spot for that geranium."

He paused, reluctantly, as if I were spoiling his fun. "Where, Mister Og?"

"Well, it's made of glass so the pollution won't hurt it. Why not plant it outside, in your window box? Who else, in this entire city, will have a red geranium in their window box blooming its heart out in November . . . and December . . . and January and every other month of the year?"

"That is a stroke of genius, Mister Og. And it can stand out there to bid you good morning, each day, as you drive into the parking lot. I shall do it. But . . . you must perform the honors."

"Honors? What do you mean?"

"You must plant it for me. Wait . . . wait . . . I'll get my trowel."

And so the two of us planted our ninety-five-dollar glass geranium. We wrestled with the ice-stuck living room window until it grudgingly moved upward and, while cold blasts of premature winter winds nearly took my breath away, I leaned out and chipped a hole in the almost frozen black dirt in the window box. Simon handed me the plant and I buried the pot, covering it with sand, so that only the plant showed. Then we stepped back to admire our landscaping as the warm light from the living room reflected off the plant's petals.

"It is beautiful, it is very special," Simon shouted. "Now I have my geranium at last. You see, he who perseveres never fails. Who but you would find such a present!"

"It's for my favorite ragpicker, that's all."

Then we drank a toast, sherry of course, to his seventy-nine years, and as we sat I could see that he was fighting to keep his emotions under control. His lips were quivering slightly and his eyes were half shut. I wondered what memory he was submerged in but I kept still. Finally he shook his head, as if to clear it, and said, "Nothing is more disgraceful than that an old man should have nothing to show to prove that he has lived long, except his years."

"I know who said that. Seneca, right?"

"Mister Og, you are too smart to be only fifty years old."

"But you have much to show for your years, Simon. Just considering only these years you have lived as a ragpicker with all those people you have helped . . ."

"Yes . . . my angels from the dump. I loved each one of them. They are my ticket to heaven . . . my passport to Lisha . . . and Eric."

"Simon, I like Henry Ford's remark about growing old better than Seneca's."

"Yes?"

"Ford said that if you took all the experience and judgment of people over fifty out of the world there wouldn't be enough brains and talent left to run it."

"But, Mister Og, Ford did not say that until after he had passed the age of fifty. And then, of course, there was the saying of that eighteenth-century German humorist, Richter. Do you know it?"

"I knew you'd top me. Go ahead."

"Richter said, 'Like a morning dream, life becomes more and more bright the longer we live, and the reason of everything appears more clear. What has puzzled us before seems less mysterious, and the crooked paths look straighter as we approach the end.'"

As if drawn by some giant magnetic force I suddenly rose from my chair, went over to Simon, and sat at his feet. I looked up into his beautiful face and said, "'The God Memorandum.' I think I'm ready for it. I would consider it an honor and a privilege for you to give it to me and I promise you that I'll do everything in my power to deliver it to the world. I can think of no time in our history when we have needed it more."

The old man sighed softly, a look of almost overwhelming relief on his face. "I was afraid you had rejected my offer or, as the months passed, had even forgotten it. Your acceptance is a greater gift than even my geranium. Still, I have had second thoughts about my offer since I made it to you."

"You mean you've changed your mind, Simon."

"No, no . . . not that. Only concern that people may

not take its message seriously, Mister Og, since it is so unsophisticated, brief, and basic. In these days it seems that the more complicated, high-sounding, and expensive one makes self-help instruction, the more people are attracted to it, while they tend to put down those such as Dale Carnegie, Dorothea Brande, Napoleon Hill, Norman Vincent Peale, and even your W. Clement Stone who offer simple but workable solutions to life's problems. Furthermore, it is one thing to advise and counsel an individual, in the flesh, prior to introducing him or her to 'The God Memorandum,' because the power of your personality hopefully adds credence to your gift. It is quite another matter for words on paper, with no preliminary, personal mind-conditioning, to be forceful enough to motivate the reader into action."

"Simon, there will always be a small group of detractors, long on education and short on experience, ready to accuse you of offering pap and simplistic solutions to what they classify as extremely complicated problems, usually requiring five years of therapy at fifty bucks a weekly visit. Yet I would like a dollar for every human who has been inspired and helped, truly helped, by reading Carnegie, Peale, Brande, Hill, Stone, and many others, without ever meeting the authors."

"Including Mandino."

"I'd join that group any day they'd have me. Simon, do you still want to multiply yourself? Do you still want to help thousands instead of only a handful?"

"Of course."

"Well, there are two ingredients necessary for 'The God Memorandum' to become a success. First, there must be a need for it and then it must have a showcase that will assure its wide distribution to those in need. I remember that Lillian Roth, in her book *I'll Cry Tomorrow*, wrote that she had been unable to rescue herself from her own living death, alcoholism, until she finally learned to say the three most difficult words she ever uttered. Those words were 'I need help.' You told me, yourself, that the best time to help people was when they had lost all hope and had no one left to turn to for support. Simon, if you listen, you can almost hear a chorus of millions from every neighborhood and status and profession in the world, crying for help. The need for your message, right now, is so great that we'll probably never be able to fill it as well as we would like. Rich or poor, black or white, beautiful or ugly, crowded or lonely . . . they all need help. There are millions who believe that life, their life, has been not heaven, but hell . . . on earth."

Simon had cocked his head and was hanging on my words as I usually hung on his. He made no reply and so I continued.

"The second ingredient to assure success is that the 'Memorandum' have the proper showcase and distribution. I haven't even read it, yet, but I promise you this . . . I will make 'The God Memorandum' a part of my next book and I will also write about you . . . and I will call the book *The Greatest Miracle In The World*. We'll show the world how to perform that miracle . . . how to recycle their own lives and come back from their living deaths."

"You would do that for me?"

"For you, of course . . . but also for all those human beings who want a chance to live and don't even realize it's still theirs for the taking."

Suddenly his booming laugh filled the apartment. "Mister Og, as I recall from my presidential days, most memorandums have carbon copies going to various individuals or departments within an organization. 'The God Memorandum' . . . should we carbon the world with it?"

"Why not? We've got four billion workers in this company of ours, all struggling for a promotion to a better life . . . or willing to struggle if they knew how. Let's give them all a chance to pull off the greatest miracle in the world and when that happens we'll have our heaven right here!"

"We'll show them how, Mister Og, we'll show them how."

"Simon, as usual when I'm with you I've lost track of the time. I must run. May I take the 'Memorandum' to read over the weekend?"

His almost imperceptible hesitation would have gone unnoticed by anyone else. "Not tonight, my friend, but soon . . . very soon, it will be in your possession."

I knew enough not to push him. "Okay. Good night, old man."

"Good night, young man. And thank you for a birthday party I shall never forget. You have truly lit a candle for me this night."

As I walked under the parking lot gate that he had held up for me in that snowstorm, nearly a year ago, I turned and looked up at his apartment window.

There, silhouetted against the warm light from his living room, swayed the dark outline of Simon's new red geranium.

Chapter VII

The thick brown manilla envelope rested ominously on my desk on that Monday that I shall never forget.

I had been away again on what I had been assured would be the final promotional tour for my book. This jaunt had consumed two weeks, twelve flights, ten cities, ten strange hotel beds, ten early wake-up calls . . . and the same endless series of questions and answers from New Orleans to Monterey.

I arrived at the office early, hoping to get an hour's jump on what I expected would be an overflowing "In" basket. The smell of freshly brewed coffee permeated the place. Only Vi Noramzyk, who had been coming in early forever, had arrived ahead of me.

I picked up the brown envelope and stared at the gentle European script on its front with a combination of horror and panic. In the upper left-hand corner, where one normally puts a return address, were the words:

A farewell gift from an old ragpicker

In the center of the envelope was my name and my business address:

Mr. Og Mandino, President
Success Unlimited Magazine
6355 Broadway
Chicago, Illinois 60660

In the upper right-hand corner stamps had been affixed . . . one dollar and twenty cents worth. They were uncanceled. There was no postmark.

I dropped the package and dashed out of the office. Just as I threw open the door leading to the hall Pat walked in. Her "welcome back" smile vanished when she saw the look on my face. "What's the matter?"

I grabbed her by her arm and almost pushed her into my office. Then I stooped to pick up the package from where I had dropped it on the carpeting, and held it up. "When did we get this?"

She took the envelope from my hand, read the message, and shrugged her shoulders. "I don't know. All your mail is on the couch. I've never seen that before. It wasn't here when I locked up on Friday. Must have come this morning. By messenger, maybe?"

I jerked the phone off its cradle and punched the digits 24 . . . our subscription department. Barbara Voigt, our subscription manager, didn't even get a chance to welcome me back. "Barbara, please ask Vi to come into my office."

Vi was soon standing uncomfortably in my doorway, her pretty cherublike face registering concern and puzzlement as to why I would want to see her. "Vi, did you open up this morning?"

"Yes, I always do."

"I know. Did anyone deliver this package to you?"

"No."

"Did you see any strangers in the hall when you arrived?"

"No. No one was around except Charlie, the janitor. I just fixed the coffee, like always, waited until the pot filled, poured myself a cup and went back across the hall. Why? What's the matter?"

"That's okay, Vi. Never mind. Thanks."

I tossed the package on my desk, grabbed my topcoat and ran out of the office. The sidewalk was beginning to turn white from Chicago's first winter snow, and I vaguely remember slipping and falling several times as I ran through the parking lot, across Winthrop Street, into Simon's apartment lobby. I didn't bother to hit the bell and leaped up the stairs two at a time. When I reached the second floor landing I turned and began pounding on the door of Simon's apartment.

The door finally flew open and I was staring at a red-faced plump woman, her hair in pin curls, holding a crying infant. Another young and grubby child was clinging tightly to the woman's faded pink nightrobe. Simon must be involved in another ragpicking mission of mercy, I thought.

"Mr. Potter, please."

"Who?"

"Mr. Potter. The old man. He lives here."

"Ain't nobody named Potter here."

"What are you talking about? He's lived here for years. Tell him Og Mandino is here."

"Look, Mac, my name is Johnson. I've lived in this dump for four years and I damn well ought to know there ain't nobody named Potter here."

She began to close the door but I stopped it with my arm and stepped in to the apartment. "Come on, lady, don't play games with me. I've been in this apartment a hundred times in the past year. An old man named Simon Potter lives here. Where is he?"

Before she could answer, my eyes swept the apartment, and I could feel the hair rising at the back of my neck. Nothing was familiar. Our two favorite talk chairs were gone. There were no books piled high along the living room wall. The braided rug had been replaced by an ugly, checkered orange-and-blue linoleum. The woman, now clutching her child closer to her breast, growled, "Mac, I'll give you just five seconds to get your ass out of here and then I'm going to start yelling and call the cops. Who the hell do you think you are breaking into my apartment, you creep! You ought to be in jail or a nut house. Get out of here!"

I felt weak in the knees. My stomach was flopping. I wanted to vomit. I backed slowly toward the door and raised my hands, helplessly. "I'm sorry, lady. Maybe I'm in the wrong apartment. Do you know Simon Potter? Old man, dark, very tall, and he has a dog, a bassett?"

"There ain't nobody like that in this building. I ought to know, I been here for four years."

"Next door?"

"That way, a little old Italian lady and her daughter. That way, there, a black man lives all alone. There ain't no guy named Potter here, I tell ya. Now scram!"

I apologized again and stepped out into the hall. The door slammed shut and I was staring at the red painted numerals with which I had become so familiar . . . 21. I still felt weak and so I sat on the stairway trying to collect my thoughts. Where was he? Was I dreaming all this? If so, what a hell of a nightmare I was having.

Any moment, I thought, Rod Serling would walk up the stairs and welcome me to another edition of "Night Gallery."

Then an idea. I ran down the stairs, past the lobby, down another flight to the basement. At the far end I could see a light and hear the drone of the oil furnace. A slight shadowy figure was leaning back in a chair under the single fly-specked light bulb. "Are you the janitor?"

"Yes, sir, yes, sir."

"Been here long?"

"All night."

"No, no . . . I mean have you worked here long?"

"Be eleven years in February."

"Is there a Simon Potter registered as a tenant in this building? Tall man, dark, long hair. Beard. Looks a lot like Abraham Lincoln. Has a dog, a bassett."

"We don't allow dogs in the building."

"Do you know the man I've described?"

"No, sir."

"Have you ever seen the man I've described, either here or outside on the street?"

"No, sir. I know everyone in the building and nearly everyone in the neighborhood. There ain't no such man here and there ain't been no such man around this block in the past eleven years, I guarantee you that."

"You're sure?"

"I'm positive."

I ran back up the steps, across the street to the parking lot and unlocked my car. Eventually I was at the Foster Avenue Police Station although I still don't remember driving there. I parked my car smack between two blue squad cars and ran into the station. I waited impatiently at the wire window until a young sergeant nodded curtly at me.

"Sergeant, my name is Mandino and I have a business over on Broadway."

"Yes, sir."

"Someone is missing. I had a friend who lived in an apartment at 6353 Winthrop Street. I've known him for more than a year. I've been away from my office for a couple of weeks and when I got back, this morning, there was a package on my desk with my name and address and some words in the upper left-hand corner to the effect that it was a farewell gift from him."

"What was in the package?"

"I don't know. As soon as I read that farewell message bit I ran to his apartment and . . ."

"And?"

"He wasn't there. Furthermore the people who were in his apartment said that he had never lived there . . . and they didn't know anyone like the man I was describing."

"You sure you had the right apartment?"

"I've been in it a hundred times. Apartment twenty-one. I talked to the janitor of the building. He didn't know anyone by the name of Simon Potter. Said there had never been such a person in the building in the past eleven years that he worked there. No Simon Potter."

"Are you all right, sir?"

"Yes, I'm all right. I'm sober and I'm no nut, honest. How the hell could I make up this kind of a crazy story?"

"We've heard crazier."

"I'll bet you have."

"What was that guy's name again?"

"Potter . . . Simon Potter. Almost eighty years old. Dark long hair. And a beard. Tall. Had a dog . . . a bassett hound."

The sergeant lit a cigarette and studied me closely for several seconds. Then he turned without saying another word and went into the back office. Perhaps fifteen minutes passed before he returned. "We haven't picked up anyone by that name or answering your friend's description in at least the past three weeks in this precinct. But this is a big city. Why don't you try Cook County Hospital?"

"Okay."

"And one other spot."

"Where?"

"The county morgue down on West Polk."

I struck out at the hospital. They were considerate and patient with me and checked back through their records for the past fourteen days. No one with Simon's name or fitting Simon's description had been brought in for any sort of treatment. They also suggested I check with the morgue. I went. There they treated my story casually . . . as if I were someone filing a complaint in a giant department store. They obviously heard similar stories, hourly, about missing fathers, sons, brothers, sisters, lovers. Methodically they checked their microfilm files and one young man finally came forward holding a small clipboard. "Sir, we have one 'unidentified' who fits the age and general description. Want to take a look?"

I nodded and followed him. As we walked along the brightly lit white antiseptic-smelling corridor he touched my arm and said, "Don't let the stench get you. They still haven't invented a deodorant to wipe out these smells."

Finally he pushed open a swinging door and we entered a chilly room with giant drawers sitting in rows like ghoulish file cabinets. He checked the number on his pad and pulled heavily on one of the drawer handles. I turned my head away, not wanting to look. Finally I forced myself and I was staring down at the nude body of a very old man, his long hair wrapped around his face and chest, his eyes still half open. My heart was thumping as I leaned forward to have a better look at this poor unclaimed nameless human who had fallen on his last junk pile.

It wasn't Simon.

Finally I tried Missing Persons on South State. Zero.

The snow was still falling as I pulled up to my parking lot. I got out, turned the key, and watched the gate move slowly toward the sky, remembering again that first day in the snow when a strange, beautiful man came into my life and held up the world in his bare hands for me. I stepped back into the car, punched the steering wheel with my fists, shifted, and slammed the car into a parking place.

I must have looked terrible. My own staff people turned away from me, as if not to notice my presence, when I reentered the office, tracking snow across the red carpet of the reception area. As I passed Pat's desk I nodded toward my office and she rose and followed me.

"Close the door, hon . . . and have a seat."

She frowned and sat facing me. Her eyes were wide with both fear and concern.

"My God, Og, what's the matter?"

"I think I must be going crazy, Pat. Now listen to me. You live on Winthrop Street don't you?"

"Yes. About a block down."

"Every morning when you walk to work do you cut through the parking lot?"

"Yes."

"Have you ever seen a strange old man around the parking lot. He wears funny old clothes and usually is feeding the pigeons. He has long hair and a beard and he always has a bassett hound with him."

Pat thought for a few moments and shook her head. "There are usually a few winos hanging around the lot, but no one like that."

"You've never seen this man? He's very tall and very old. Sometimes he wears a wooden crucifix around his neck?"

"Never. What's the matter, Og. What's happened?"

"It's okay, hon. I'll tell you later. Thank you. Oh . . . hold my calls until I tell you."

After she closed the door I just sat there and tried to collect my thoughts . . . chasing elusive and ephemeral butterflies of irrational images . . . trying to ignore the pain in my head . . . and in the pit of my stomach. Was I cracking up? Was this how a nervous breakdown climaxes in the frightening inability to connect one rational thought with another? Is this what all those executive seminars and books warn you will happen if you push your body and mind to their limits and beyond, while trying to compress several lives into one in your mad dash for success? Does the mind finally switch channels on you and force you to participate in a fantasyland of acts and conversations with characters dredged from some long-forgotten childhood storybook? Is this the ultimate escape when pressures and responsibilities grow too big to handle?

Was Simon just a dream? Impossible. Still, if Simon was nearly always around the parking lot each morning why hadn't Pat ever seen him? And what about his apartment? Was somebody playing some sort of macabre joke on me? Yet, why had I never discussed him with anyone? And what about all his lectures . . . those priceless hours of inspiration and knowledge and hope? And how about the ragpicker thing . . . pulling dropouts from the human race off the junk pile . . . showing people how to perform the greatest miracle in the world . . . dear God, I couldn't have made all that up in my wildest creative moments.

I snapped back to some semblance of sanity when I suddenly realized that I had been turning the brown envelope over and over in my hand. The brown envelope —my only link to the truth . . . my only link to Simon . . . my proof that he really existed! I found myself rubbing the package as if, like some genie's lamp, my touch would cause the old man to reappear. I relaxed a little. If he had sent the package then I wasn't crazy. Simon existed!

"Simon, Simon . . . where the hell are you? Don't do this to me. I don't deserve this from you!"

I must have been close to the edge of shock . . . as I yelled toward three empty orange chairs that faced me across my desk. Finally, I turned over the brown en-velope, ripped open the flap, reached in and removed several sheets of typewritten paper held together with a paper clip.

As I did so a small object rolled from the envelope on to my desk. I picked it up . . . a tiny safety pin attached to a small piece of white rag measuring approximately half an inch square.

I pushed the pin aside. Attached to the paper clip that held the pages was a letter to me in the same handwrit-ing as the envelope.

The letter was undated. . . .

Chapter VIII

Dear Mr. Og,

I am ill-prepared to deal with the specific and time-consuming legalities of drawing up a last will and testament. Let this letter suffice.

During the past year you have brought love, companionship, laughter, and good conversation, not to mention an immortal red geranium, into the life of an old ragpicker.

Ragpickers, by the very nature of their chosen profession, are not accustomed to being on the receiving end of life's finer gifts, nor is it wise to become too closely attached to those whom one desires to help. Still there are times when teachers must be taught, doctors must be cured, lawyers must be defended, comedians must be amused, and even ragpickers must be loved.

I know you have loved me, as I love you.

It is fitting and right, therefore, that I bequeath the enclosed master copy of 'The God Memorandum' to you, not only to fulfill my promise but also to bring to a culmination that long series of seemingly miraculous coincidences between your book's great salesman and myself.

Perhaps after you have benefited from much introspection and thought regarding our relationship, you will be able to put the past twelve months in their proper perspective and even come to the eventual conclusion that it was not as difficult a task for me to write a memorandum from God as it is for you to accept its existence.

Since I know you to be an impetuous man I am certain that long before you have reached this portion of my letter you have already sought me out, in vain, and are now tormented with grief and concern for my well-being. Fear not. Banish all worry from your mind. In the words of another ragpicker, I now ask you to grieve no more . . . for where I go you cannot follow me now, but one day you will.

Do not forget that we have a contract, you and I. 'The God Memorandum' is now in your possession and it is my desire that you share it, eventually, with the world, but only after you apply its principles to your own life, consonant with my instructions.

Remember that the most difficult tasks are consummated, not by a single explosive burst of energy or effort, but by consistent daily application of the best you have within you.

To change one's life for the better, to resurrect one's body and mind from living death, requires many positive steps, one in front of the other, with your sights always on your goal.

'The God Memorandum' is only your ticket to a new life. It will do nothing for you unless you open your mind and your heart to receive it. By itself it will move you not one inch in any direction. The means of transportation, and the power to break your inertia, must be generated by forces long dormant but still alive within you. Follow these rules and your forces will self-ignite:

1. First, mark this day upon your calendar. Then, count forward one hundred days and mark that day. This will establish the length of your mission without the necessity of your counting each day as you live it.

2. Next, in this envelope you will find a small safety pin to which has been attached a tiny piece of white rag in the shape of a square. This combination of pin and rag, two of the most common and unprepossessing materials in the world, is your ragpicker's secret amulet. Wear your amulet on your person in a place visible to you as a constant reminder, during the next hundred days, that you are trying to live as you are being instructed to live in 'The God Memorandum.' Your pin and rag are symbols . . . a sign that you are in the process of changing your life from the pins and rags of failure to the treasures of a new and better life.

3. Do not, under any conditions, divulge the meaning of your amulet to those who may inquire during your hundred-day mission.

4. Read 'The God Memorandum' before you retire,

each night, for one hundred nights . . . and then sleep in peace, while the message you have read gradually seeps down into your deep mind that never sleeps. Let no reason or excuse force you to forego the reading for even one night.

Gradually, as the days become weeks, you will notice great changes in yourself . . . as will those around you. By the hundredth day . . . you will be a living miracle . . . a new person . . . filled with beauty and wonder and ambition and ability.

Then, and only then, find someone who, like your old self, needs help. Give him two things: your ragpicker's secret amulet . . . and 'The God Memorandum.'

And one more thing give to him . . . as I have given to you . . . love.

I have a vision wherein I can see thousands upon thousands wearing our ragpicker's amulets. People will encounter each other in the marketplace, on the street, in their places of worship, in their public conveyances, in their schools, and on their job and they will look upon each other's insignificant pin and rag and smile at their brothers and sisters . . . for each will know that the other is embarked on the same mission, the same dream, with a common purpose . . . to change their own life for the better and thus, joined together, change their world.

Still, I prophesy many difficult situations ahead for you, Mister Og. Should you eventually decide to make 'The God Memorandum' part of a future book you will inevitably be asked, by your publisher, to make promotional tours as you have in the past for your other books. How will you explain 'The God Memorandum' since it will be impossible for you to either produce or even prove that its creator, its author, ever existed? Severe challenges will be made on your integrity and perhaps your sanity by those who will refuse to believe your story if you recount it as we have experienced it. And who can blame them? It has not been so long since humans were crucified, beheaded, or burned for far less than you will be required to say in order to be absolutely truthful about me and the 'Memorandum.'

Nevertheless, I leave it in your care with complete faith that you will tend it as you would a beloved child. I know how much you enjoy a dare and so I dare you to use it, yourself. I dare you to publish it, and I dare you to share it with the world.

Once you said you had a premonition about me. As you read these words you know that we shall not see each other again for a long time. There will be no more hours together when we can sip our sherry in the peace and warmth of a loving friendship that knew no boundaries of time or space. And I leave you, for now, not with sadness but with satisfaction and joy that we came together and walked, arm in arm, through this brief moment of eternity. Who could ask for more?

Someday, when the world closes in on you, as it will from time to time, pour yourself a glass of sherry and think of your old ragpicker. My blessings are with you always, and my only injunction to you is that you continue with your writing no matter what circumstances befall you. You have much yet to say. The world needs you. The ragpickers need you. I need you.

One of my dear friends, Socrates, in his last moments, said, "The hour of my departure has arrived, and we go our ways . . . I to die, and you to live. Which is better, God only knows."

Mister Og, I know which is better.

To live . . . is better.

Live in happiness . . . and everlasting peace.

With love,
Simon

I dropped his letter and stared at the pages of type.

I picked up the small safety pin with its wisp of white rag and pinned the amulet to my jacket lapel.

I reached across the desk and drew my five-year calendar toward me.

I circled the date and counted forward one hundred days, bringing me well into the new year.

I circled the hundredth day.

Tonight, before I turned off my bedside light I would read 'The God Memorandum' as he had instructed.

My hands were clenched together tightly. I lowered my head to my desk until my forehead touched it.

Why was I crying? Was it because Simon had left me? Was it because I had suspected, too late, his true identity? Or was it because I knew that my life, my dreams, my world, would never be the same again, now that he had placed his hand upon them. . . .

Chapter IX

The God Memorandum

TO: YOU
FROM: GOD

Take counsel.

I hear your cry.

It passes through the darkness, filters through the clouds, mingles with starlight, and finds its way to my heart on the path of a sunbeam.

I have anguished over the cry of a hare choked in the noose of a snare, a sparrow tumbled from the nest of its mother, a child thrashing helplessly in a pond, and a son shedding his blood on a cross.

Know that I hear you, also. Be at peace. Be calm.

I bring thee relief for your sorrow for I know its cause . . . and its cure.

You weep for all your childhood dreams that have vanished with the years.

You weep for all your self-esteem that has been corrupted by failure.

You weep for all your potential that has been bartered for security.

You weep for all your individuality that has been trampled by mobs.

You weep for all your talent that has been wasted through misuse.

You look upon yourself with disgrace and you turn in terror from the image you see in the pool. Who is this mockery of humanity staring back at you with bloodless eyes of shame?

Where is the grace of your manner, the beauty of your figure, the quickness of your movement, the clarity of your mind, the brilliance of your tongue? Who stole your goods? Is the thief's identity known to you, as it is to me?

Once you placed your head in a pillow of grass in your father's field and looked up at a cathedral of clouds and knew that all the gold of Babylon would be yours in time.

Once you read from many books and wrote on many tablets, convinced beyond any doubt that all the wisdom of Solomon would be equaled and surpassed by you.

And the seasons would flow into years until lo, you would reign supreme in your own garden of Eden.

Dost thou remember who implanted those plans and dreams and seeds of hope within you?

You cannot.

You have no memory of that moment when first you emerged from your mother's womb and I placed my hand on your soft brow. And the secret I whispered in your small ear when I bestowed my blessings upon you?

Remember our secret?

You cannot.

The passing years have destroyed your recollection, for they have filled your mind with fear and doubt and anxiety and remorse and hate and there is no room for joyful memories where these beasts habitate.

Weep no more. I am with you . . . and this moment is the dividing line of your life. All that has gone before is like unto no more than that time you slept within your mother's womb. What is past is dead. Let the dead bury the dead.

This day you return from the living dead.

This day, like unto Elijah with the widow's son, I stretch myself upon thee three times and you live again.

This day, like unto Elisha with the Shunammite's son, I put my mouth upon your mouth and my eyes upon your eyes and my hands upon your hands and your flesh is warm again.

This day, like unto Jesus at the tomb of Lazarus, I command you to come forth and you will walk from your cave of doom to begin a new life.

This is your birthday. This is your new date of birth. Your first life, like unto a play of the theatre, was only a rehearsal. This time the curtain is up. This time the world watches and waits to applaud. This time you will not fail.

Light your candles. Share your cake. Pour the wine. You have been reborn.

Like a butterfly from its chrysalis you will fly . . . fly as high as you wish, and neither the wasps nor dragonflies nor mantids of mankind shall obstruct your mission or your search for the true riches of life.

Feel my hand upon thy head.

Attend to my wisdom.

Let me share with you, again, the secret you heard at your birth and forgot.

You are my greatest miracle.

You are the greatest miracle in the world.

Those were the first words you ever heard. Then you cried. They all cry.

You did not believe me then . . . and nothing has happened in the intervening years to correct your disbelief. For how could you be a miracle when you consider yourself a failure at the most menial of tasks? How can you be a miracle when you have little confidence in dealing with the most trivial of responsibilities? How can you be a miracle when you are shackled by debt and lie awake in torment over whence will come tomorrow's bread?

Enough. The milk that is spilled is sour. Yet, how many prophets, how many wise men, how many poets, how many artists, how many composers, how many scientists, how many philosophers and messengers have I sent with word of your divinity, your potential for godliness, and the secrets of achievement? How did you treat them?

Still I love you and I am with you now, through these

words, to fulfill the prophet who announced that the Lord shall set his hand again, the second time, to recover the remnant of his people.

I have set my hand again.

This is the second time.

You are my remnant.

It is of no avail to ask, haven't you known, haven't you heard, hasn't it been told to you from the beginning; haven't you understood from the foundations of the earth?

You have not known; you have not heard; you have not understood.

You have been told that you are a divinity in disguise, a god playing a fool.

You have been told that you are a special piece of work, noble in reason, infinite in faculties, express and admirable in form and moving, like an angel in action, like a god in apprehension.

You have been told that you are the salt of the earth.

You were given the secret even of moving mountains, of performing the impossible.

You believed no one. You burned your map to happiness, you abandoned your claim to peace of mind, you snuffed out the candles that had been placed along your destined path of glory, and then you stumbled, lost and frightened, in the darkness of futility and self-pity, until you fell into a hell of your own creation.

Then you cried and beat your breast and cursed the luck that had befallen you. You refused to accept the consequences of your own petty thoughts and lazy deeds and you searched for a scapegoat on which to blame your failure. How quickly you found one.

You blamed me!

You cried that your handicaps, your mediocrity, your lack of opportunity, your failures . . . were the will of God!

You were wrong!

Let us take inventory. Let us, first, call a roll of your handicaps. For how can I ask you to build a new life lest you have the tools?

Are you blind? Does the sun rise and fall without your witness?

No. You can see . . . and the hundred million receptors I have placed in your eyes enable you to enjoy the magic of a leaf, a snowflake, a pond, an eagle, a child, a cloud, a star, a rose, a rainbow . . . and the look of love. Count one blessing.

Are you deaf? Can a baby laugh or cry without your attention?

No. You can hear . . . and the twenty-four thousand fibers I have built in each of your ears vibrate to the wind in the trees, the tides on the rocks, the majesty of an opera, a robin's plea, children at play . . . and the words I love you. Count another blessing.

Are you mute? Do your lips move and bring forth only spittle?

No. You can speak . . . as can no other of my creatures, and your words can calm the angry, uplift the despondent, goad the quitter, cheer the unhappy, warm the lonely, praise the worthy, encourage the defeated, teach the ignorant . . . and say I love you. Count another blessing.

Are you paralyzed? Does your helpless form despoil the land?

No. You can move. You are not a tree condemned to a small plot while the wind and world abuses you. You can stretch and run and dance and work, for within you I have designed five hundred muscles, two hundred bones, and seven miles of nerve fibre all synchronized by me to do your bidding. Count another blessing.

Are you unloved and unloving? Does loneliness engulf you, night and day?

No. No more. For now you know love's secret, that to receive love it must be given with no thought of its return. To love for fulfillment, satisfaction, or pride is no love. Love is a gift on which no return is demanded. Now you know that to love unselfishly is its own reward. And even should love not be returned it is not lost, for love not reciprocated will flow back to you and soften and purify your heart. Count another blessing. Count twice.

Is your heart stricken? Does it leak and strain to maintain your life?

No. Your heart is strong. Touch your chest and feel its rhythm, pulsating, hour after hour, day and night, thirty-six million beats each year, year after year, asleep or awake, pumping your blood through more than sixty thousand miles of veins, arteries, and tubing . . . pumping more than six hundred thousand gallons each year. Man has never created such a machine. Count another blessing.

Are you diseased of skin? Do people turn in horror when you approach?

No. Your skin is clear and a marvel of creation, needing only that you tend it with soap and oil and brush and care. In time all steels will tarnish and rust, but not your skin. Eventually the strongest of metals will wear, with use, but not that layer that I have constructed around you. Constantly it renews itself, old cells replaced by new, just as the old you is now replaced by the new. Count another blessing.

Are your lungs befouled? Does the breath of life struggle to enter your body?

No. Your portholes to life support you even in the vilest of environments of your own making, and they labor always to filter life-giving oxygen through six hundred million pockets of folded flesh while they rid your body of gaseous wastes. Count another blessing.

Is your blood poisoned? Is it diluted with water and pus?

No. Within your five quarts of blood are twenty-two trillion blood cells and within each cell are millions of molecules and within each molecule is an atom oscillating at more than ten million times each second. Each second, two million of your blood cells die to be replaced by two million more in a resurrection that has continued

402

since your first birth. As it has always been inside, so now it is on your outside. Count another blessing.

Are you feeble of mind? Can you no longer think for yourself?

No. Your brain is the most complex structure in the universe. I know. Within its three pounds are thirteen billion nerve cells, more than three times as many cells as there are people on your earth. To help you file away every perception, every sound, every taste, every smell, every action you have experienced since the day of your birth, I have implanted, within your cells, more than one thousand billion billion protein molecules. Every incident in your life is there waiting only your recall. And, to assist your brain in the control of your body I have dispersed, throughout your form, four million pain-sensitive structures, five hundred thousand touch detectors, and more than two hundred thousand temperature detectors. No nation's gold is better protected than you. None of your ancient wonders are greater than you.

You are my finest creation.

Within you is enough atomic energy to destroy any of the world's great cities . . . and rebuild it.

Are you poor? Is there no gold or silver in your purse?

No. You are rich! Together we have just counted your wealth. Study the list. Count them again. Tally your assets!

Why have you betrayed yourself? Why have you cried that all the blessings of humanity were removed from

you? Why did you deceive yourself that you were power-
less to change your life? Are you without talent, senses,
abilities, pleasures, instincts, sensations, and pride? Are
you without hope? Why do you cringe in the shadows, a
giant defeated, awaiting only sympathetic transport into
the welcome void and dampness of hell?

You have so much. Your blessings overflow your
cup . . . and you have been unmindful of them, like a
child spoiled in luxury, since I have bestowed them upon
you with generosity and regularity.

Answer me.

Answer yourself.

What rich man, old and sick, feeble and helpless,
would not exchange all the gold in his vault for the blessings you have treated so lightly.

Know then the first secret to happiness and success—
that you possess, even now, every blessing necessary to
achieve great glory. They are your treasure, your tools
with which to build, starting today, the foundation for a
new and better life.

Therefore, I say unto you, count your blessings and
know that you already are my greatest creation. This is
the first law you must obey in order to perform the greatest miracle in the world, the return of your humanity
from living death.

And be grateful for your lessons learned in poverty.
For he is not poor who has little; only he that desires
much . . . and true security lies not in the things one
has but in the things one can do without.

Where are the handicaps that produced your failure? They existed only in your mind.

Count your blessings.

And the second law is like unto the first. Proclaim your rarity.

You had condemned yourself to a potter's field, and there you lay, unable to forgive your own failure, destroying yourself with self-hate, self-incrimination, and revulsion at your crimes against yourself and others.

Are you not perplexed?

Do you not wonder why I am able to forgive your failures, your transgressions, your pitiful demeanor . . . when you cannot forgive yourself?

I address you now, for three reasons. You need me. You are not one of a herd heading for destruction in a gray mass of mediocrity. And . . . you are a great rarity.

Consider a painting by Rembrandt or a bronze by Degas or a violin by Stradivarius or a play by Shakespeare. They have great value for two reasons: their creators were masters and they are few in number. Yet there are more than one of each of these.

On that reasoning you are the most valuable treasure on the face of the earth, for you know who created you and there is only one of you.

Never, in all the seventy billion humans who have walked this planet since the beginning of time has there been anyone exactly like you.

Never, until the end of time, will there be another such as you.

You have shown no knowledge or appreciation of your uniqueness.

Yet, you are the rarest thing in the world.

From your father, in his moment of supreme love, flowed countless seeds of love, more than four hundred million in number. All of them, as they swam within your mother, gave up the ghost and died. All except one! You.

You alone persevered within the loving warmth of your mother's body, searching for your other half, a single cell from your mother so small that more than two million would be necessary to fill an acorn shell. Yet, despite impossible odds, in that vast ocean of darkness and disaster, you persevered, found that infinitesimal cell, joined with it, and began a new life. Your life.

You arrived, bringing with you, as does every child, the message that I was not yet discouraged of man. Two cells, now united in a miracle. Two cells, each containing twenty-three chromosomes and within each chromosome hundreds of genes, which would govern every characteristic about you, from the color of your eyes to the charm of your manner to the size of your brain.

With all the combinations at my command, beginning with that single sperm from your father's four hundred million, through the hundreds of genes in each of the chromosomes from your mother and father, I could have created three hundred thousand billion humans, each different from the other.

But who did I bring forth?

You! One of a kind. Rarest of the rare. A priceless

treasure, possessed of qualities in mind and speech and movement and appearance and actions as no other has ever lived, lives, or shall live.

Why have you valued yourself in pennies when you are worth a king's ransom?

Why did you listen to those who demeaned you . . . and far worse, why did you believe them?

Take counsel. No longer hide your rarity in the dark. Bring it forth. Show the world. Strive not to walk as your brother walks, nor talk as your leader talks, nor labor as do the mediocre. Never do as another. Never imitate. For how do you know that you may not imitate evil; and he who imitates evil always goes beyond the example set, while he who imitates what is good always falls short. Imitate no one. Be yourself. Show your rarity to the world and they will shower you with gold. This then is the second law.

Proclaim your rarity.

And now you have received two laws.

Count your blessings! Proclaim your rarity!

You have no handicaps. You are not mediocre.

You nod. You force a smile. You admit your self-deception.

What of your next complaint? Opportunity never seeks thee?

Take counsel and it shall come to pass, for now I give you the law of success in every venture. Many centuries ago this law was given to your forefathers from a mountain top. Some heeded the law and lo, their life was filled with the fruit of happiness, accomplishment, gold, and peace of mind. Most listened not, for they sought magic means, devious routes, or waited for the devil called luck to deliver to them the riches of life. They waited in vain . . . just as you waited, and then they wept, as you wept, blaming their lack of fortune on my will.

The law is simple. Young or old, pauper or king, white or black, male or female . . . all can use the secret to their advantage; for of all the rules and speeches and scriptures of success and how to attain it, only one method has never failed . . . whomsoever shall compel ye to go with him one mile . . . go with him two.

This then is the third law . . . the secret that will produce riches and acclaim beyond your dreams. Go another mile!

The only certain means of success is to render more and better service than is expected of you, no matter what your task may be. This is a habit followed by all successful people since the beginning of time. Therefore I saith the surest way to doom yourself to mediocrity is to perform only the work for which you are paid.

Think not ye are being cheated if you deliver more than the silver you receive. For there is a pendulum to all life and the sweat you deliver, if not rewarded today, will swing back tomorrow, tenfold. The mediocre never goes another mile, for why should he cheat himself, he thinks. But you are not mediocre. To go another mile is a privilege you must appropriate by your own initiative. You cannot, you must not avoid it. Neglect it, do only as little as the others, and the responsibility for your failure is yours alone.

You can no more render service without receiving just compensation than you can withhold the rendering of it without suffering the loss of reward. Cause and effect, means and ends, seed and fruit, these cannot be separated. The effect already blooms in the cause, the end pre-exists in the means, and the fruit is always in the seed.

Go another mile.

Concern yourself not, should you serve an ungrateful master. Serve him more.

And instead of him, let it be me who is in your debt, for then you will know that every minute, every stroke of extra service will be repaid. And worry not, should your reward not come soon. For the longer payment is withheld, the better for you . . . and compound interest on compound interest is this law's greatest benefit.

You cannot command success, you can only deserve it . . . and now you know the great secret necessary in order to merit its rare reward.

Go another mile!

Where is this field from whence you cried there was no opportunity? Look! Look around thee. See, where only yesterday you wallowed on the refuse of self-pity, you now walk tall on a carpet of gold. Nothing has changed . . . except you, but you are everything.

You are my greatest miracle.

You are the greatest miracle in the world.

And now the laws of happiness and success are three.

Count your blessings! Proclaim your rarity! Go another mile!

Be patient with your progress. To count your blessings with gratitude, to proclaim your rarity with pride, to go an extra mile and then another, these acts are not accomplished in the blinking of an eye. Yet, that which you acquire with most difficulty you retain the longest; as those who have earned a fortune are more careful of it than those by whom it was inherited.

And fear not as you enter your new life. Every noble acquisition is attended with its risks. He who fears to encounter the one must not expect to obtain the other. Now you know you are a miracle. And there is no fear in a miracle.

Be proud. You are not the momentary whim of a careless creator experimenting in the laboratory of life. You are not a slave of forces that you cannot comprehend. You are a free manifestation of no force but mine, of no love but mine. You were made with a purpose.

Feel my hand. Hear my words.

You need me . . . and I need you.

We have a world to rebuild . . . and if it requireth a miracle what is that to us? We are both miracles and now we have each other.

Never have I lost faith in you since that day when I first spun you from a giant wave and tossed you helplessly on the sands. As you measure time that was more than five hundred million years ago. There were many models, many shapes, many sizes, before I reached perfection in you more than thirty thousand years ago. I have made no further effort to improve on you in all these years.

For how could one improve on a miracle? You were a marvel to behold and I was pleased. I gave you this world and dominion over it. Then, to enable you to reach your full potential I placed my hand upon you, once more, and endowed you with powers unknown to any other creature in the universe, even unto this day.

I gave you the power to think.
I gave you the power to love.
I gave you the power to will.
I gave you the power to laugh.
I gave you the power to imagine.
I gave you the power to create.
I gave you the power to plan.
I gave you the power to speak.
I gave you the power to pray.

My pride in you knew no bounds. You were my ultimate creation, my greatest miracle. A complete living being. One who can adjust to any climate, any hardship, any challenge. One who can manage his own destiny without any interference from me. One who can translate a sensation or perception, not by instinct, but by thought and deliberation into whatever action is best for himself and all humanity.

411

Thus we come to the fourth law of success and happiness . . . for I gave you one more power, a power so great that not even my angels possess it.

I gave you . . . the power to choose.

With this gift I placed you even above my angels . . . for angels are not free to choose sin. I gave you complete control over your destiny. I told you to determine, for yourself, your own nature in accordance with your own free will. Neither heavenly nor earthly in nature, you were free to fashion yourself in whatever form you preferred. You had the power to choose to degenerate into the lowest forms of life, but you also had the power, out of your soul's judgment, to be reborn into the higher forms, which are divine.

I have never withdrawn your great power, the power to choose.

What have you done with this tremendous force? Look at yourself. Think of the choices you have made in your life and recall, now, those bitter moments when you would fall to your knees if only you had the opportunity to choose again.

What is past is past . . . and now you know the fourth great law of happiness and success . . . Use wisely, your power of choice.

Choose to love . . . rather than hate.

Choose to laugh . . . rather than cry.

Choose to create . . . rather than destroy.

Choose to persevere . . . rather than quit.

Choose to praise . . . rather than gossip.

Choose to heal . . . rather than wound.

Choose to give . . . rather than steal.

Choose to act . . . rather than procrastinate.

Choose to grow . . . rather than rot.

Choose to pray . . . rather than curse.

Choose to live . . . rather than die.

Now you know that your misfortunes were not my will, for all power was vested in you, and the accumulation of deeds and thoughts which placed you on the refuse of humanity were your doing, not mine. My gifts of power were too large for your small nature. Now you have grown tall and wise and the fruits of the land will be yours.

You are more than a human being, you are a human becoming.

You are capable of great wonders. Your potential is unlimited. Who else, among my creatures, has mastered fire? Who else, among my creatures, has conquered gravity, has pierced the heavens, has conquered disease and pestilence and drought?

Never demean yourself again!

Never settle for the crumbs of life!

Never hide your talents, from this day hence!

Remember the child who says "when I am a big boy." But what is that? For the big boy says, "when I grow up." And then grown up, he says, "when I am wed." But to be wed, what is that, after all? The thought then changes to "when I retire." And then, retirement comes, and he looks back over the landscape traversed; a cold wind sweeps over it and somehow he has missed it all and it is gone.

Enjoy this day, today . . . and tomorrow, tomorrow.

You have performed the greatest miracle in the world.

You have returned from a living death.

You will feel self-pity no more and each new day will be a challenge and a joy.

You have been born again . . . but just as before, you can choose failure and despair or success and happiness. The choice is yours. The choice is exclusively yours. I can only watch, as before . . . in pride . . . or sorrow.

Remember, then, the four laws of happiness and success.

Count your blessings.

Proclaim your rarity.

Go another mile.

Use wisely your power of choice.

And one more, to fulfill the other four. Do all things with love . . . love for yourself, love for all others, and love for me.

Wipe away your tears. Reach out, grasp my hand, and stand straight.

Let me cut the grave cloths that have bound you.

This day you have been notified.

YOU ARE THE GREATEST MIRACLE IN THE WORLD

Chapter X

I believe all office Christmas parties should be abolished! There's just no way to prevent at least one poor soul from trying to work off his or her pent-up repressions or holiday melancholia in a fit of drinking that either ends up in a scene that will be regretted later or climaxes in a fight over someone's right to get into an automobile and kill himself or some innocent soul. I know. I've acted the fool myself a couple of times . . . long ago.

Furthermore, that "Cold Duck" leaves permanent scars on office carpeting that no cleaning fluid has ever completely removed.

Each year I resolve, usually on the first work day following Christmas, that next year there will be no party in our office. We'll give that foolishly spent money to some needy-family fund instead. And each year, when committees begin to form to plan "the party," I weaken, plead "no contest," and allow it to happen again.

So . . . I had a couple of drinks and tried to smile

through the silliness of the grab-bag exchange while someone's record player monotonously abused a scratchy version of "White Christmas." Then I walked around, patting shoulders and kissing cheeks, feeling like a house detective, constantly reassuring myself that everyone would make it home without any spontaneous motel stops or drunken-driving violations.

Finally the wine ran out and the office emptied swiftly, leaving in its wake a collection of debris that would only be removed if I left a twenty-dollar bill for our cleaning man. It was already in a Christmas card, propped up on Pat's desk where he wouldn't miss it.

I carried my last glass of wine into my office and fell wearily onto the couch, setting the glass into a standing ash tray. The glass. I found myself staring at it, almost hypnotized. Simon. All those sherry glasses we filled and emptied together. Simon. Simon. Where are you?

Suddenly I reached a decision and went to my desk. I punched "F" on my telephone index gadget and found Fred Fell's home phone number. I dialed it. He recognized my voice as soon as I said, "Happy Holidays."

"Og, how wonderful to hear from you. How are you? How's the weather in Chicago?"

"We've got snow."

"Here it's been raining for two days. I think Long Island is sinking."

"So head for Miami."

"I think it's too late. What's going on with you?"

"We've just had our Christmas party in the office. . . ."

". . . and you've had a few drinks and got a little sentimental and remembered your old publisher?"

"All that . . . and one more reason."

"Tell me."

"I'm ready to do another book."

"I don't believe what I'm hearing. I was beginning to think you were so busy counting your money and making like Gore Vidal on all those talk shows that there was no time for writing anymore. What do you want to do? What's the book about?"

"I'm not going to tell you. There's no way I can explain it, either on the phone or in person. I'm just going to do it."

"Does it have a title?"

"*The Greatest Miracle In The World.*"

"I like it already. What's the big miracle?"

"Don't ask."

"Will it be another like *The Greatest Salesman In The World?*"

"Better. I don't have to make this one up."

"Okay, Og. I know better than to push you. You want a contract?"

"No hurry. Whenever you get around to it."

"Same terms as before?"

"Fine."

"What should I put down for delivery date of manuscript?"

"Make it . . . January thirty-first, nineteen-seventy-five."

"That's a year and a month from now. You need that long?"

"Yes."

"Very well. Consider it done. What a relationship we have! I wonder how many other publishers contract for books like this, without even knowing what they're buying?"

"Mailer's publisher, Wallace's publisher, Updyke's publisher, Fowles's publisher, Michener's publisher, Herriot's publisher. . . ."

"Merry Christmas, Og."

"You too, Fred. Love you."

"I love you, too."

It was very dark and still snowing when I left the office and laid down a row of footprints all the way to the parking lot. I felt a burning emptiness inside me and I knew why. Across the lot I could see the dark shadows of the apartment where I had spent so many happy hours, its silent hulk checkered here and there with squares of light blinking through the falling snow.

Right about now we'd be wishing each other "Merry Christmas" and touching glasses and his beautiful voice would be washing over me as he opened whatever silly gift I would have brought. Simon. Simon.

"I miss you. I miss you very much." I was speaking aloud . . . to the wind and the snow flakes. Then I was fighting back sobs that seemed to start deep in my gut. I felt absolutely alone . . . and lost.

Finally I forced myself to shape up. I had to get home.

There was still some shopping to do. Life does go on.

I fumbled for the car keys and unlocked the door. As I turned the key in the ignition I had the sudden compelling urge for another drink. But I knew what would happen: one would lead to twenty . . . and no matter in how many bars I looked I wouldn't find Simon.

I backed the car and cut it sharply toward the exit gate, its tires crunching noisily on the newly fallen snow. I rolled down my window and reached out to turn my key in the gate-release slot. The gate creaked and rose slowly toward the sky. I shifted into "drive" and accelerated slowly over the small asphalt mound under the gate. The front of my car pointed upward slightly as it reached the crest of the mound and the headlight beams swept across a second-floor-apartment window that was dark.

I blinked my eyes and shook my head. I looked again.

My headlight beams had converged in a single shaft of light on a window box.

My God!

In the box was a plant—tilting gently in the blowing snow. . . .

. . . A beautiful plant!

. . . A blue-ribbon plant!

. . . A red glass geranium.